The Reasons Teachers Stay

The Reasons Teachers Stay

Lessons from High-Retention Schools, Districts, and Communities

DOUGLAS B. LARKIN
SUZANNE POOLE PATZELT
HARVARD EDUCATION PRESS
CAMBRIDGE, MASSACHUSETTS

HARVARD EDUCATION PRESS
CAMBRIDGE, MASSACHUSETTS

Paperback ISBN 9798895570425

Cataloging-in-Publication Data available from the Library of Congress.

Published by Harvard Education Press,
an imprint of the Harvard Education Publishing Group

Harvard Education Press
8 Story Street
Cambridge, MA 02138

Cover Design: Jackie Shepherd Design
Cover Image: Ivonne Wierink (corkboard), Inspiration GP (paper), Duntrune Studios (index card), CHALERMCHAI99 (sticky notes), and Irina Gutyryak (clips and tacks); all via Shutterstock

The typefaces in this book are Adobe Garamond Pro and Myriad Pro.

Contents

INTRODUCTION

If I had to say the number one reason why I didn't move, it is because of the people I work with and the department. . . Just having those relationships with those people.

—High school science teacher, Wisconsin

This is a book about teacher retention—specifically why teachers seem to stay longer in some schools and districts than they do in others. Of course, remaining in a job as a teacher is no guarantee of professional growth, effectiveness, or flourishing, but it is a precondition for all of those things. In public discussions about teacher shortages, there is a tendency to focus on aspects of the job that push teachers into leaving, such as low pay, impossible workloads, lack of autonomy, and issues with the overall school and work environment. All of those issues and many others remain vital in any consideration of teachers' work lives. And yet, it seems to us that the most interesting questions about teacher retention concern the reasons that teachers choose to *stay*, particularly when they might have made the decision to leave a particular job or the teaching profession altogether.

The work presented in this book is the product of a six-year study funded by the National Science Foundation (NSF) and conducted by our research team at Montclair State University, which investigated the factors related to successful teacher retention in the United States.[1] School settings are an important aspect of this project because they are the places where teachers work, so we aimed to capture the range of public-school contexts that exist across the nation. This required attending to both demographic and geographic diversity, as well as the types and sizes of schools. Rural, suburban, and urban schools were included in our selected sites, as were charter and vocational schools. Just as important, we learned from places where teachers of color appeared to thrive, and we investigated why teachers stayed in high-need schools or districts that were otherwise similar to locations with a significantly higher teacher attrition rate.[2]

The story we tell about why teachers stay turns out to be unexpectedly complex. Initially, we anticipated that our study would primarily concern mentoring and induction practices aimed at novice teachers. Very quickly, however, we learned that in order to put forward a more accurate accounting of teacher retention, our study would need to be more expansive. Our investigation led us to draw upon the theoretical framework of *job embeddedness* to understand how teachers' decisions to stay in their current positions were shaped by how well they fit into their organization, profession, and community, as well as how strongly they connected with others, and what they valued about where they were. We will discuss this framework and our modification of this theory into *teacher embeddedness* in chapter 3.

The aim of this book is to provide tangible suggestions and existence proofs to school leaders and policymakers who work to sustain teachers in their jobs, and aim to shape the experiences of newly hired teachers in particular. In the chapters that follow, we will discuss our study in detail, but as avid consumers of educational research who appreciate clear findings up front, we begin with a summary of what we learned. The following is a list of ten factors—ordered by prevalence across our case studies—that we identified as most important in the districts where teachers were retained at rates well above average in their state:

1. supportive relationships with colleagues
2. school- and district-level systems and culture of support
3. compensation
4. teacher autonomy
5. specialness of place
6. availability of resources for teaching
7. opportunity and agency for professional growth
8. district- and school-level race consciousness
9. affordances related to school size
10. personal satisfaction and the rewards of being a teacher

Over the course of this book, each of these factors will be illustrated with case study data and discussed in conversation with the wider scholarship on teacher retention.[3] Though our research has some obvious limitations, the findings suggest possibilities for practice and policy that we hope will be taken up by administrators, school communities, educational stakeholders, and—of course—teachers. One of the most compelling findings of the study is the role played by colleagues in influencing teachers' decisions to stay. This book aims to shift the teacher-retention conversation away from solutions grounded in oversimplified notions of job satisfaction and toward a vision of teacher retention that acknowledges the roles of colleagues, community, resources, administrators, the school organization, and most importantly, the role played by teachers themselves about their own individual decisions to stay.

We write as teacher educators and scholars who were once teachers in K-12 settings, and this study was conceived out of a sense that, by focusing primarily on those who leave, research on teacher retention was missing something important. We still see ourselves as educators, even though the principals and school boards that once employed us as newly certified teachers have long since hired our replacements. Our identities were critical to how we conceptualized and conducted this study. We sought to elevate the voices of teachers and administrators in our case study sites as they shared their own ideas about the comparatively higher rates of teacher retention in their schools and districts. Indeed, this study is grounded in the belief that researchers can learn about retention from teachers and school leaders themselves, who are experts in their own career choices precisely because they have lived them. Consequently, the claims we make in this book are also drawn from the practical wisdom of those who were and may still be involved in efforts to retain teachers across a broad array of school contexts. We have made no attempt to conceal our empathy for the work of teaching and remain grateful to all of the educators who participated in this project at every stage.

DESCRIPTION OF THE IMPREST PROJECT

The scholarly basis for this book is the Induction and Mentoring Programs for the Retention of Science Teachers (IMPREST) project funded by a National Science Foundation Noyce Track 4 Research grant from 2017–2023. As we will discuss, our research initially focused on just secondary science teachers but over time grew to encompass district-wide teacher-retention efforts in each site. The primary question we investigated in our research was: In places that have demonstrated comparatively more successful teacher retention for novice science teachers, what are the factors that relate to such retention? In short, the task we set for our research was to identify districts that were doing a very good job in retaining science teachers and then visit those districts to learn from teachers, administrators, and other school leaders about what they were doing that might be a factor in teacher retention there.

Most of the data analysis to identify districts that were retaining secondary science teachers at a high rate (top 10 percent in each state) was undertaken during the first year of this project with publicly available staffing data. Recognizing that state teacher policies were likely to have an impact on teacher retention, we selected four states with different policy contexts and available teacher-staffing data for this research: New Jersey, Pennsylvania, North Carolina, and Wisconsin. Over the course of the next four years, we carefully selected individual school districts for participation.[4] In choosing these districts, we sought to balance our opportunity to learn by including a number of factors, such as the district's geographic location in the state, districts that demonstrated success in retaining science teachers of color, and the demographic profile of the school, which included the percentage of students receiving free/reduced lunch or were designated limited English proficiency.[5] These districts were promised anonymity so that the participants could speak freely about their experiences. As a consequence, the names of participants are not shared and all districts were assigned pseudonyms. We discussed the project with district administrators prior to seeking research approval from the relevant school board authorities. Ultimately, we ended up with thirteen participating districts across the four states.

The evidence used to make claims in this book comes from two main sources. The first is from interviews with teachers and administrators in these districts where we conducted the case studies. While our conversations with practitioners were wide ranging and interesting, often the most informative answers came from asking directly why they believed their district was able to retain teachers well-above the state average. Some of the interviews were one-on-one, but many were in focus groups of two to five teachers each. In these discussions, interviewees often triggered memories and ideas for one another, creating a rich and robust data set. All interviews were transcribed and analyzed, and each district case study was written by a lead author on the team and then shared with participants for feedback. The second data source was a cross-case analysis of all thirteen cases, in which we sought to identify factors salient to teacher retention that districts had in common. We used web-based qualitative software to identify themes, and we analyzed the frequency of the factors across districts. While not every factor appeared in every district, there was sufficient overlap to make claims about the set of cases as a whole.

A Nonrepresentative Sample

Throughout this book, we make the inductive leap from interviewing secondary science teachers about their reasons for retention to generalizing these findings in order to make claims about retention factors for teachers across grade levels and subject areas that we did not study. We fully recognize the possibility of error in our reasoning and would likely agree with critiques that our samples were not representative of the teacher populations in the schools and districts we studied. A critic may reasonably ask: By what logic can we claim that factors underlying the retention of biology, chemistry, physics, and earth science teachers ought to be applicable to those teaching kindergarten, middle school music, French, physical education, etc.?

We have two responses to such a question. The first is that many of the retention factors we describe in this book are structural or local in nature and did not seem to be closely connected specifically to science teaching at all. This finding came somewhat as a surprise to our research team—composed primarily of former science teachers—because we expected that districts doing a good job at retaining science teachers would be doing something special for them. Of course, there were a few science-specific factors that did arise in our interviews with teachers—these will be discussed as they appear. In most cases, however, even these science-specific efforts reflected a broader approach to supporting teachers' needs. As we aim to show through the cases in this book, it was clear that the retention factors we identified were simply not unique to secondary science teachers.

Our second response is that in many ways, our sample of science teachers was indeed generalizable, both as a defined subgroup of teachers within their district and as individuals. When we consider all of the characteristics that science teachers have in common with the broader population of teachers—including education level, certification, demographic factors, and connections to their school community—there are certainly more similarities than differences. While we freely concede that some of these differences may be important, it was the act of identifying a single group for these case studies that made this research possible at all. At this writing, five-year retention statistics are simply unavailable for all teachers at the school and district level for most states. Indeed, the time and effort in this project to identify retained science teachers and determine which districts were more successful in retaining them was a substantial undertaking.

We are intentionally up-front about this methodological choice and recognize the validity of critiques against the claims we make in this book as a result. However, as case study researchers, the problem of generalizability is a familiar one to us. It is rare for qualitative research in schools to claim truly representative samples, and we follow in the footsteps of other case study researchers who have faced similar situations.[6] In communicating the findings of this study, we hope that we have left ample room for others to challenge or add nuance to our conclusions. We have pointed out a few areas along the way where the findings might be different for others in the districts who are not secondary science teachers. We also hope that future research on teacher retention can benefit from advances in data quality and transparency in order to further refine distinctions across grade levels, subject areas, and certifications when it comes to understanding the reasons teachers stay.

The Organization and Ethos of this Book

In the opening chapter, we begin with a general discussion about job retention before looking specifically at the current framing around teachers staying or leaving. We will set the problem of teacher retention as understanding why teachers stay and detail a framework for describing teacher retention. In chapter 2, we provide an overview of the research on teacher retention that informed our approach, including the retention of specific groups that were important to us in our study—such as teachers of color and secondary science teachers. In chapter 3, we introduce the teacher embeddedness framework as our theoretical lens and demonstrate its explanatory power as well as its usefulness in conducting research on teacher retention.

In each of the next four chapters, we select a single district—each from a different US state—to examine the specific factors and state policies that impacted teacher retention there. Chapter 4 describes the case of the Mulberry School District in New Jersey, where the retention rate for teachers of color was the highest across all of the districts in the four states we studied. In chapter 5, we present the case of the Granite County Technical School in Pennsylvania, where collegial relationships presented a compelling story about teacher retention. In chapter 6, we share the case of the Pompano School District in Wisconsin, where teacher autonomy in an uncertain and changing policy environment was highly valued. In chapter 7, we close out the case studies with the Kingfisher School District in North Carolina, where the story of teacher retention can only be told with close attention to the ties of kinship and community.

In chapter 8, we draw from the cases presented in those chapters and others from the study to discuss the ten retention factors presented in this introduction and examine the role that teacher mentoring and induction programs in these places appeared to have impacted teacher retention. In chapter 9, we conclude with a look at some of the findings from the state comparisons of retention and make specific suggestions for education leaders who work on issues of teacher retention and the next generation of researchers studying this issue. Three appendices describe the methods of the study, the national teacher policy context, and a brief discussion on the role of state policy on teacher retention.

In the opening paragraphs, we mentioned the importance of our identities as teachers and the value we place on the contributions and insights of educators throughout this project. Now that we have set the stage for presenting our findings in the chapters to come, we wish to conclude this introduction by sharing the reasons that we embarked on this project in the first place. Of all the things that we could have spent six years of our lives doing, why study teacher retention?

Our answer can be found within the principles of equity and justice that drove us to become educational researchers and faculty in teacher preparation programs in the first place. We believe that schools ought to be humane places, not only for learning but also for working. All students deserve high quality teachers, and we have seen what is possible when novice teachers are provided the necessary supports that permit them to become more effective teachers over time. Yet, opportunities to learn are limited for many K–12 students because they are in schools where teachers are not retained, and the teaching expertise that could have been developed and deployed in the classroom is lost instead. This is only one dimension of the vast array of inequities that still impact schools in the United States and poor children of color most acutely.[7] It is therefore no accident that issues of equity are central in some way to each of the teacher-retention stories from the schools and districts that we studied. Our sincere hope is that by sharing the cases in this book and the overall findings of this study, we are able to provide educators with new tools and ways of thinking about teacher retention that will benefit their students and the teaching profession as a whole.

CHAPTER 1

Posing The Problem of Teacher Retention

As an educational issue, teacher attrition and retention refers to the need to prevent good teachers from leaving the job for the wrong reasons.

—*Geert Kelchtermans*[1]

Jobs, as we know them today, are a relatively recent innovation in human history. Many people in the modern world are integrated into a global economic system that requires compensation for daily labor as a resource for survival. For most adults, jobs are an essential way to exchange labor for pay and other benefits and may take up a significant fraction of one's waking hours. Jobs vary in duration, demand, and reward; the farm worker who is hired for two weeks to help harvest a ripened crop has a very different job from a salaried judicial officer with a lifetime appointment and a pension. Some people derive immense satisfaction from their jobs, which serves as an additional benefit, while others do not particularly enjoy their jobs at all. Some people hold one job, while others juggle many. The duties of a job can be deeply intertwined with one's personal life, be demarcated into completely separate spheres, or exist somewhere in between as the ties formed in the workplace drift outward into an employee's wider social world. Some jobs are considered difficult, and the prospective pool of individuals who can reasonably be expected or permitted to do them is limited by the knowledge, skills, and credentials required. Consequently, such jobs are demanding in many ways and frequently offer greater social status, compensation, and/or security. As long as there is work to do and compensation to offer, employers tend to prefer retaining well-performing employees because recruiting, selecting, and training new workers requires additional resources. Employees, all things considered, tend to remain in their jobs when the reasons to stay outweigh the reasons to leave. A decision to change jobs is often dependent upon a wide array of factors that include personal circumstances and the social context.

Conventional wisdom suggests that the explanation for why people stay in their jobs is primarily connected to job satisfaction and the economics of the labor market. If an individual is generally satisfied with their job and compensation, this reasoning goes, then there is little motivation to leave. By this same logic, if a worker perceives that a different, available job opportunity (or just leaving) would be more satisfactory, then they leave. This explanatory framework of job satisfaction for retention is quite fragile, however. It only takes the briefest of thought experiments to imagine why someone who is very unsatisfied with their job might stay. After all, a job is often a financial lifeline that many are unable or unwilling to put at risk. Alternatively, it is not difficult to consider a scenario where someone who is very satisfied as an employee might decide to leave in order to pursue further career ambitions, such as teaching internationally or attending graduate school.[2]

Researchers have expended a significant amount of time and effort researching job satisfaction and its relationship to *attrition*—a word which is often used interchangeably with an individual quitting, resigning, or leaving a job but is more properly applied as a categorical description of employees exiting a given workforce.[3] The counterintuitive finding from this body of scholarship is that measures of job satisfaction actually have very little power to predict worker attrition, a finding confirmed across different categories of workers.[4] Because employers typically prefer a stable and adequately qualified workforce, figuring out what makes workers unsatisfied remains an important question. The logical argument is that if employers make reasonable changes to working conditions to make workers more satisfied, then they will ultimately be able to retain more workers. Of course, workers themselves may seek to address the causes of their dissatisfaction by pressing their employers for change, either individually or collectively. Ensuring employee satisfaction remains a key aspect of creating a sustainable working environment across many professions, and any employer who cannot keep workers satisfied will likely have problems in meeting their organization's goals. And yet, the reasons workers stay may not simply be the absence of reasons to leave.

TEACHERS WHO LEAVE AND TEACHERS WHO STAY

We share these observations about the nature of work because they can easily be overlooked when discussing the employment and retention of teachers. For many years, research on teacher retention focused on identifying the reasons why teachers leave the profession, with the goal of pointing toward interventions that might reduce unwanted teacher attrition. These efforts uncovered some of the systemic difficulties faced by teachers and provided important empirical support for improving the work lives of teachers and the experiences of the students they teach. The problem of teacher attrition is of greatest interest to those who are charged with ensuring there is a "good teacher in every classroom," and few concerns are more vexing to school administrators than staffing shortages.[5] In the United States, this is particularly true in areas of perennial teacher vacancies, such as in science, mathematics, world languages, and special education, where there is no guarantee that an open position can be filled in a timely manner.[6] The act of teachers leaving is the key problem to be solved in this framing of the problem of teacher attrition.

Teaching has always been a demanding profession, and as noted above, in our current era there are many challenges. These include keeping up with rapid technological change, navigating politicized debates over curriculum, and attending to the mental and physical health concerns of students and teachers alike. Many teachers struggle to plot the course of their work lives as they make choices about whether to continue in a particular school or even in the teaching profession. Such pressures undoubtedly contribute to the number of novice teachers who make the difficult decision that teaching is not the career for them.

We recognize that teachers have always been at the frontlines of crises; the literature is saturated with research about the reasons teachers choose to leave the profession, as we will demonstrate in the following chapter. Plenty has also been written about promising strategies to recruit and retain teachers in schools. And yet, the field of educational research has only recently begun to unearth the reasons why some teachers choose to stay in their jobs and their profession even in the face of such challenges. Our premise is that the retention of teachers—the fact of their staying—is the more promising phenomenon of interest. As we will show, the reasons that teachers stay in their schools, which are multiple and complex, cannot be characterized as just the opposite or inverse of the reasons why others may leave. By examining the reasons why teachers choose to stay where they do, we look to highlight factors within districts, schools, departments, and communities that offer lessons to others who seek solutions to the issue of teacher retention. We also seek to follow in the tradition of qualitative education researchers like Sara Lawrence-Lightfoot, Gloria Ladson-Billings, and John Goodlad, who find value in researching what is good and what is working in education, as opposed to taking an approach that seeks to diagnose pathologies in individuals or school settings.[7]

When a teacher leaves a teaching position, there can be many reasons why. A teacher's circumstances outside of school may have changed, such as starting a family or following a partner's job to another part of the country. Sometimes the reasons are connected to the school or location in some way, such as when a teacher takes a new position closer to where they live or seeks to find better working conditions at a different school or district. There are also times when teachers do not choose to leave, but the choice is made for them. For example, a district may choose not to renew the contract of a first-year teacher for performance reasons, or a teacher may be let go as part of a reduction in force due to a drop in student enrollment.[8] Alternately, teachers may choose to pursue career advancement in some way—perhaps as an administrator, counselor, or college professor—or just leave the profession to try something else.[9]

There are as many reasons to leave teaching as there are teachers who choose to leave. There has long been an implicit assumption among education policymakers and researchers—informed by the logic described above—that understanding the reasons why teachers leave will provide guidance on what to do in order to dissuade them from leaving. For example, if teachers leave because salaries are too low and they can get other higher-paying jobs elsewhere, then one obvious solution is to increase salaries. Or, if new-teacher attrition is driven by difficulties in managing students in a classroom, then providing support to teachers in their first years to help them with classroom management skills is likely to be of some benefit. Even though teacher retention may have much to do with being personally and professionally satisfied, measuring teacher satisfaction in a way that is predictive of retention turns out to be notoriously difficult, not just in teaching but in many lines of work. [10]

Schools are complex systems embedded in larger social and economic structures. Even with attention, input, and engagement from a broad range of stakeholders, it turns out to be rather difficult to give teachers extra preparation periods, raise their salaries, or adequately make provisions for ongoing long-term and sustained high-quality professional development. Like many issues in education, there are no quick fixes to the problem of teacher retention.[11]

WHAT DO WE MEAN BY TEACHER RETENTION?

What does it mean for a teacher to be retained? To the school or district administrator who hires a teacher for a particular position, retention means having that person available to teach in the coming year.[12] From the perspective of the teacher, however, retention may refer to the profession of teaching rather than to an individual school or district. An even more expansive definition of retention would also include those who continue in the field of education in capacities other than as a classroom teacher, such as an administrator, guidance counselor, university professor, or museum educator. Clearly, retention is in the eye of the beholder, so to work with the concept in a research study such as ours, it was important to establish an operational definition.

However, arriving at such a definition is complicated, as the following example will show. Imagine the following trajectory: a newly certified teacher is hired as a one-year-leave replacement in district #1 for another teacher on family leave. After successfully finishing out the school year, the teacher is offered a job in district #2 and teaches there for the next four years. Personal circumstances then require leaving that job for one full year, but conditions align the following year to permit that teacher to return to district #2 and resume their career. How does the concept of teacher retention apply to such a situation? The teacher was not retained by district #1 but was certainly retained in the profession. A measure of teacher retention at the five-year mark likely would have categorized this teacher as leaving, which would be erroneous in the longer view.

Teachers make up the third largest group of public-sector workers in the US economy. From the perspective of economists who examine trends in the labor workforce with a focus on human capital, such detail on the personal lives of the 2.5 million elementary, middle, and secondary school teachers in the US is largely irrelevant.[13] It is useful for these researchers to use a simple definition of retention—as a teacher continuing to teach in the same position the following year—when examining issues such as teacher shortages, pension reform, and other policy-related concerns.[14] However, such distinctions did matter in our study because our focus is on the experiences of the teachers themselves in choosing to stay.

Our definition of retention requires transcending the narrow economic terms used to describe whether a position is vacated or not.[15] Though quite common in the economics of education literature, we have avoided the phrase *teacher turnover* because of its conceptual imprecision. It is our view that teacher turnover statistics for a given setting or context generally serve to obscure the nature of the reasons for teacher movements in the workforce. For example, both a high-performing school district with an ample supply of applicants for teaching positions and a struggling school with difficult working conditions may both have a high teacher turnover rate but for very different reasons. In fact, the language used in the field of teacher retention is full of similar conceptual baggage, so it is worth examining the terms and metaphors commonly used in research and public discourse to describe the work lives of teachers.

CHARACTERIZING TEACHER RETENTION, ATTRITION, AND MOBILITY

There are a wide variety of terms used to characterize the attrition, retention, and mobility of teachers. While some labels are self-evident, others are less useful because they lack not only categorical definition but the descriptive precision to characterize changes in location, position, and duration. For example, Thomas Smith and Richard Ingersoll used the term *leavers* to describe "beginning teachers who leave the teaching occupation at the end of their first year." They defined *movers* as those teachers who remain in teaching but "move to a different school at the end of their first year" and *stayers* as those who not only remain in the profession but "stay in the same school to teach a second year."[16] Such language serves a specialized purpose for looking at what happens to teachers at the conclusion of their first year but falls short in the long-term as career trajectories become complicated and questions about staying where and for how long become increasingly important.

Similarly confounding are the words *returning* or *returner*, which may be used to characterize teachers who leave the profession for a period of time and then re-enter the teacher workforce. Paradoxically, this same word is also often used in the literature to describe a teacher who comes back to the same school for a second year. To make matters more confusing, some research studies even use these words to describe individuals who return to the district or even the school where they graduated to become a teacher.

Unless data systems carefully track individual teachers across different local educational authorities or states, it is not easy for labels such as *leaver* or *returner* to distinguish between a teacher who switches schools within a district, a teacher who leaves one district for another, a teacher who puts a teaching career on hold for a year or more, or a teacher who leaves the profession altogether. Consequently, it is quite easy for various forms of teacher mobility to be mischaracterized as attrition. And yet, such labels continue to be applied to teachers in the workforce as if they had conceptual or explanatory power.

Metaphors serve a foundational role in human cognition and are important in scaffolding learning by connecting the unknown to the known.[17] Yet, as commonly deployed in the retention literature, the uncritical use of metaphors may contribute to continuing conceptual imprecision in the field. For example, discussions of employment often draw upon survival metaphors—such as sinking or swimming—where being retained is analogous to remaining alive.[18] The use of the word *migration* fits into this category as well, because the term implies that in order to continue to survive, an organism must travel to a new location.[19] The analogue in teaching is that someone will not be able to remain in the teaching profession in their present place of employment, and that movement to a new school presents an opportunity to exist—and perhaps thrive—in a more hospitable environment. Some are used to evoke the movement of a person through physical space, such as the revolving door metaphor that describes teachers who are hired and then quickly leave a specific position or the profession altogether.

Economic metaphors for retention evoke systems and mechanisms, with teachers as a product for which there is turnover, as well as supply and demand. The sectors of agriculture and manufacturing give us the notion of a *reserve pool*—a term for crops or products that are set aside during a period of low demand—to refer to certified teachers who are currently not teaching.[20] Relatedly, the term *grow your own* refers to a strategy by which a school or district seeks to impact retention rates (among other goals) by hiring teachers who have been carefully cultivated from graduates of that district.[21]

TOWARD A NEW TERMINOLOGY FOR TEACHER RETENTION

The uncritical use of metaphors in the teacher retention literature may be responsible in shaping inadequate conceptions about professional trajectories. Clearly, leaving the teaching profession is not dying, and walking through a revolving door is not the same as putting one's career on hold to start a family. As tools for sensemaking, metaphors and analogies often work best when their limitations are recognized. One of those limitations may be seen in the problematic labeling of individuals from the terminology described above. When categorical descriptors like stayers, leavers, movers, and returners are used to identify groups, these labels easily become applied to individual teachers all too easily. Some researchers justify this slippage from the categorical to the individual by making extensive theoretical usage of categorizations in their work. For example, Martin Haberman divided the urban teachers he studied as either stars, failures, or quitters, while Marilyn Cochran-Smith categorized teachers by their career pathways using the terms leaders, learners, lovers, and dreamers.[22] While we have encountered many variations of these labels and identifiers in our research on this project, rarely have any served a useful purpose in better understanding the phenomenon of teacher retention.

In the empirical literature however, such labels often appear to reflect a distillation, explanation, or even a statement of value about the people in a given category while obscuring important differences. This can create imprecision in both directions. If someone is labeled a stayer, this designation may imply that staying is the same as being retained, even if there is no clarity about whether the individual has stayed in the same school or district. Such language may also carry an implication that staying is desirable, even though it might not be so. It also seems possible that someone who finds themselves labeled as a leaver could resist such a categorization, particularly if the act of leaving implies a nonexistent sense of agency or otherwise has a negative connotation. In eschewing labels like movers, leavers, and stayers, we aim to avoid the potential for imprecise and potentially condescending euphemisms. We have found modern guidance and reporting standards provided by professional research organizations with regard to bias-free, person-first language to be particularly helpful in making thoughtful decisions about using specific terminology in teacher retention research in this study.[23]

This study began using the categories developed by Richard Ingersoll and his colleagues, as noted above (e.g., movers, leavers, etc.), to describe the career trajectories of the science teachers in the state data sets we used to identify our high-retention districts for this study. Yet, the conceptual and empirical imprecision in these labels—particularly in distinguishing between mobility and attrition—posed a significant problem for us. Ultimately, our research team found such terms to be insufficient for our purposes, and we developed more appropriate and descriptive terminology in the framework to use for this study, to which we now turn.

THE PERSON-POSITION FRAMEWORK

To the district personnel who must hire a teacher to replace one who has left, little distinction is likely to be made between someone who leaves the profession and someone who takes a position in another school or district, because either case leaves a vacant position that must be filled. The key insight, as noted above, is that the characterization of the vacancy depends on the frame of reference of the observer, a distinction often overlooked in the teacher retention literature.

In our work, we have found it important to distinguish between the action of the person and the effect on the position, leading us to refer to this as a *person-position framework*. Figure 1.1 shows the four elements needed to characterize the working lives of teachers that we used: employment status, action, effect on position, and retention descriptors.[24] Of greatest value to the present study is the retention descriptor, which we note must always be accompanied by a duration.

EMPLOYMENT STATUS

We suggest that only three descriptors are necessary to describe employment status. *Active teachers* are those who are currently working as teachers in schools. If there remains a possibility that an individual could one day return to employment as a teacher, they are described as *reserve teachers*, or collectively as the *reserve pool*.[25] Individuals who are not actively teaching may be described as *attritted* if they are no longer willing or able to be employed as a teacher. In practice, it may actually be very difficult to distinguish between individuals in the reserve pool and those who have attritted, primarily because the designation hinges on a return to teaching that may or may not ever happen in the future. For this reason, it may be prudent to categorize an individual in a sample as attritted only when a standard of reasonable certainty is met (e.g., as establishment in another occupation, loss of teaching license, or death).

Action

There are six possible actions that can impact employment status: retention in position, retention with reassignment, transfer, break in service, advancement, and the aforementioned attrition. Regardless of whether years or some other

FIGURE 1.1 The person-position framework for teacher retention research

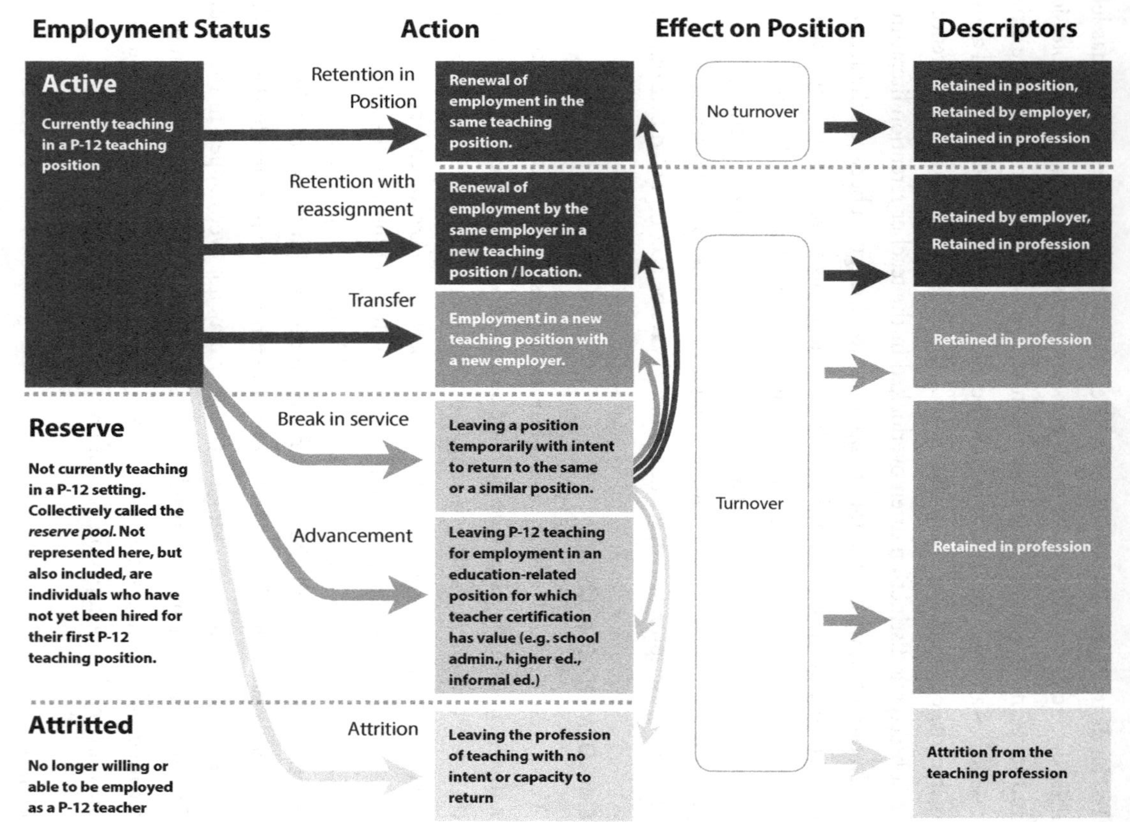

duration is used to track employment, one of these six actions must take place at the end of one interval and before the beginning of the next. All are viewed from the perspective of the employee. *Retention in position* is the renewal of employment in the same or an equivalent teaching position at the same location. *Retention with reassignment* happens with the renewal of employment by the same employer but in a new teaching location.

We categorize an action as a *transfer* when a teacher starts employment in a new teaching position with a new employer. Though the term *migration* has been sometimes used to describe a teacher's move from one employer to another, we have chosen to use the term *transfer* instead to avoid confusion with the category of teachers who cross international borders—migrating in a truer sense of the word—for employment as a teacher.[26]

Of all the terminology used to describe teacher employment, none appears to have caused more conceptual confusion in the literature than those used to describe teachers who leave a position temporarily with the intent to return to the same or a similar position. Less common in the teacher retention literature, but more widely used elsewhere, is the concept of a *break in service*, which is typically used for pension and benefit calculations by US governmental agencies. For clarity, we use this term and consider it synonymous with a leave of absence from the profession (i.e., not just a school district) in which someone is not teaching for one or more years but then returns to an active teaching position.

The literature on teacher retention has been inconsistent in its characterization of individuals who leave employment as a teacher for work in other education-related positions. For example, many teachers earn additional credentials to continue working in their current school district in a different capacity, such as a school administrator or counselor. By this framework, these teachers would not be considered retained because they would not be in a teaching position, yet it would be incorrect to say that they have attritted. Drawing from the work of teacher education scholars who frame this career trajectory as not only positive but necessary for the field of teaching, we use the term *advancement* here to indicate that teacher certification has value that may be recognized and built upon for an individual's subsequent employment.[27] Other forms of advancement may include (but are not limited to): work as an informal or museum educator, positions in higher education, education-adjacent employment (such as educational publishing or test preparation), and governmental service. Advancement does not necessarily imply a hierarchy or status within education, rather, it describes a movement to the next stage in a career trajectory from the perspective of the person to whom it applies.

EFFECT ON POSITION

In contrast to the above framework element of action, the effect on position takes the perspective of the immediate employer of the teacher. As discussed above, use of the term *teacher turnover* has been both wide and imprecise, impeding comparisons between studies in the empirical literature on teacher retention. Our recommendation is to limit the use of the term *turnover* strictly to descriptions of the position itself, rather than as a referent to groups of individuals who may in fact have widely divergent pathways in the profession. When turnover is applied solely to positions, rather than to people, it becomes apparent that turnover happens only when an individual leaves a given teaching position. A person who is reassigned to a new school within a district and leaves an administrator the task of hiring someone new for that position contributes to turnover. From this perspective, the only action on employment status that does not count as turnover is retention in position.

It is fair to argue that the general concept of turnover remains essential from a human resources perspective and ought not to be abandoned completely. Indeed, understanding how many positions need to be filled in a given school or district is often one of the highest priorities of administrators throughout the school year. Even so, there remains a conceptual volatility to the term *turnover* that emerges whenever it is modified. The phrase teacher turnover is worth highlighting as problematic because of the way it conflates the problems of a vacant position with the reasons why a given teacher is no longer in that position. Teachers do not turn over, positions do, and therefore we do not use the phrase teacher turnover for the sake of conceptual clarity. In the person-position framework, turnover only ever refers to a position.

RETENTION DESCRIPTORS

The literature is inconsistent when it comes to defining the duration of time required to be considered retained, and this seems to be an artifact of the measures and data available to researchers, rather than a theoretically informed demarcation of a certain employment interval. Some studies define retention as first-year teachers becoming second-year teachers, while many other studies frame teacher retention as extending beyond the second year.[28] In several studies, a teacher was considered "beginning" if they had fewer than six years of experience, implying a retained teacher is one who exceeds the six year mark.[29] Other longitudinal studies have marked teacher retention for even longer.[30]

Some suggest a more cautious view of retention, viewing the process of some teachers leaving and others arriving as part of an ongoing and regular cycle, and that in many circumstances, the retention of a teacher in a school or in the profession may not be desirable; others argue that attrition is inevitable because mobility between careers within and beyond education has increased over past decades.[31] There may only be subjective answers to the question of how long teachers must teach until they are considered retained.

Our view is that in order for comparisons to be made to other groups of teachers, one must be specific about where a teacher has been retained and for how long. A teacher who is *retained in position* is someone who is working for the same employer in the same (or similar enough) position at two different points of time. In describing such individuals, we would say that they have been retained-in-position for (t) years.

If research were conducted on teacher mobility within positions across a large school district, such a measure would likely be the most appropriate. Note that such a description need not be concerned with breaks in service. While reasonable objections to this definition can certainly be raised, we claim that defining retention in this manner is consistent with viewing retention from the perspective of the person being retained. Simply having one's position held during a break in service is itself a form of retention. A teacher who was reassigned to a new position or location by their employer would then be described as retained by employer for (t) years because the employer did not change. In our study, we measured retention with an even more refined metric: retained by employer for four of the first five years of teaching. This was the most beneficial unit of analysis in characterizing individual-teacher employment trajectories from our state-level data sets, because it was often difficult to distinguish between temporary and permanent teaching assignments, particularly during a new teachers' first year of employment.[32]

The descriptor *retained in profession* encompasses those retained in position and by employer, those who move to new districts, as well as teachers in the reserve pool who either hold out the possibility of returning to teaching or are advancing their careers beyond the foundation of their work as P–12 teachers.[33] For teachers in the reserve pool, this categorization features the same uncertainty that troubles the boundary between attrition and a break in service, and any analytical decision to categorize someone as retained in the profession is almost certain to contain some instances of false positives and false negatives.

With this person-position framework established to clearly describe the ways in which teachers move through their careers as teachers, we now take a look at how teacher retention has been understood and studied over the past century and take stock of what is now known about why some teachers stay in their jobs or in the profession while others do not.

CHAPTER 2

What We Know about Teacher Retention

In the early history of public education in the United States, teacher retention was primarily viewed as part of the process of sorting and selecting the quality of teachers, whereby desirable teachers would be rehired while undesirable teachers would not. In 1901, the superintendent of New Bedford Public Schools in Massachusetts put it this way: "The superintendent, by his attitude toward the selection and retention of teachers, influences the whole school system in a matter that is of supreme importance to its efficiency, and moreover, affects the well-being of every good teacher in it."[1] Teachers themselves often exerted agency over this process, which caused no small degree of consternation to school leaders, because the task of filling teacher vacancies was so onerous and time-consuming. In 1935, one frustrated superintendent—in a statement that leaves a great deal to unpack from the perspective of our current time—lamented the attrition of "pretty teachers" from Delaware schools: "No sooner do they get settled down in their jobs than they leave to get married. Something has to be done about it."[2]

In this chapter, we first look across the historical and current literature to understand the phenomenon of teacher retention and its causes, with particular attention to the data sources used to investigate both teacher attrition and retention. We follow this with a review and summary of the teacher attrition literature as a starting point to compare and contrast the way teacher attrition and retention have been framed. Next, we examine the literature on the retention of novice teachers specifically and devote particular attention to the research on mentoring and induction. We conclude this chapter with a brief look at the literature on the retention of teachers of color and teachers in high-need schools and districts.[3]

TEACHER SUPPLY AND TEACHER SURVIVAL

Research studies on teacher recruitment, supply, and retention began to appear in the 1920s and 1930s, as the need for a more systematic study of the workforce grew along with the number of public schools. Of particular concern was the oversupply and undersupply of teachers for various positions and the extent to which they received sufficient preparation as teachers.[4] Over the next few decades, research on teacher supply and demand became commonplace, and scholarly inquiry turned to the more novel question of how long teachers were remaining in their jobs and why some were leaving the profession.[5]

In 1958, Marion B. Folsom—the Secretary of Health, Education, and Welfare under President Eisenhower—gave an address to a national gathering of school administrators in which he expressed concern about how few beginning teachers planned on making teaching their "life work."[6] In this talk, he shared a finding from a recent national survey, noting, "Half the young men and women who began teaching in the United States in 1957 expected to leave the profession within five years."[7] This line became notable as an enduring trope in teacher retention discourse, even if it was not always true. It is worth noting that Folsom was reporting a projection from teachers' stated intentions rather than outcomes from actual data that tracked career trajectories.

The first actuarial approach to studying teacher retention was undertaken in the mid-1960s by Joy Whitener, who used data from ten school districts in the St. Louis area to calculate the "survival" of teachers over a ten-year period. This groundbreaking study was later described by another teacher retention researcher, Werrett W. Charters Jr:

> In an exploratory study, he obtained lists of all teachers entering employment in ten Missouri school districts during the calendar years of 1951, 1952, and 1953—a total of 937 teachers—and recorded their lengths of service at the time they terminated employment in the district, if they did, through a ten-year period. These data were converted into a survival curve, showing the proportions of the cohort still in employment at yearly intervals.[8]

From this study, Whitener found empirical backing for the claim that half of all new teachers left the classroom within their first five years. Others, like Charters and Jerome Ryscavage, reproduced his analytical techniques with different teacher populations and obtained similar results.[9] In the early 1970s, this methodology was widely adopted by other researchers, who sought to better understand "teacher survival" and its factors across various district and state contexts. Notably, few appeared to replicate Whitener's ten-year time frame for examining survival, with many opting for a more pragmatic five-year analysis instead.

A 1978 review of the teacher survival research by Jonathan H. Mark and Barry D. Anderson on this body of research cast doubt on the "half of all teachers leave in five years" statistic and showed that some five-year teacher survival rates were as high as 60 percent and as low as 35 percent. Perhaps more importantly, Mark and Anderson showed how this teacher survival rate varied over time, even in the same setting. Such findings dimmed the optimism of those who had hoped to forecast staffing budgets with greater accuracy, assuredly the driving force behind this program of research.[10]

TEACHER TURNOVER AND THE ROLE OF NATIONAL SURVEYS

The phrase "teacher survival" did not quite survive long itself, and by the 1980s the issue of teachers' continued employment was more neatly framed as teacher turnover, with similar emphasis as before on the need to replace teachers who leave a position for whatever reason. As a new round of educational reforms that focused on teacher quality and effectiveness took hold in the wake of the 1983 *A Nation at Risk* report, renewed concern over teacher vacancies and "out-of-field" teaching served to draw attention to the question of why teachers chose to leave their teaching job in a particular school or leave the field altogether.[11] Persistent questions about supply and demand receded slightly but never quite went away.[12]

However, the widespread idea that the United States was somehow falling behind in educational outcomes out of a failure to produce enough teachers was about to be refuted with a very different explanation for teacher shortages. Methodological improvements, including the use of technological tools like survey automation and computational analysis, paved the way for a new generation of research on school staffing throughout the 1980s and 1990s. In 1987, the National Center for Educational Research—part of the US Department of Education—launched the first School and Staffing Survey (SASS), a comprehensive survey that included questions about teaching experience, preparation, qualifications, teaching assignments, and course load. These questionnaires sought to capture a representative sample of educators in the fifty states and the District of Columbia and typically surveyed tens of thousands of public and private school teachers. Between 1987 and 2011, the survey was administered seven times, and a supplement—the Teacher Follow-up Survey (TFS)—was sent a year later to individual teachers who had completed the survey.[13]

When sociologist Richard Ingersoll and his colleagues first began examining the SASS and TFS survey data in the early 1990s, it became readily apparent that the supply of new teachers was actually keeping pace with population growth and should have been adequate. The more startling finding, a topic to which Ingersoll would return in publications throughout his career, was that the loss of teachers from the positions where they had been hired was a much more significant driver of teacher shortages.[14] Ingersoll's scholarship over the next few decades brought clarity to policy debates over teacher recruitment, preparation, and retention by highlighting the role of teacher attrition and its relationship to individual and organizational factors, as well as the conditions of teaching.

Reckoning with this scholarship on teacher attrition is important because of the contours it provides in mapping the landscape of the closely-related problem of teacher retention. Surely, there is some relationship between the reasons some teachers leave and the reasons others stay, but it is hardly self-evident. And so, we now turn to the task of reviewing this substantial body of work on teacher attrition to see what it can tell us about teacher retention.

WHAT WE KNOW ABOUT TEACHER ATTRITION

Richard Ingersoll and Henry May looked across data from five separate SASS reports from 1988 to 2005 for all teachers in their US sample and found that the annual attrition rate for all teachers varied between 3.5 percent and 9 percent of teachers per year.[15] A more detailed study of the TFS data suggested that only 17 percent of new teachers leave the profession within their first five years, a far lower figure than reported elsewhere.[16] Our own analysis of science teachers hired in the state of New Jersey in 2010 found that 35 percent had left the profession after five years.[17] A similar range of teacher attrition rates have been reported as well outside of the United States. For example, a sixteen-country survey by the Organization for Economic Co-operation and Development in 2021 reported annual teacher attrition rates varied widely: from 3.3 percent in Israel to 11.7 percent in Norway.[18] One of the recurring themes of this literature is that attrition rates are highly variable, context dependent, and rather difficult to predict.

In the last few decades, there have been a wealth of studies on teacher attrition and its underlying factors, and a number of reviews of this literature have been done to summarize their findings. A well-regarded meta-analysis of the quantitative attrition literature was conducted by Geoffrey D. Borman and N. Maritza Dowling and published in 2008. Subsequently, an updated and expanded meta-analysis by Tuan D. Nguyen, Lam Pham, Matthew G. Springer, and Michael Crouch was conducted and published in 2019.[19]

Each of these works serves as a suitable source for summarizing what is known about the relationship of various factors affecting teacher attrition. Although Nguyen et al. confirmed many of the claims previously reported by Borman and Dowling, they also modified or refined certain other findings through the inclusion of newer studies and using improved methodological techniques in their review. Ingersoll's work with colleagues—along with a review of recent National Center for Educational Statistics surveys by Desiree Carver-Thomas and Linda Darling-Hammond in 2019—provided additional perspective on claims of attrition correlates.[20] We note that this body of research is primarily survey-based and quantitative and that measures and retention probabilities are calculated from one year to the next.

In this section, we share the broad strokes of the findings from these studies, divided into the categories of personal correlates and school and district organization correlates. This slightly awkward phrasing is needed because these represent correlates of teacher attrition, not causal factors.[21] This is a crucial distinction because while an attribute (e.g., salary) may correlate with teacher attrition or retention, it may not be the proximate cause. Certainly, there is nothing in the data collected in these studies that we might use to claim that salary level is the only or even main reason for a teacher's decision to leave or stay. Indeed, it is much more helpful to view the correlate itself as just a clue to the way that the particular combination of factors in a particular setting operate to impact attrition and retention.

Personal Correlates

This section details the relationship of personal and categorical attributes of individuals, such as age, gender, race, ethnicity, measures of career satisfaction, as well as other teacher attributes that may reasonably be assigned to an actual individual rather than their context. One of the clearest findings is also the most well-known: many young teachers leave their school (though perhaps not the profession) within a few years of starting to teach. Experienced teachers are less likely to leave than novice teachers, and older teachers are slightly less likely to leave than younger teachers.[22] Put another way, it is much more likely that a tenth-year teacher will return for their eleventh year than a first-year teacher will return for their second.

Studies from the 2000s and earlier typically found a relationship between gender and attrition, in that women were more likely to leave than men. However, the analysis by Nguyen et al., which included thirty-seven recent studies that examined this relationship, found no difference between male and female teachers in their likelihood to leave. Whether or not this is a true shift in the attrition pattern—perhaps driven by a range of societal and policy factors—is unknown.

Race and ethnicity were often conflated in studies undertaken with data gathered prior to 2013 and so are reported together here.[23] There was little evidence that the attrition rates for Black teachers were any different from White teachers in the meta-analysis. Non-White minority teachers were slightly less likely to leave than White teachers; however, Hispanic teachers had a far lower attrition rate than White teachers (over 50 percent). The commonly held notion that non-White teachers have a higher rate of attrition was not borne out by the available evidence.[24] It is worth remembering that, even if the rates of attrition are similar for different racial groups—such as in a comparison between teachers who identify as White and those who identify as Black—this leaves little indication concerning the *reasons* for that attrition, which may be quite different for each group. Notably, the likelihood of attrition was lower in schools with a more racially diverse staff.[25]

In terms of teacher qualifications, there was no statistical difference in the Nguyen et al. meta-analysis between the attrition rates of teachers with undergraduate degrees and those with graduate degrees. However, teachers with higher academic achievement—as measured by standardized test scores or grade point average—were slightly more likely to leave. Teachers with a standard certification, as compared with those who were provisionally certified or not certified at all, were half as likely to leave. Notably, teachers of specialized subjects like science, math, or special education were also identified as slightly more likely to leave.

Full-time teachers were significantly less likely to leave in comparison to part-time teachers. And perhaps unsurprisingly, teachers who indicated satisfaction with teaching as a career were less likely to leave. An earlier review of the attrition research by Cassandra M. Guarino, Lucrecia Santibanez, and Glenn A. Daley investigating teacher mobility patterns noted that teachers tended to move toward higher salaries, improved working conditions, and greater opportunities for intrinsic rewards. These could be other teaching positions, nonteaching jobs in education, or even activities outside of a teaching career.[26]

School and District Organization Correlates

It has long been recognized that the conditions and experiences of teachers in their school settings, often situated in the larger context of a district-wide organization, impact teacher decisions to stay or leave. Such characteristics include grade-level assignments, locale classification (e.g., urban, rural, etc.), student demographics, available resources, salary, school size and facilities, school type (e.g., traditional, charter, vocational, etc.), and the presence and nature of professional development programs, including those for the support of new teachers. It also includes less tangible conditions, such as the severity of discipline problems in the school, perceptions of administrative strength, the extent to which teachers collaborate with one another, and the demographic congruence between teachers, students, and administrators. Certainly, many correlations between school-level characteristics and attrition have been found, while other commonly held assumptions or conventional wisdom about attrition in certain settings are not supported by the available evidence.

For example, middle and secondary school teachers have been found to leave at higher rates compared with elementary teachers, and charter school teachers leave at approximately twice the rate of their noncharter-public-school counterparts. However, school size does not appear to correlate with attrition, and somewhat surprisingly, neither does class size or the presence of in-class support. While attrition did not appear to be impacted by locale, rural teachers were slightly more likely to switch schools than urban teachers.

As might be expected, teachers were less likely to leave schools when the working environment was more favorable. Nguyen et al. note that teachers were slightly more likely to leave when there were fewer reported disciplinary issues, less violence, and less school problems overall. Teachers were also less likely to leave when schools had higher student achievement, better facilities, stronger administrative support, and new-teacher programs for mentoring and induction, which we discuss in greater detail in the section on retention below. Increased measures of teacher relationship and collaboration, which we note are often associated with support for new teachers, are associated with lower teacher attrition.[27] Teacher evaluation and assessment itself is not associated with increased attrition. Teachers in settings with union membership were also found to be slightly less likely to leave.

In our experience, the question of the relationship between the student population and teacher attrition is perhaps one of the most commonly discussed factors.[28] Drawing on evidence from the SASS, Carver-Thomas and Darling-Hammond report on a finding that appears well-documented:

> Consistent with previous research, we found that, controlling for school size and student poverty rates, those teaching in schools with 25% or more students of color were more likely to move or leave teaching than teachers in schools with fewer students of color, all else being equal.[29]

And yet, there are clear differences in the interpretation of available evidence. In their meta-analysis, Nguyen et al. write:

> In terms of the characteristics of the students in the schools, we observe the relationships between percent Black or percent Hispanic students and teacher attrition are not significant. However, the odds of teacher attrition for a percent increase in minority students at the school level are statistically significant, but only with a five percent reduction. In terms of percent free or reduced priced lunch (FRPL), percent individualized education plan (IEP), and schools with the majority of students classified as low socioeconomic status, the results are statistically insignificant. In short, there is little evidence that these factors greatly influence teacher attrition.[30]

We note that the mixed messages sent by these two reports are not unusual in educational research. As might be expected, most research on this topic urges further study—but for us, it is sufficient to note that these findings disrupt simplistic narratives about why certain teachers leave certain schools.

There has been increasing interest in the role of demographic congruence in teacher attrition (i.e., teachers and principals identifying similarly by race/

ethnicity), but the evidence is so far inconclusive and appears to be highly contingent on the school context, at least with respect to the quantitative data in the attrition literature.[31] However, we will return to this notion of demographic congruence in discussions of retention factors, particularly for teachers of color, later in the book.

Looking across eighteen different studies, Nguyen et al. found that an increase in salary decreased the likelihood of attrition. Though statistically significant, the effect size was small. It is worth remembering that the determinants of salary typically include degree and experience and may be set by state policy, local supplements, or negotiated contracts with set salary guides. Opportunities for extra assignments, bonuses, or merit pay may vary significantly across settings.[32]

THE ATTRITION LITERATURE VS. THE RETENTION LITERATURE

These studies on teacher attrition have sought to provide clear data on how many people actually leave teaching as well as to characterize the reasons why people leave a job or the profession altogether. One aim of this research literature is to provide information upon which policymakers and education leaders might act in order to reduce unwanted teacher attrition. For example, when teachers' attrition is found to correlate with lower salaries, one possible action is to raise salaries in order to make teachers less likely to leave.[33] However, there are two issues with this reasoning. First is that raising salaries is no easy task, and the necessary levers of change may simply not be available to policymakers and educational leaders for such action. Second is that the adjustment of any single factor may not, in fact, be sufficient to change an employment outcome. For example, raising the salary of a teacher who works in a school where they perceive the school environment to be problematic may not sway one's decision to leave.

Nevertheless, this body of attrition research has had an impact. By focusing attention on issues such as school climate, teacher autonomy, and the role of standardized testing on teacher attrition, this body of research has provided the field of education with empirical support for improvements in the work lives of teachers and likely in student outcomes as well.[34] This research also has brought attention to important distinctions in teacher attrition across different categorical groups and their intersections, such as teachers of color, science teachers, and teachers in fast-track preparation programs.

Moreover, a new generation of literature on teacher attrition has emerged over the past two decades, as more qualitative approaches have enriched the inquiry into teachers' career decisions by using ethnographic methods and narrative data sources. A great deal of this work has examined teachers of color and teachers in urban, underfunded, or high-need schools. The scholarship of researchers like Lynette Mawhinney, Carol Rinke, and Andrew Brantlinger has sought to elevate the stories of teachers who made the choice to leave. This work has highlighted the nature of teaching as an exploratory career and offered nuanced understandings of the ways in which racism and marginalization continue to impact teachers' career trajectories.[35] Similarly, scholars like Rita Kohli, Travis Bristol, and others have documented the ongoing impact of racial hostility—and microaggressions in particular—on the decisions of teachers of color to leave the classroom.[36] Doris Santoro has documented the demoralization of teachers more generally, highlighting the divergence between daily experiences and motivations for selecting teaching as a career in the first place.[37] Much of this research is qualitative in nature and centers the experiences and perspectives of teachers.[38]

It is fair to state that the qualitative literature on teacher attrition, by its very nature, skews toward the pathological; nearly all are stories about problems.[39] For example, Lisa Scherff quotes one English teacher named Toni who left teaching early in her second year, both because of the overwhelming demands of her job and feelings of professional isolation:

> I just want to cry out, "Why are you driving us away!?" Why have you left us alone, fending for ourselves among a sea of IEPs, screaming students, angry parents, micromanaging superiors, and unfeeling co-workers? Here we are, stripped of our sense of purpose. Our plans trampled. I remember sitting on my husband's lap practically yelling about all the great plans I had. This year was going to be great! I knew my stuff, I had files, I had plans, I had experience. I could handle it! And if it didn't work out, we would find a new job for me the next year. Instead, I'm looking for a job now. [40]

The anguish in the above quote may be familiar to those who have worked with novice teachers who are considering leaving. Although quantitative data and stories about teacher attrition help to shape an understanding of why teachers leave, they often fall short in providing actionable guidance that school leaders and policymakers could use—paraphrasing Kelchtermans—to keep from losing good teachers for the wrong reasons.[41] In other words, just understanding the reasons that teachers leave may not be enough to help them stay.

Conversely, the retention literature—to which we now turn—can be characterized as more actionable and generative of solutions. As noted in chapter 1, retention and attrition are not quite reciprocal categories, even if they have been treated as complementary in public discourse. We also wish to emphasize that a focus on retention does not mean ignoring the pathological. Rather, following the medical metaphor, it is more about maintaining the health of an individual in a particular environment. In the following section, we finally turn to this empirical literature to see what it tells us about what matters for teacher retention.

Retention Factors

Much like we saw with the studies on attrition, the retention literature offers a distinction between attributes of the teacher and those of the school and organization in categorizing the reasons why teachers stay. Yet, there is also an inclusion of factors related to the community in which the school is located, which was less apparent in the scholarship on attrition. It is worth remembering—particularly in the search for commonalities, factors, and correlates in teacher retention data—that the intersection of teachers' lives and their institutional contexts are complex, and the decisions teachers make to stay or go are deeply personal.[42] And yet, although we may not be able to whittle them down to a handful of factors applicable to all teachers, there are a number of clear findings in the retention literature that are relevant to the present study.

The literature on teacher retention is wide-ranging and overlaps significantly with the attrition literature described in the previous section. Certainly, many retention studies simply identified correlates for retention that are the complement of corresponding attrition studies, such as the finding that teachers who went through teacher preparation programs with a field experience (e.g., student teaching) or other specific pedagogical components tended to be retained at a higher rate than those who did not.[43] Some of these personal characteristics that correlate to retention are possible to nurture, such as a sense of equity, social justice, or inquisitiveness about one's own teaching.[44] Others point toward professional pathways to be followed in the future, such as teachers who have ambitions to become school leaders.[45]

The presence of a satisfactory school culture, adequate physical facility, and professional working environment each appears to be important to teacher retention, as does having a supportive administration.[46] Teachers have consistently reported that school and district factors positively influence their retention. For example, the sufficiency of salary, benefits, and supplemental pay are all cited as reasons for remaining in teaching.[47] A number of studies also reported the positive effect of professional development opportunities on retention.[48] One study noted that secondary teachers with fewer classes for which to prepare (i.e., teacher who teaches one class of ninth-grade English and four classes of tenth-grade English would have two "preps") were more likely to be retained.[49]

As we will discuss in greater detail in the next chapter, the degree to which a teacher's values and goals align with their school and district, known as *person-organization fit*, also correlates with their retention.[50] This person-organization fit is often seen to be higher in *hometown teachers*, those who are hired to work at—or in proximity to—the schools they attended.[51] Research confirms the conventional wisdom that such hometown teachers are retained at significantly higher rates in some settings, though this is certainly likely to differ across contexts.[52] Studies also show that retention is greater for teachers with higher measures of a sense of self-efficacy, autonomy, and engagement in meaningful work.[53]

The retention research is clear and consistent on the connection between the presence of collegial and collaborative relationships in the workplace and the choice to remain in a teaching position.[54] Similarly, connections within networks internal to a school or externally across a district or local community appear to positively influence teacher retention as well by fostering social relationships and reducing social isolation, a factor commonly linked to attrition.[55] Such community-network influence on retention may include romantic relationships as well.[56]

The impact of mentoring and teacher induction programs run by schools and districts for novice teachers has been extensively studied for the past two decades. Much of this research has sought to examine such programs for evidence of their effect on teacher practice, teaching effectiveness, job satisfaction, and of course, teacher attrition.[57] However, studies focusing specifically on the impact of mentoring and induction on novice-teacher retention have been decidedly mixed.[58]

It is worth noting that many published studies about both attrition and retention conclude with a call for more targeted support of newly hired teachers, and yet, the goals of such support are rarely made explicit. Our own view is that, if there is any consensus in the literature about mentoring and induction, it is that their structure, activities, and overall operation appears highly dependent on both individual teachers and their teaching contexts. For example, researchers like Julie Luft and her colleagues have engaged in an ongoing program of research on the specific components of mentoring and induction for newly hired secondary science teachers, and it may be the case that such fine-grained analysis will ultimately be necessary across grade levels, subject areas, and geographic regions to more fully understand the relationship between mentoring, induction, and teachers' career trajectories.[59] We will return to this question after examining mentoring and induction in the cases of this project.

Retention Factors for Teachers of Color

There is a substantial body of research that documents the markedly different experiences teachers of color have in US schools, as compared with their White counterparts. These experiences, which range from encounters with microaggressions to the effects of institutional and systemic racism, have been reported by teachers of color across the professional continuum, including during teacher preparation.[60] Given broader social aims of ensuring demographic parity between student and teacher populations, there has been a great deal of research specifically on recruiting, preparing, and retaining teachers of color in recent years.[61]

The findings from this program of research both reinforce and contradict what we know about patterns in teacher retention across the population of US teachers. For example, the research suggests that the retention effects of ties to local communities are even stronger for teachers of color and homegrown teachers in particular.[62] Teacher autonomy, collaboration, and collective decision-making by teachers are also associated with higher rates of retention.[63] The influence of the student population is also more pronounced for teachers of color. For example, in a decade-long study of teacher retention in North Carolina, researcher Min Sun noted that teachers who were identified as Black were more likely to stay in schools that served a larger proportion of Black students.[64] Additionally, if a Black teacher did choose to leave one school for another, they were more likely to move to a school that served a higher proportion of Black students.

And yet, the factors we described earlier with respect to retention may be experienced quite differently by teachers of color than their White counterparts.[65]

For example, Travis Bristol describes a group of teachers of color he terms *loners*, whose retention decisions are more influenced by the better working conditions of their schools, despite having negative interactions with colleagues.[66] Ain Grooms, Duhita Mahatmya, and Eboneé Johnson examined the retention of teachers of color in Iowa and found that the racialization of a school climate could influence the retention of teachers of color both positively and negatively, by either increasing or decreasing teachers' sense of self-efficacy and race-based stress.[67]

Given the diversity of the population categorized under the umbrella of the term *teachers of color*, any generalization about these findings warrants caution. However, the history of the struggle for nonmajority groups to obtain education in the United States is well-documented, and therefore, it is not unreasonable to suggest that there are categorical differences in the ways that different groups conceptualize the role of a teacher and the aims of education.[68]

Retention Factors for High-Need Schools

The term *high-need school* has been used by the federal government since 1965 to identify settings where recipients of various federal loans and grants may teach to fulfill their obligations. Though the precise definition changed slightly over time, a school is often considered high-need if more than 20 percent of its students come from low-income families and there are persistent teacher vacancies. The conditions within a school or district may fluctuate of course, and so it is possible that a school or district's high-need designation may change from one year to the next, but it is not an exaggeration to say that teacher retention is always a clear concern in such schools.

The research on retention factors in high-need schools mirrors that of teachers of color in many ways. Satisfactory working conditions, collegial relationships, professional autonomy, and self-efficacy (as it relates to students) have all been shown to encourage teacher retention in high-need schools.[69]

SUMMARY OF THE RESEARCH ON TEACHER ATTRITION AND RETENTION

Over the past century, the way school administrators, education researchers, the general public, and teachers themselves think about teacher attrition and retention has changed a great deal. Like many questions investigated by the educational research community, the task of better understanding teacher retention has been aided by systematic approaches to investigation, the improvement of data sources, new technologies, and consideration of the issue from multiple perspectives. One thing that has not changed is the need for principals to fill vacancies with qualified teachers before the start of every school year, a challenge that can be exacerbated by teacher attrition or eased by teacher retention.

We know that teachers tend to be retained when working conditions are good, when they feel they have autonomy over their classroom and agency over the path of their professional career. We know that good relationships with colleagues and students matter, as does support from administration, opportunities to collaborate, and a shared sense of the aims of teaching. We know that mentoring and induction matter in specific contexts, but beyond that, it is difficult to say exactly how such efforts impact retention. We know that the social relationships within a school and in the surrounding community matter a great deal, and that teachers who return to the places where they themselves were students are more likely to stay. We know that all of these things matter even more for teachers of color and for teachers in high-need schools. And finally, we know that teachers of color are more likely to stay when the racial climate inside of a school offers a layer of protection from the ongoing harms of racism.

Above all, we know that efforts to predict and control retention have been stymied by the sheer unpredictability and complexity of the task, and that existing frameworks for understanding teacher retention have had limited utility. This complexity requires thinking about teacher retention in new ways, a task we take up in the next chapter.

CHAPTER 3

Our Research Framing

From Job Satisfaction to Teacher Embeddedness

In early 1995, at what is now the Foster School of Business at the University of Washington, Tom Lee and Terry Mitchell met for their weekly meeting, a practice they had started a few years earlier, which would continue for many more. The main topic of discussion, as always, was their shared interest in researching employee turnover. Mitchell and Lee were regularly joined by other faculty, and even students, who were interested in being part of these ongoing conversations. Miriam Erez, a visiting scholar, had recently started attending, as had a doctoral student named Brooks Holtom. At this particular meeting, the group had been reading and discussing articles about involuntary turnover, selected in part because of their growing dissatisfaction with the theoretical model they had been developing. In a 2014 account of the meeting, Tom Lee described what happened next:

> Lee noted that conversations focused almost exclusively on the question, why do people leave? He asked whether it might be more interesting and useful to instead consider, why do people stay? Almost instantly, Mitchell commented that he had been at Washington since 1969, and Lee responded that he had been at Washington since 1983. In jest, Mitchell then said that they knew more about staying than leaving. Almost in the same breath, Mitchell added that he stayed at Foster because of fit or comfort with the University of Washington and

> city of Seattle, his many links to doctoral students and the community (e.g., his accumulating seniority with Seattle Seahawk season tickets), and the sacrifices that leaving entailed (e.g., forgoing the accumulated Washington- and Foster-specific human and social capital; hardships to his many doctoral students). At that moment, the construct of what was later to be known as *job embeddedness* was born.[1]

The resulting paper from this working group was titled: "Why People Stay: Using Job Embeddedness to Predict Voluntary Turnover," and when published in 2001, it heralded the beginning of a new program of research and a long overdue reconfiguring of existing paradigms about employee turnover.[2] Over the next two decades, as the colleagues from the initial weekly group extended and deepened their original work, the theory of job embeddedness became one of the most widely used theories in the field of organizational behavior and a mainstay of graduate courses and programs of research around the world.[3]

The insights from the theory of job embeddedness have gradually been incorporated into research on teacher retention over the past two decades. In this chapter, we begin with a review of the theory of job embeddedness as an alternative to the explanations of attrition and retention based on notions of job satisfaction. We then share our research team's small but necessary iteration of this theory, which we differentiated by terming it *teacher embeddedness*, as a framework for thinking about and researching teacher retention specifically.

DISSATISFACTION WITH JOB SATISFACTION

In the 1970s, research convincingly showed that job satisfaction played a real, yet uncertain, role in employee turnover. In a now classic 1977 paper, William H. Mobley published a flowchart model of the employee decision process that led to an ultimate decision to quit or stay.[4] One of the key elements of this linear and rational model of decision-making was the employee's search for alternatives as a consequence of job dissatisfaction. Mobley's paper, which contained suggestions for the ways such a model could be tested and improved over time, would come to set the field's research agenda for the next two decades.

One of the mysteries later investigated by the University of Washington group in the early 1990s concerned the ways in which employee decisions to leave a job unfolded over time, hence the name given to their framework—the *unfolding* model of voluntary turnover—which was a clear descendent of Mobley's work.[5] Their model more closely resembled a decision tree, with two main pathways leading to possible voluntary turnover.[6]

The first pathway dealt with the downstream consequences of a "shock," which they defined as a jarring event that initiated a series of decisions and actions. The second pathway concerned the accumulation of dissatisfaction over time, with either path initiating the process of leaving. In their detailed analyses, the group numbered and dissected the five different pathways for leaving. The pathways in which the employee ultimately stayed were left unlabeled. Lee and Mitchell's group produced a number of papers based on empirical tests of their model from employee survey data, and with each study made, ongoing refinements to increase its predictive power.[7]

One problem however, was that while the model certainly appeared to have some degree of predictive power, it was impractical for real-world use and offered little guidance to managers, policymakers, and others who might want to forecast employee turnover. There was also the inconvenient finding that some employees seemed more resistant to shocks than others, something the model was unable to explain. Sometimes employees who indicated high levels of job satisfaction were unable to overcome shocks and ultimately chose to leave. Similarly, high job dissatisfaction did not always begin the cascade of actions, like searching for a new position or accepting an available alternative position, that the model implied would occur. Under their emerging theory of job embeddedness, however, these anomalous outcomes would become explainable.[8] So it is to the details of that theory we now turn.

JOB EMBEDDEDNESS

As noted previously, the defining feature of the theory of job embeddedness is an emphasis on attending to why people stay in a job rather than on why they leave. Instead of tracing deliberations through a cascade of decision forks, a focus on embeddedness shifts attention to the strength of the individual strands of the social web that connect the various parts of a person's life.[9] The more connections in one's metaphorical web, the more embedded, or "stuck," that individual becomes. Mitchell, Holtom, Lee, and their colleague argued that an individual's job embeddedness grows over time as they make more connections to their job and the broader community, and therefore, the longer one remains at a job, the harder it becomes to leave.[10] From this perspective, retention is a function of embeddedness. If shocks occur, embeddedness determines how much an individual will be buffered to its effects. If job dissatisfaction rises, the degree of an employee's embeddedness may influence a decision to stay or leave.

The building blocks of job embeddedness are the concepts of *links, fit,* and *sacrifice*, each operating in two distinct domains: the *organization* and the *community*. These were described succinctly in the 2001 paper:

> The critical aspects of job embeddedness are (1) the extent to which people have links to other people or activities, (2) the extent to which their jobs and communities are similar to or fit with the other aspects in their life spaces, and (3) the ease with which links can be broken—what they would give up if they left, especially if they had to physically move to other cities or homes. We labeled these three dimensions "links," "fit," and "sacrifice," and they are important both on and off the job. This three-by-two matrix suggests six dimensions: links, fit, and sacrifice associated with an individual's organization and with his or her community.[11]

Links are a shorthand for the formal and informal relationships that an individual has within an organization or larger community. Many of an individual's links within an organization can be described as coworkers or colleagues, but links can also be formed with individuals or activities throughout an organization. Outside of work, links can also include family, religious affiliations, and social connections within the community. Studies using the job embeddedness framework have observed similarities between links and the concept of *ties*, as used in social network analysis.[12]

Fit within an organization can be most simply described as the perception of how an employee's goals, values, and worldviews align with that of their place of employment. The basic idea is that the more a person feels connected to their job due to their personal values, the more likely they will remain in their current position. The concept of person-organization fit predates the theory of job embeddedness and is itself a foundational concept in organizational theory.[13] Measuring person-organization fit has long been of interest within the area of human resources, especially in making employee hiring decisions. As a component of job embeddedness, fit also refers to how comfortable and compatible an individual feels within the broader community, encompassing emotional attachments and aspirational commitments both inside and outside of work environments.[14] The fit of an individual with respect to their community takes into consideration many factors, which may include job location, cost of living, the cultural environment, local geography, and even climate. Combined, these different strands of fit serve to weave the webbing that embeds an individual within an organization and community.

The third factor of the framework is sacrifice. Though characterized in the original paper as the breaking of links, job embeddedness research later emphasized this component as the perceived costs of organizational departure.[15] In Mitchell's hypothetical leaving of Seattle, a departure from his university to go elsewhere would entail a great deal of both tangible and intangible losses. Indeed, the job embeddedness literature typically describes sacrifice in terms of the material or psychological cost of loss. Within the workplace, such a potential loss could be an office with a view, medical benefits, a pension plan, or the promise of advancement. In the community, a decision to leave could cost a short commute, a vibrant neighborhood, childcare-providing relatives, or a weekend softball league. We note here that this inclusion of sacrifice in the theory of job embeddedness serves as a remnant of Mobley's flowchart and Lee and Mitchell's unfolding decision tree, requiring the creation of—and deliberation about—a hypothetical scenario in which employees imagine themselves leaving.

Methodologically, employee retention studies have measured job embeddedness through employment surveys and quantitative analysis. Such surveys have been adapted for various contexts and purposes and used in a wide variety of professions, including education.[16] Although many of these studies have used job embeddedness as a predictor of turnover, some have used job embeddedness as a framework for studying teacher retention, employing the survey methodologies, tools, and analytical techniques that have become commonplace in the field.[17]

TOWARD A THEORY OF TEACHER EMBEDDEDNESS

It is always a good question to ask what work a theoretical framework does in a given research study. What new insights does it provide? What new explanations does it offer? In educational research, as elsewhere, a good theoretical framework helps researchers organize observations and other data into coherent interpretations and credible predictions. The usefulness of a theoretical framework grows when the explanations it provides are both plausible and consistent with other findings as well as when its predictions are confirmed over time.

In our own study, job embeddedness was an obvious theoretical framework to use for thinking about and better understanding the reasons teachers stayed. Yet, the framework had some shortcomings as we thought about answering our research questions. First, surveys designed for quantitative analysis typically constrain participants' communication to a selection of set responses, and we were committed to elevating the voices of educators through the richness of qualitative methods. Second, as educators with experience across a wide variety of school settings, we recognized the importance of context in making meaning from findings. Job embeddedness research is often limited to single organizations or industries and typically strips away the kind of context and nuance that we knew would be critical for interpreting our qualitative data about teacher retention. Perhaps most importantly, in our aim to make sure that good teachers did not feel compelled to leave their job for the wrong reasons, it was important to us that our study produced actionable and pragmatic advice for how to support them. For us, this meant recentering the focus of job embeddedness on the needs of employees—namely, teachers—rather than that of their employers.

The job embeddedness components of links and fit were quite adaptable to the work we wanted to do. Both are defined in a positive sense with existing and identifiable indicators, and we could transform these concepts rather naturally into interview questions. However, qualitatively researching sacrifice posed problems, because asking questions about sacrifice required introducing the idea of leaving to the conversation. We recognized early on that the creation of a conditional negative in such questions such questions activated emotions and was likely to shift the discussion away from retention.[18] However, reframing our questions in terms of *assets*—defined as tangible and intangible things that have value—permitted us to probe for the positive and identifiable indicators we sought. Being forced to give up assets is a reasonable definition of sacrifice, and we saw this minor shift in framing as a reasonable fine-tuning of the job embeddedness theory for our purposes. Finally, we needed to account for those teachers who stayed in the profession of teaching even if they did not remain in a particular job. We gave this adjusted and now qualitative-research-friendly framework the name of *teacher embeddedness* in order to avoid confusion with

TABLE 3.1 The teacher embeddedness framework

Component	*Domain: Organization*	*Domain: Profession*	*Domain: Community*
Fit	The comfort and compatibility of an individual with respect to the local educational context. This includes the degree to which the aspirations, career goals, values, culture, and worldview of the teacher are aligned with the environment of the school or district in which an individual works.	The comfort and compatibility of an individual with respect to the local educational context. This includes the degree to which the aspirations, career goals, values, culture, and worldview of the teacher are aligned with those of the teaching profession in local, national, or even global contexts.	The comfort and compatibility of an individual with respect to the community. This includes the degree to which the aspirations, career goals, values, culture, and worldview of the teacher are aligned with the environment of the local community in which an individual works.
Links	Personal relationships and connections made with colleagues, students, and others within the local educational context.	Personal relationships and connections made with educators in other settings, professional associations, universities, and others within the teaching profession.	Personal relationships and connections made with individuals and groups within the community, which may include family, consumer, religious, and other social affiliations.
Assets	The sum of the tangible and intangible benefits from a job to an individual in terms of perceived material and psychological value. Such assets may include salary, health benefits, workplace space, resources and materials, perquisites, established patterns of working, and support for professional growth.	The sum of the tangible and intangible benefits from a job to an individual in terms of perceived material and psychological value. Such assets may include certifications, state pensions and benefits, products of professional collaborations (e.g. published materials), and status.	The sum of the tangible and intangible benefits from a community to an individual in terms of perceived material and psychological value. Such assets may include housing, sense of place, established patterns of living, personal safety, favorable commutes to work, and other aspects of one's quality of life influenced by the community.

Note: This table has been adapted from the work of Holtom, Terence R. Mitchell, and Thomas W. Lee. "Increasing Human and Social Capital by Applying Job Embeddedness Theory." *Organizational dynamics* 35, no. 4 (2006): 316–31. https://doi.org/10.1016/j.orgdyn.2006.08.007.

the methods, tools, and analytical techniques of the broader job embeddedness research community. Our final theoretical framework—with the domain of the profession added—is shown in table 3.1, with examples of embeddedness shown in figure 3.1. As we designed and carried out our study, this framework of teacher embeddedness shaped what we looked for, what we learned, and how we learned it.

In the next four chapters, we share the products of our investigation. Each begins with an overview of the state-policy context followed by a brief description of the district. We then provide a detailed review of each of the factors behind teacher retention in the district revealed by our study. Each chapter concludes with a look at mentoring and induction programs that were designed to support and retain newly hired teachers in the district.

FIGURE 3.1 Examples of Teacher Embeddedness

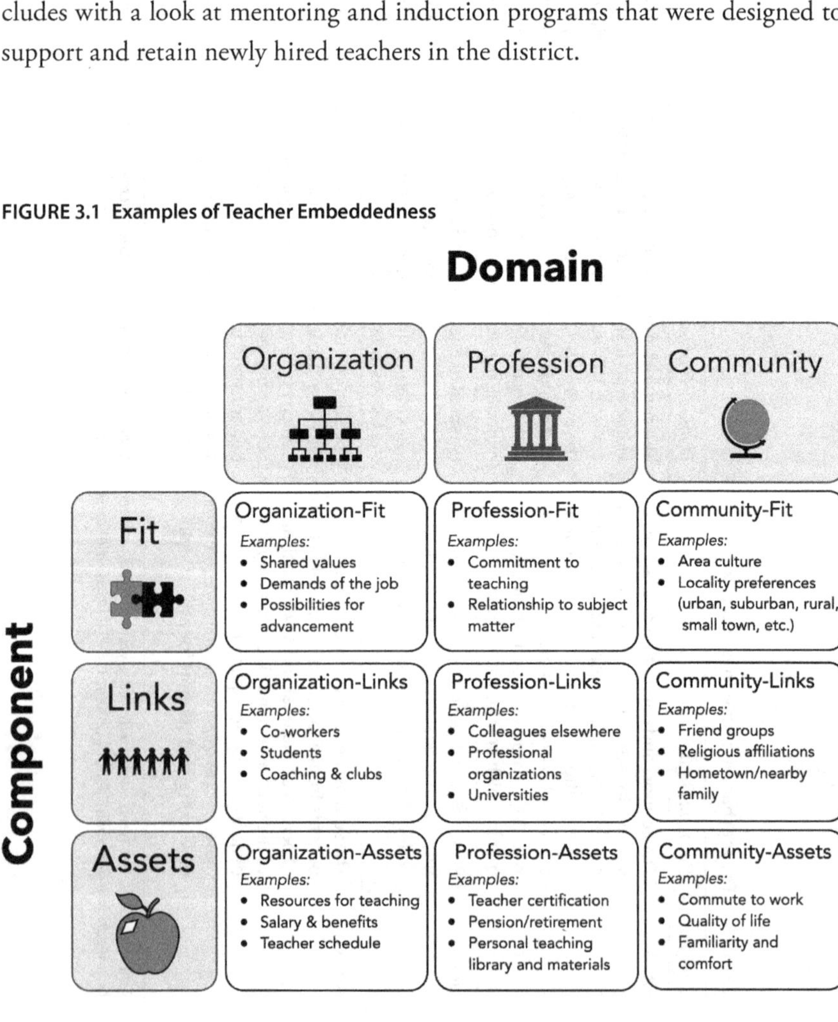

CHAPTER 4

Where Teachers of Color Stay and Flourish

The Case of Mulberry School District

The Mulberry School District in New Jersey, which serves approximately 10,000 students and employs almost 800 teachers, possessed several characteristics that influenced its selection for this study. Most importantly, it maintained one of the highest five-year retention rates among novice teachers that we studied. In a state where approximately 85 percent of teachers identify as White, Mulberry was somewhat unique in that the vast majority of teachers and administrators working there identified as Black or African American. When we examined the retention of novice science teachers of color, no other district in New Jersey came close. Given the attention to the issue of retaining teachers of color both statewide and nationally, our research team saw an opportunity to learn from the Mulberry School District about the factors driving the district's notable high teacher retention rate for teachers of color, even as we explored the reasons for retention across the district generally.

As this chapter will show, what we came to call the *culturally protected environment* of the Mulberry School District played a key role in both the recruitment and retention of teachers of color. Like other districts in this study, Mulberry teachers also cited their colleagues as a primary reason for continuing to teach in the district. Other reasons shared by teachers included the belief that their compensation was fair and locally competitive, their opportunities for

FIGURE 4.1 Mulberry School District Fact Sheet

Mulberry School District, New Jersey

About the community

Community total population:	~65,000
Total households:	~24,000
Median household income:	~$48,000
Households with broadband Internet:	~80%
Housing structure type	
House:	~20%
Apartments/other:	~20%

NCES Locale type

Suburban – Large: Territory outside a principal city and inside an urbanized area with population of 250,000 or more.

About the district

Total Students:	~9,000
Classroom Teachers (FTE):	~700
Student/Teacher Ratio:	13:1
Per pupil spending (2018):	~$29,000
Grades served:	preK–12
Total Schools:	~20
Total Certified Science Teachers:	~30
Avg. HS Science Department Size:	~10
Starting salary 2007–08:	~$48,000
Starting salary 2017–18:	~$54,000

Mulberry School District Demographics

Race/ethnicity	Teachers	Students	Admins.
White	20%	<1%	0%
Hispanic	10%	10%	0%
Black	60%	90%	90%
Asian	10%	<1%	10%
Other	<1%	<1%	0%

Category	Students
Economically Disadvantaged Students	80%
Students with Disabilities	20%
English Learners	10%

Note: All school and district names in this report have been changed to pseudonyms to protect the confidentiality of study participants. The "Mulberry" School District is a K–12 public school district, serving a single municipality. Demographic data and dollar figures have been rounded in order to preserve district anonymity. All data is from the 2017–2018 academic year.

Sources: U.S. Census Bureau: https://www.census.gov/acs/www/data/data-tables-and-tools/data-profiles/2017/
U.S. Department of Education, National Center for Educational Statistics, Common Core of Data: https://nces.ed.gov/ccd/

professional growth, and the degree of professional autonomy granted to them in their work.

NEW JERSEY TEACHER POLICY BACKGROUND

The modern history of teacher policy in New Jersey began in 1875, with an amendment to the state constitution that read, "The Legislature shall provide for the maintenance and support of a thorough and efficient system of free public schools for the instruction of all children in the state between the ages of five and eighteen years."[1] Over the next century and a half, the phrase "thorough and efficient" would serve as the legal cudgel for racial integration in the schools, gender equity in educational outcomes, school finance reform that led to the creation of a state income tax in 1971, and a series of lawsuits (collectively known as *Abbott v. Burke*) and State Supreme Court judgements concerning the adequacy of state funding for public education.[2] For the last fifty years, the issues of ensuring teacher quality and educational equity have been at the forefront of discussions about the state's teacher policy.

All teachers in New Jersey are required to have at least a bachelor's degree and the equivalent of a major or minor in the content area in which they teach. The state has two pathways to initial teacher certification, a *traditional* and an *alternate route certification*. Traditional certification is characterized by learning to teach in a program with a field-based internship, enrollment in an approved university-based teacher education program, and the completion of a full-time supervised field experience in a classroom lasting at least one semester. In contrast, alternate route certification programs allow teachers to complete their requirements for certification as paid teachers of record in a classroom. In 1984, when the alternate-route-certification program was established in New Jersey, it operated primarily through the state's extensive community college system, but over time it expanded to four-year institutions and some private providers as well. Approximately one third of all NJ teachers become certified through an alternate route program.[3]

Like most other states, New Jersey requires all new teachers to pass professional and subject matter tests of knowledge to obtain licensure and requires teachers to complete a state-approved educator preparation program. Although requirements for teacher licensure in New Jersey were already some of the strictest in the nation, a new set of policy reforms in 2015 mandated increased time in field experiences, additional proficiency tests, coursework on students with disabilities, and increased minimum-grade-point requirements.

New Jersey's professional teaching labor force has historically enjoyed high rates of union membership—with active local chapters of the American Federation of Teachers (AFT) and the New Jersey Education Association (NJEA)—and educators are among the most unionized profession in the state.[4] These professional organizations have played an important role in shaping educational policy in the state through their legislative outreach efforts.

New Jersey's mentoring requirements for new teachers have changed little since they were enacted in 1984 with the establishment of the Provisional Teacher Program (PTP), designed to increase teacher retention by assisting novice teachers during their first years of teaching. Teachers in both alternate route and traditional pathways are required to receive thirty weeks of mentoring by a mentor teacher, with payment made directly to mentors through funds deducted from the novice teacher's salary, though school districts may elect to cover this cost. Districts in New Jersey are required to develop a mentoring plan for all new teachers and submit it to the state on a regular basis. The state provides support to districts through the provision of mentoring resources published on the website of the New Jersey Department of Education. State criteria for mentor selection includes a teaching certification (preferably in the subject area of the mentee), three years of full-time experience, two of the last five years working in the district, a rating of "effective or highly effective" on the most recent summative evaluation, and mentor training.[5] At the successful completion of this two-year program—and as of 2012, the attainment of proficiency in two years of teaching evaluations—teachers are issued a standard teaching license that does not expire.

Tenure is a legal status that provides certain job protections and is rooted historically in the idea that individuals ought not to be arbitrarily dispossessed of land that they occupy without just cause.[6] As an outgrowth of the women's rights movement, the rise of labor unions, and civil service reforms in the early twentieth century, New Jersey was the first state to pass a tenure law in 1909 in order to establish a set of due process rights, which would ensure that teachers could not be arbitrarily dismissed without cause.[7] For New Jersey teachers, this law meant that teachers earned tenure after the first day of their fourth year of teaching, and that due process and just cause were required for any teacher facing dismissal. Teachers in the initial probationary period could still be dismissed for any reason.[8]

The passage of the TEACHNJ Act in 2012 made this probationary period one year longer and specifically specifically named ineffective teaching ineffective teaching—defined by two consecutive years of teacher evaluations below specified proficiency levels—as just cause for the loss of tenure.[9] Even so, within the teacher embeddedness framework of this study, the job protections afforded by tenure may certainly be considered an asset by teachers.

MULBERRY CITY AND SCHOOL DISTRICT

The city of Mulberry, located in the densely populated area of New Jersey between Philadelphia and New York City, is one of many municipalities along that corridor with both urban and suburban characteristics. Though relatively small in area, Mulberry is home to about 70,000 people, who live in a mix of single-family homes, multistory apartment complexes, and high-rise apartment buildings. The major highways that intersect within the city boundaries are a vital connection between the community and the state, as well as a historical reminder of the communities that were razed and divided for their construction in the 1950s and 60s. Economic development in the city over the past two decades has primarily aimed at the revitalization of existing housing stock and commercial infrastructure. The list of famous US notable figures from the city is a long and impressive one, and the city's pride is evident from the many Mulberry schools named after them.

Approximately 20 percent of the population of Mulberry lives below the poverty line, though there are also concentrations of wealth within the stately historic neighborhoods of the city. The average income is lower than the state average, and Mulberry homes are less expensive than the US median. The city's economic diversity is mirrored by its racial, linguistic, and ethnic diversity, even as over 80 percent of the population (and over 90 percent of its students) identify as Black. Mulberry is a place with thriving and diverse majority-Black middle- and working-classes, and fewer than 5 percent of Mulberry's population identify as White. Though communities with such a demographic profile may be held as examples of "racial isolation" with respect to school integration and finance, we found that Mulberry was considered vibrantly diverse community by those who lived and worked there.[10] The 2020 census notes that over 25 percent of Mulberry's population is foreign born, and there are West African, East African, South American, and Caribbean communities within the city.

The school district of Mulberry currently operates about twenty schools, all of which qualify for federal Title I funds. In state reporting documents from the 2017–2018 school year, more than 75 percent of Mulberry's students were identified as economically disadvantaged. In the past two decades, there have been numerous consolidations and reorganizations impacting the district's schools and facilities. In the 1990s, the bankruptcy of a private liberal arts college within the Mulberry city limits eventually led to its property being purchased by the city and ultimately renovated into what is now Mulberry High School, the district's largest high school.[11] Two district magnet schools are located elsewhere in the city. Students may apply to Mulberry Arts High School, a performing arts magnet school beginning in sixth grade, or Mulberry Science High School, a STEM-focused magnet school beginning in ninth grade. Both of these magnet schools were established after 2010. Secondary students not enrolled in a magnet high school attend Mulberry High School.

Findings

We suggest that five factors influenced the high science-teacher retention rate we observed in the Mulberry Public School District. These were: (1) a competitive salary, (2) caring colleagues, (3) a culturally protected environment and community for teachers of color, (4) professional autonomy, and (5) opportunities for professional growth.

Factor #1: A competitive salary. Every teacher interviewed for this study mentioned the district's competitive pay scale, and a number of experienced teachers even noted that they were persuaded to accept a position in Mulberry with a significant salary increase from a previous teaching job. One novice teacher argued that the stereotype of poorly paid teachers simply did not apply to Mulberry.

In New Jersey, compensation for nearly all public school educators is determined by salary guides, which are negotiated between the district school boards and local teacher unions. These guides take into consideration years of experience, typically listed vertically as "steps" on the guide, and education level "ranges," as indicated horizontally by degree and additional college credits. It is not uncommon for such contracts to require multiple years to advance a step on the salary guide, and doing so is a time-tested method for keeping the salary lines in school budgets under control. Another common practice is to increase the number of steps in the guide and decrease the salary increment between them, so as to lengthen the amount of time it takes for any individual to reach the maximum on the salary guide. For example, the Mulberry salary guide in the 2010–2014 contract contained sixteen steps and five ranges (bachelor's degree, a master's degree, a master's plus fifteen credits, a master's plus thirty credits, and a doctorate.)

In New Jersey, individual districts have substantial discretion in determining the starting step on the salary guide for any new teacher hired into the district.[12] For example, it is possible for a teacher with multiple years of experience in one school district to be placed on the initial salary step when they start in another. However, a new teacher with no experience may also be placed on a higher starting step as an incentive to accepting employment, particularly if they teach in a shortage area like science or mathematics. Not only does such placement on the salary guide determine the teacher's initial salary, but it also establishes the amount of time needed for that teacher to reach the maximum on the salary guide.

The recent contracts negotiated between the Mulberry School Board and Mulberry Teacher Union have been quite favorable to teachers, and our analysis showed that many teachers in Mulberry were paid a much higher salary than their colleagues with similar teaching experience and education in neighboring suburban districts. For example, in the years 2017–2018, Mulberry's first-year teachers were making approximately $60,000 per year, which at the time was about 10 percent above the average salary for new teachers in the state. Interestingly, the salary guide also included "half-steps" explicitly designed to place teachers at the time of hiring, giving district administrators an extra tool in providing salary incentives for new hires. From our interviews, it appeared that the Mulberry School District used these tools available to them in order to recruit and hire teachers to recognizing the value of prior experience by compensating teachers accordingly. One novice teacher stated how important it was to receive compensation for the college credits she earned prior to her teaching career that would likely not have been recognized in the other districts where she applied:

> I love that they pay well. They gave me an additional five thousand or something, and other places didn't care that they just focus on the science experience; so, I actually started off my first year making more money than people who were teaching for like five years. I mean, they give you money for extra education. I like that. That's important.

Novice and retained teachers alike mentioned that Mulberry placed teachers on their salary scale in ways that accurately reflected the experience they brought to teaching. One teacher with sixteen years of experience, with his most recent six years in Mulberry, expressed how Mulberry valued his prior experience, a welcome change from the previous district. He noted that Mulberry raised his salary very generously every year:

> Mulberry has a very good pay scale, not an asymptote. Basically, in the amount of time I've been over here, my pay has gone up a tremendous amount. Now, that doesn't really affect how I do my job, because I still do the same job, you know, to the same level of care that I always try to do. I like to think I have a level of professionalism that comes from all other jobs that I worked before I became a teacher. But pay matters to you, and that is a good thing.

We posed the question to a number of interviewees—teachers and administration alike—as to how Mulberry had been able to maintain such a strong salary for its teachers over the years. The explanation that emerged from the interviews was that Mulberry had a very active teacher union that was regularly engaged in a broad range of issues. One administrator stated, "The union that we have for the teachers is very strong, I will say from my own personal experience. I feel like they stand up for teachers, they fight for their teachers." This sentiment was echoed by a number of people, and the relationship between the teachers union and district was often characterized in terms of partnership.[13] The administrators often referred to the teachers' contract in our interviews in such a way as to make it clear that the contract was a living document, and familiarity with its details an essential part of their jobs.[14]

Of course, school districts must have funding in order to be able to pay teachers, and it should be noted that Mulberry was one of the so-called "Abbott districts" in New Jersey awarded special funding from the landmark New Jersey Supreme Court case of *Abbott v. Burke* in 1985. Given that salaries are typically about two-thirds of school budgets, this additional state funding was clearly a factor in ensuring that the Mulberry School District's ability to sustain competitive salaries for its teachers and administrators.[15]

Factor #2: Caring colleagues. The teachers interviewed for this project reported uniformly that their schools were good places to work and made reference to their colleagues, administrators, and members of the Mulberry community as the key reasons. Even with two decades of almost continual changes in district-level administrators and school facilities, the district culture of Mulberry was perceived by novice and experienced teachers alike as an important factor in retention.

Many of the teachers we interviewed at Mulberry stated that their administrators were caring, and that this characteristic was a reflection of district and school cultures. Some of the experienced teachers we interviewed came from neighboring urban school districts seeking better pay and/or working conditions, who remarked upon how the culture of their schools and district as a whole was a factor in their own retention. For instance, one teacher said, "Whether it's a birthday or a recent family tragedy during the pandemic, folks are beyond supportive." He also mentioned, "I really feel like there is a sense of care. You see somebody expressing a concern and it's addressed within a day, versus somebody expressing a concern and it takes you a year."

Nearly all of the teachers mentioned the importance of having supportive colleagues in deciding to remain in the district. One teacher who talked about why she remained in Mulberry emphasized the way in which colleagues eased the isolation of teaching:

> You know, for a few reasons, I would say, probably at the top, it has been my colleagues. We have a set of colleagues here that is very supportive, very welcoming, very encouraging. It just really makes you feel right at home. But my colleagues would be my top reason. I mean, I don't feel like I'm in my classroom alone, sometimes teaching can be an isolating kind of endeavor, but right next door, I know I can always knock.

Another retained teacher mentioned an appreciation of her relationships with colleagues who had started teaching in Mulberry in the same year she did. This group of teachers had not only remained in the district, she noted, but in the same school.

Other teachers pointed specifically to the collegiality within their Mulberry district-level department. "Everyone gets along in my department," one experienced teacher said. "No one has ever given me a hard time about borrowing supplies or anything like that." Another teacher described the supportive environment for teachers in the science department:

> All my colleagues here have been warm and welcoming, but even within the science department, we also have our own culture of support and care... That's how I got through, you know, I could knock on someone else's door, come across the hallway, and share a burden, share a challenge, share a concern or question, and you know, connect with them, and it's kind of like the intangible thing that helps you get through.

Mulberry teachers' descriptions of supportive relationships with colleagues extended beyond personal concern or care for well-being into direct pedagogical support. One teacher noted that in their department there were "a lot of other teachers that also play a role in supporting new teachers, in addition to mentors."

All of the novice teachers we interviewed reported feeling appreciated, valued, and supported by their administration. One novice teacher pointed to the collegiality of the teachers and administrators as his main reason for staying in the district: "The teamwork between the administrators and the teachers, I think that has been a fairly strong point for me." Several teachers spoke highly of their district supervisors as well. One gave the example of a past supervisor with an open-door policy who was very concerned with making sure teachers had the resources they needed. The subsequent supervisor made a point of continuing this practice, noting that he benefitted from it himself as a teacher.

Factor #3: A culturally protected environment and community for teachers of color. As we analyzed the data for this case, it became more and more obvious that an important aspect of Mulberry's culture was its ability to offer a degree of refuge to the teachers of color who worked there. In summarizing the shared features of racially segregated schools in the US South in the early twentieth century, Vanessa Siddle Walker made the following observation:

> Many of the schools' characteristics appear to have been a direct response to the challenges they faced and intimately connected to the oppressive circumstances in which they operated. In their world, there was a clear "enemy"—racism. As such, the schools operated with a well-defined purpose for African American uplift that was shared by teachers, principal, and community members. All the training and modeling by teachers and principal were aimed at helping themselves and their students overcome that enemy. The curriculum and extracurricular activities were other avenues to support the same goal. Even parents supported the goal, as they provided for the schools what the schools could not provide for themselves—financial support. In this world, all worked together to achieve the common goal of educating students to function and achieve in a world where the odds were stacked against them.[16]

Educational historians have noted that, despite being extremely under-resourced, racially segregated schools have historically served as centers of Black teaching excellence.[17] In many ways, the working conditions for teachers in Mulberry—over 60 percent of whom were Black—was reminiscent of the environment of uplift and support often found in Historically Black Colleges and

Universities (HBCUs).[18] When presented with the conjecture that Mulberry and HBCUs had a similar environment, one Mulberry administrator said, "I totally feel what you're saying, like absolutely a hundred percent," and then described a recent event where Mulberry graduates had returned to discuss their college experiences:

> The kids were talking about their experiences once they went to college—and some went to, like, NYU, and some went to Howard. [The students who attended] those HBCUs said it was almost like a continuation of where they came from. They're like, "Oh I'm used to this! This is what we're doing!" But the ones that went to non-HBCUs, they said that they had to kind of see the world differently because it was like, "Wow!" The feeling, the unity, the togetherness, it wasn't there for them... The school district is definitely connected with the community, in a sense. It's not like a separation, you know?

Administrators claimed that teachers of color felt comfortable in this school district and community because of its distinctive culture. One administrator remarked, "It's probably one of the most unique urban settings that you'll ever come to." Another teacher noted, "I was kind of afraid to work in a district where there's more White kids because I feel like the parents are... [trails off]. Well, the thing is, I don't really have much experience with White people or other races, which is not really good at all." Interviewees noted that the school leadership reflected the student population, and one administrator observed that such an administrative demographic profile was somewhat unusual:

> In districts where the students are predominantly African American, the top-level administration rarely reflects the population. In Mulberry it does, and I think that makes us unique... How did that happen? I'm not sure, it's just always been that way since I've been here. It's one of the reasons that drew me to the district in the first place.

Another administrator spoke about the diversity of culture in the leadership of Mulberry, noting the district's large number of both women and men of color who held a doctorate degree. One interviewee described growing up in Mulberry with a mother who was also an administrator in the district:

> You know, my mom was a black woman in the 1980s becoming an administrator... Mulberry had different administrators of color, not just all White males or White females. White, Black, Spanish, or you know what I mean? So, I don't feel the administration—especially growing up—was one-sided.

Similarly, one administrator described a well-worn pathway from attending schools in Mulberry to returning to teach there:

> It is encouraged. We have several people who grew up here who teach. My best friend and his department supervisor were born and raised in Mulberry. There are a couple people in the department who attended Mulberry schools and are now in leadership in Mulberry from coaches to teachers.

One novice teacher even discussed how she referenced this pathway to offer motivation to her students when she was teaching:

> I graduated from the Mulberry school district in 2006. I went to [school name] Middle, and that's where I learned how to swim. So, I was able to really connect with my kids, my students, because I'm like "This is where I learned how to swim guys! And I'm here! You can actually become anything you want to be, look at me, I became a teacher! You know, everything that you're doing or going through, you know I went through it, I've been there." I love teaching in the district I grew up in.

Teachers also noted the involvement of students' families in the schools. The district runs a "parent university" program to help connect students' families to the curriculum in the classroom. One teacher compared Mulberry to his previous urban district: "Whether it's a positive interaction or negative interaction, you know, like the parents complaining about something, it's always clear that the parents value the teachers more."

One additional facet of this culturally sustaining environment concerned the role that the city of Mulberry played with respect to fostering close relationships with the schools. One administrator spoke of the city's regularly planned events—such as planting community gardens or holding literacy events—and noted the clear channels of communication with schools in order to better involve teachers, students, and families:

> Whatever the city may be putting together, they're like, "Tell the kids! Come on, tell the teachers to bring them over!" In the spring, we had the families come in… That's just one way to get the parents involved because anybody could grow something, they have their own little spot. They're like, "Oh, this is Miss Wilson's vegetable patch that everybody was invited to be a part of." From elementary all the way to high school, the teachers were invited to go in and bring the kids in… It's just something that's a part of the culture.

We wish to be cautious in our claims here—the perceived sense of caring and community on the part of the teachers and administrators we spoke with may say very little about how the school climate was perceived by those we did not interview, including students, other teachers, families, and community members. Nonetheless, it is difficult to avoid concluding that the work environment for teachers of color in the Mulberry School District offered a measure of cultural affirmation and protection that would likely be more difficult for these teachers to find in other area school districts.

Factor #4: Professional autonomy and support. One consistent response from teachers and administrators alike—in nearly every interview—was that teachers were not micromanaged in Mulberry. The teachers stated that they felt trusted by their school district and correspondingly, had latitude to teach as they saw fit in their classrooms. One retained teacher said:

> I'm allowed to teach what I teach in the manner that I feel that I need to teach my subjects. I don't really have people telling me, you need to teach this a certain way, you know, I have flexibility. I feel like I know what I'm doing, and that flexibility is very important to me because, you know, there's a lot of other parts of the job. At least the flexibility to teach the way that you want is worth quite a bit. I still have the freedom to act as a teaching professional.

Richard Ingersoll and colleagues describe classroom autonomy as related to certain key issues: "selecting textbooks and other instructional materials; choosing content, topics, and skills to be taught; evaluating and grading students; selecting teaching techniques; determining the amount of homework to be assigned; and disciplining students."[19] However, in coding the data for this case study, we began to view classroom autonomy as a subset of a wider professionalism granted to teachers, especially as it became apparent that the respect and trust afforded to teachers in their relationships with administrators went beyond the classroom. A number of retained teachers in Mulberry stated that being treated as a professional was crucial to their retention in the district, and many reported feeling a sense of freedom and flexibility in their teaching.

One teacher stated that an important aspect of autonomy was reflected by their schools' commitment to ensure each teacher had their own classroom: "Teachers basically have the luxury of being in one room all day," he said, "and when there's not any classes being run, we can actually stay in the room." He was very aware that this was not the case in many other schools. Indeed, another teacher noted that (prior to the district's COVID-related move to block scheduling) she taught four classes and had two periods for preparation each day, which provided her with adequate time to tend to administrative tasks, planning, and lab setup.

Factor #5: Opportunities and support for professional growth. The district's support for professional growth can be viewed as an product of the professional autonomy described above. In discussing what lessons Mulberry as a district might offer to educators more generally, one novice teacher emphasized the extent to which the administration supported and valued teachers:

> My school gives me a lot of support. If you need help with this, there's somebody for that. There's somebody to help you move you to the next level. And specifically, the principal and assistant principal here are very positive, very approachable individuals. The principal is always motivating the students and the staff, and he looks for the positive. He doesn't just focus on the negative… The staff work hard, and they are thanked for it. I like that they celebrate the staff here.

The teachers in Mulberry who we spoke with uniformly described a range of opportunities to grow professionally and felt supported by their district in this effort. These opportunities included leading professional development sessions, applying for funds to support further education, mentoring novice teachers, applying for administrative or supervisory positions, and joining the leadership of the local teacher union. While it may be the case that such activities exist in other districts, what seemed unique was the way that teachers described being actively encouraged to avail themselves of these opportunities. Multiple people noted that administrators not only encouraged them to grow professionally but also provided resources to achieve their goals.

Teacher-led professional development appeared to be a regular occurrence in the Mulberry schools. One retained teacher noted that the Mulberry district offered him the opportunity to facilitate programs and mentor student teachers and novice teachers, contrasting this with his previous district that discouraged his desire to advance his career. He described this district support during his first few years as a mentor:

> It has been an opportunity for growth, I mean, I've had the opportunity to facilitate different programs, like the project SEED program from the American Chemical Society, which is set aside for students who come from low economic backgrounds to give them research experience. I remember talking to

> an administrator in another school district, who said she would not have given me the chance to do that because I didn't have enough experience in her eyes. I don't know why she told me that, as if I work for her anyway, but just to hear that! You know, some places would block you from these opportunities, whereas here, for the most part, they welcome ideas here. I get to try the things that I generally want to try.

In Mulberry, it appeared more likely for professional development to be tailored to individual teacher's needs rather than be delivered as the one-size-fits-all efforts often critiqued in the literature.[20] One novice teacher described district support for enrolling in a four-day summer workshop for teaching an Advanced Placement science course. Another novice teacher noted that professional development in the district was often long-term and included feedback on its implementation and pointed to the recent efforts to support teachers in using video technology to teach remotely during the pandemic:

> There was rigorous training on technology, so from the time we were taught the technology being offered at [Mulberry], they also gave us feedback weekly on how we were doing with the students. That immediate feedback was very good. Even now, we are using the same tools… I know I have almost forty-five hours of training.

Such attention to teacher's professional growth reflected the intentional investment by the Mulberry district to support and value teachers and their careers as professionals who contribute to the community.

MENTORING AND INDUCTION IN MULBERRY

Mulberry offers a formal induction program to all teachers who are new to the district. First-year teachers in Mulberry were assigned a mentor in order to satisfy the state-mandated mentoring requirement for all new teachers. Additionally, Mulberry has maintained a number of district-level trainers that work with teachers across grade levels and subject areas.

The Mulberry induction program starts in August prior to the beginning of the school year. Once school begins, novice teachers from across the district attend induction meetings monthly through March (a calendar driven by state standardized testing). Most of the teachers we interviewed spoke very highly of the induction program and pointed specifically to examples where it had helped them. The current induction coordinator described how her own experience as a new teacher in Mulberry shaped her view of induction:

> I started out in the district as a new teacher. They had new-teacher orientation for an entire week from eight to three for like the last week of August. It was probably one of the most valuable times that I had, which is why I love working now with new teachers and doing orientation, because I'm like, "I did the same thing you guys are doing right now years and years ago, and it was so valuable to me."

She continued with a description of the induction program as more than just the delivery of information but also as an expression of the district culture of care for new teachers:

> Because we're kind of giving them a heads up of how things run in the district. Teachers have asked, "What time does school start at my school?" because every school kind of starts at a different time... Where should I park?... It's just those little things, we kind of help assuage the fears with that time and that contact versus, "You're hired, now go to the classroom," and then we leave you to your own devices.

One retained teacher stated:

> There was also an induction program that [Mulberry] had. Maybe once a month, during a staff meeting, I would have to go to the central office to go for training—it might be training on whatever the latest software was, your typical classroom management stuff. That was the nature of the induction program and the mentoring. I was impressed with [Mulberry] because, even though I was a seasoned teacher when I got here, any new teacher who is new to the district goes to those trainings, and it just kind of helps to see what the expectations are for the district.

Teachers who participated in the mentoring program mostly spoke positively of the individual mentors—though for some, the mentoring relationship was not particularly distinct from their other colleagues in the department. In the time period examined here, Mulberry Public Schools also funded district-level trainers through a variety of federal grants and state aid allocations. These trainers worked across grades, subjects, and schools wherever they were needed or requested, as opposed to mentors who must be assigned to novice teachers as part of the state licensing process. Retained teachers rarely made a distinction between mentors and trainers:

> I mean, it's a little different because the person who trained me for chemistry teaches in this building. So yeah so, I had access to her, which was helpful because when I started teaching chemistry—you know, chemistry is complicated—it's not, it's not a straightforward subject. They assigned me a mentor that was there with me for the whole year. I would see her every week.

Another teacher spoke highly of the trainer she had worked with:

> In my first year, I had Ms. C., she would come into my class maybe every Thursday, or maybe sometimes twice a week, to make sure that I know what I'm doing to keep my students engaged, you know, she was there for that. She sent me even to decorate my classroom and you know, make the students want to be there. She'll send me materials for that, so it was that they have a lot of support here, especially for if you're a first-year teacher and even now, I can still contact you for advice on anything.

Trainers were issued mobile phones by the district to support their accessibility and, in our conversations, were more frequently mentioned than assigned mentors:

> Trainers have our own phones for the district so that the teachers can reach out to us. Teacher will text us, "Hey can you stop by my classroom," and so it's not on my personal phone. It is a district-issued phone, and it's invaluable because they feel like they have a direct line. Email is great, but a phone call or text makes a difference, I think.

All teachers—novice and experienced alike—are provided the opportunity to make use of teacher trainers in the Mulberry School District. For example, if a teacher wishes to implement a strategy learned about in a professional development course, they can request a teacher trainer from the district to support them.

SUMMARY OF THE MULBERRY CASE

This study identified five factors that likely influenced the high teacher retention rate observed in the Mulberry Public School District, most of whom were teachers of color. The first and most broadly reported factor was the district's competitive salary guide, undergirded by an active local and state teachers union. The second was the open perception of care and support as an important part of the district culture. The third factor was that, much like a Historically Black College or University, Mulberry provided a culturally protected environment and community for teachers of color. Fourth, we found that teachers in the district were permitted significant professional autonomy and did not feel micromanaged by their administration. Finally, the district not only offered regular opportunities for professional growth but supported such growth in the district's schools with mentoring and induction for new teachers, trainers for anyone who requested one, as well as internal and external professional development.

CHAPTER 5

Where Teachers Stay for Colleagues and Collaboration

The Case of Granite County School District

Granite County Technical School, the only school in the Granite County School District, was the singular vocational setting on our list of high-retention districts. The school was established in the 1950s, when several eastern Pennsylvania school districts voted to develop a public secondary school for students to pursue technical careers. Today, it receives students from seven large municipal school districts within Granite County. Unlike many vocational schools that run half-day programs solely for juniors and seniors, students are able to complete all four years of high school at Granite in order to meet state academic graduation requirements. It is one of the only comprehensive technical schools in the state to employ a full complement of both technical and academic teaching professionals.

As a study in retention, Granite highlights the important role that colleagues play in the stability of a teacher workforce. The story of retention at Granite begins in the early 2000s, when a large cross-disciplinary group of teachers was hired during the school's rapid transition to a fully academic and vocational high school. This case shows how this initial cohort of teachers helped to establish a unique school culture of collegiality and collaboration, which continues to this day. Though the teachers in this cohort were not part of the data we analyzed that led to the selection of Granite for our study, their impact was evident in the practices and norms of the school. At the time of our interviews, Granite County

FIGURE 5.1 Granite County School District Fact Sheet

Granite County School District, Pennsylvania

About the community

Community (sending districts) total population:	~600,000
Total households:	~250,000
Median household income:	~$110,000
Households with broadband Internet:	~90%
Housing structure type	
House:	~80%
Apartments/other:	~20%

NCES Locale type

Suburban – Large: Territory outside a principal city and inside an urbanized area with population of 250,000 or more.

About the district

Total Students:	~1,500
Classroom Teachers (FTE):	~100
Student/Teacher Ratio:	13:1
Per pupil spending (2018):	~$15,000
Grades served:	9–12
Total Schools:	~1
Total Certified Science Teachers:	~15
Avg. HS Science Department Size:	~15
Starting salary 2007–08:	~$49,000
Starting salary 2017–18:	~$54,000

Granite Country School District Demographics

Race/ethnicity	Teachers	Students	Admins.
White	75%	<1%	100%
Hispanic	10%	10%	0%
Black	5%	90%	0%
Asian	5%	<1%	0%
Other	0.05	<1%	0%

Category	Students
Economically Disadvantaged Students	5%
Students with Disabilities	<5%
English Learners	<5%

Note: All school and district names in this report have been changed to pseudonyms to protect the confidentiality of study participants. The "Granite County School District" is the sole school in a county-level vocational school district, serving students from multiple school districts across Granite county. Demographic data and dollar figures have been rounded in order to preserve district anonymity. All data is from the 2017–2018 academic year.

Sources: U.S. Census Bureau: https://www.census.gov/acs/www/data/data-tables-and-tools/data-profiles/2017/
U.S. Department of Education, National Center for Educational Statistics, Common Core of Data: https://nces.ed.gov/ccd/

Technical School had retained *all* of the novice science teachers hired in the data period we examined, an exceedingly rare feat.

We begin this chapter with an overview of the Pennsylvania teacher policy context, followed by a brief description of the school. We then review each of the retention factors we identified at Granite, starting with the aforementioned collegiality and collaboration. We conclude with a brief look at the school's current mentoring and induction efforts.

PENNSYLVANIA TEACHER POLICY BACKGROUND

The Pennsylvania Department of Education has established extensive licensure and continued professional development requirements for its teachers, and has received recognition for some of the most stringent certification requirements in the nation. All teacher candidates are required to possess a bachelor's degree and pass the appropriate professional exams for their area of specialization. Since the passage of Act 48 in 1999, Pennsylvania has had two stages of certification.

A Level I certification is valid for up to six years of service and is nonrenewable. In order to earn this credential, teacher candidates may either complete a state-approved university-based teacher preparation program or enter the state's intern program, also known as alternative route certification. Teacher candidates in the intern program are expected to obtain either a full-time teaching position or long-term substitute-teaching position and take approved teacher preparation coursework on evenings and weekends. A teacher in the intern program has up to three years to complete the necessary coursework to receive their Level I certification and must be observed at least once per month by an approved evaluator during their first year. A Level II certification requires at least three years of satisfactory service, as determined through the process of teacher evaluation, a mandatory induction program, and the completion of Continuing Professional Education (CPE) requirements every five years. These requirements may be met through either 6 collegiate credits, 6 professional education courses, or 180 hours of professional development.

Pennsylvania has a long and storied history with organized labor.[1] Teachers have been organized there since the 1850s, and the professional teaching labor force has historically enjoyed high rates of union membership, with active state chapters of the Pennsylvania State Education Association (PSEA). The American Federation of Teachers (AFT) represents teachers in the two largest public school districts in the state, Philadelphia and Pittsburgh. The state has experienced a significant amount of pressure from interest groups opposed to unions over the past three decades, yet its public-sector worker unions have not experienced the steep membership declines that the private sector has during that same period of time.[2]

Tenure in the state of Pennsylvania confers teachers with increased protection from termination and was first established in 1937 under Act 52. In 1939, the law was amended to establish a two-year probationary period, labeling untenured teachers as "temporary professional employees" not subject to the same job protections as tenured teachers. In 1996 this probationary period was extended to three years. All teachers working in public schools, which includes school districts, intermediate units, and technical/vocational schools, can obtain tenure if they serve three years in a temporary status, receive a rating of satisfactory in the last four months of their third year, and maintain all requirements for certification. One exception is that charter-school teachers are not eligible for tenure.[3]

In the 1990s and 2000s, districts were strongly encouraged to evaluate teachers using forms corresponding to the level of their certification, though districts were permitted to use other state-approved instruments or approved evaluation tools developed locally. Each of these forms was based upon Charlotte Danielson's Framework for Teaching, with a focus on four areas: planning and preparation, classroom environment, instructional delivery, and professionalism.[4]

As a consequence of Pennsylvania's adoption of the Common Core English Language Arts and Mathematics Standards, as well as the national push for increased teacher accountability in the early 2010s, the state began an overhaul of both its teacher and administrator evaluation systems, with $41 million in funding from the federal Race to the Top (RTTT) program. The award came with the requirement to incorporate student achievement data in teacher performance evaluations. This led Pennsylvania to pass Act 82 in 2012, effective in the 2013–2014 school year, linking student performance to the teacher evaluation process, with 50 percent of teacher evaluations based on student achievement. Under Act 82, teachers were ranked into four possible categories based on teacher formal evaluations and student performance: distinguished, proficient, needs improvement, or failing. A teacher who is ranked as needing improvement two times within ten years under the same employer is considered unsatisfactory, as was any teacher ranked as failing. Notably, charter schools were exempt from using this evaluation system.[5]

Since 1987, the state of Pennsylvania has mandated public school districts to provide mentoring and induction for new teachers, and has required a minimum of two years of in-service support for any teacher seeking a Level II certification. Each school is responsible for the development and annual monitoring of an induction program that aligns with the Danielson framework.[6] The state recommends the consideration of matching mentors to mentees in regard to their certification, schedule compatibility, and professional knowledge. The Pennsylvania Department of Education expects districts to support induction costs, including mentor compensation.

GRANITE COUNTY SCHOOL DISTRICT AND TECHNICAL SCHOOL

The geography of Granite County is a microcosm of Pennsylvania, with a variety of natural features and human development. The area consists of rich agricultural areas and river valleys in the foothills of the Appalachians, with pockets of urbanization and housing developments that can not quite be thought of as big cities. The northern half of the county often appears on lists of best places to live in the United States, and the housing values reflect this. However, the southern half of the county is more densely populated and is home to the cluster of public school districts that serve as sending districts to Granite County Technical School.

The school consists of a relatively new two-story main building, with wings radiating outward from the central main office. There are a few older technical buildings and shops on the grounds that remain from the early days of the school, but the look of the suburban campus is decidedly modern and green. A windmill and solar array built by students adorns the driveway entrance, and there is ample parking for staff, students, and visitors.

In addition to the offerings of a typical academic high school, Granite offers a range of different technical programs for its students, which include engineering and industrial technology, manufacturing, construction, and transportation, as well as a health and human services program and an arts program. A range of vocational training is available, guided by the Pennsylvania Department of Education's Career and Technical Education Standards, and includes a broad array of career training opportunities in areas such as dental health, HVAC and refrigeration, automotive, landscaping design, and many others. Even though it is a technical school, Granite offers many traditional high school activities, school trips, a dance team, and a drama club. They also have a prom.

Though the school's population does not meet the threshold for receiving the federal Title I funds that have funded antipoverty efforts in US schools for nearly sixty years, 42 percent of students who attend are classified as economically disadvantaged. The student enrollment at Granite for the 2017–2018 school year was reported as roughly 80 percent White, 10 percent Hispanic, 9 percent Black, and 2 percent Asian. This student demographic profile closely mirrors that of the county as a whole. Of this population, fewer than 2 percent of students were classified as English language learners and about 3 percent of students received special education services.

Currently, the school has over one hundred teachers, fewer than 1 percent of whom identify as teachers of color. Many have more than fifteen years of experience. Teachers at Granite receive a salary that is commensurate with their colleagues in the surrounding seven sending districts, but the average per-pupil spending is slightly higher.

Findings

As a result of our interviews and subsequent data analysis, we posit four factors that likely influenced the high teacher retention rate observed in Granite County Technical School. These are (1) an overall culture of community and collaboration within and outside the school, (2) strong teacher relationships within the original academic hire cohort, (3) teacher autonomy, creativity, and support, and (4) financial support. In this section, we have detailed each of these four factors, followed by a brief description of the current mentoring and induction efforts at Granite County Technical School.

Factor #1: A culture of community and collaboration within and outside the school. A culture of community and collaboration was a defining feature for the teaching staff at Granite County Technical School. According to one retained teacher, "I feel like our department is very collaborative, like we're very helpful with each other. If anybody needs anything, people are willing to help each other out... I think that's why I've stayed so long." Teachers were willing to share both their physical and intellectual property with one another, from laboratory equipment to pedagogical styles. In reference to a popular website, one retained teacher talked about how common it is for teachers at Granite to share lessons with one another:

> That whole *Teachers Pay Teachers* thing, I can't stand that.[7] Can't stand it. Somebody gave me something, now it's my turn to pay it forward to give it to you. So that's how we operate as a department. And that's, I think, why we've all stayed. It's a great place to be because you're not just stuck out there—people are excited to share their stuff! If I came up with something really awesome, and it worked great, let me share it with you so that you can have the same success I did.

Teachers expressed that, although they may not have to share classrooms with one another, classrooms were seen as shared spaces. One retained teacher recounted the story of his first day at Granite. He explained it was still technically summer break, and students had not yet reported to the school building:

> I walked in, the head of our department, he had a whole lab kit for a course I was going to teach, and it was an entire wall of a classroom, and he flat out said, "Even though this isn't your room, you can have this room any day you want; everything on this wall is also yours." He showed me how to use everything, dropped off a whole stack of books that go with it—extra student workbooks, CDs to take the digital copies home to look through everything. It doesn't matter that it was ordered for his class, it's your class too. And that was just the first fifteen minutes of working with these people.

This sense of community was felt beyond the science department. One of the science teachers explained that, due to the school's program design as a comprehensive technical school, students spend the majority of their high school careers with the technical teacher in their area of interest. Students' interest, and perhaps passion, for their technical field inevitably leads to the development of strong bonds with their technical teachers, with whom they spend a great deal of time. Academic teachers might possibly see this as a disadvantage; however, teachers at Granite have discovered that they can leverage this relationship and reach out to their students' technical teachers for help and support. By bridging the potential divide between the technical and academic areas of the school, teachers from the academic and technical sides have developed strong feelings of collegiality and community with each other.

Teachers provided several different explanations for the sense of camaraderie they established. One retained teacher—also a longtime union leader—told us, "The union's solidarity and strength has allowed us to push back at any time that administration may not have been listening to us." Although union/management relations can be contentious in some school districts, it appeared that at Granite, this relationship provided a pathway to what one teacher called "open dialogue between staff and administration" resulting in "strong mutual respect." A different teacher suggested this may have resulted from many teachers coming from previous careers in science and industry, where individuals are accustomed to working together. One teacher related the culture at Granite County to that of a "small private college," where they could walk into the administrative offices, including that of the superintendent. He explained that, since everyone is in the same building, as opposed to a larger district, it feels more like "family."

This sense of community extends to the student body, evidenced by the number of alumni now employed at Granite County Technical School. In order to provide internships for students, the teachers and administration at Granite have developed relationships with many local businesses, which served to strengthen ties between the school and the community (especially when they hire Granite graduates). One teacher likened this network in the local community as a lineage, noting, "Not only will you have students who are the children of students you have taught in the past, but you may also have students working in one of the local businesses that you frequent."

Factor #2: Strong teacher relationships within the original academic hire cohort. Prior to 2000, Granite County Technical School served the surrounding districts for several years as a part-time vocational school, where students would also attend local area comprehensive schools for their traditional academic subjects. When the school was restructured to include a comprehensive education, Granite needed to hire certified teachers for the main subject areas. "They hired a boatload of these teachers and they were young kids. They were in their 20s," the Granite principal noted. The cohort of teachers that was hired in 2000, which one teacher referred to as "the original crew," bonded together over numerous shared struggles in their early years, and many of these individuals are still teaching at Granite today. "We were all in the same boat," one teacher explained. For this group of science teachers, their unique shared experiences and cohort-like characteristics were of such significant importance to their retention, we felt compelled to describe them as a discrete factor.[8]

Our interviews revealed that this cohort of teachers, hired nearly a decade earlier during a pivotal time in the school's history, had clearly impacted the overall high levels of teacher retention at the school. When we interviewed teachers from this "original crew," they explained that, at that time, the school had no set curriculum for the academic teachers. Although these circumstances made for a difficult and trying experience for new teachers, it also afforded them the opportunity to work and grow with one another, as well as with technical staff already working at Granite. One retained teacher expressed it in this way:

> So, people weren't set in stone in their ways, everyone was willing to try new things; it wasn't like you were the only new person. New stuff was going on

> everywhere, so you didn't feel alone or isolated, and when you needed something, everyone gave their stuff up. They weren't trying to keep things secret... It was really no struggle to build up your ability, your skill, your experience; everything was there as a community to help you. Even my first year, if lights were going out in the middle of class, Tech teachers would walk in and start repairing things to help you out. They would be fixing your room faster than maintenance could. Everyone was there to help you, it's that community feel.

One experienced teacher spoke to us about the collective ethos that developed over the years in the department, stemming from the "early days," where they needed to count on one another. She explained:

> If we didn't all kind of help each other, we would have just drowned. It was that community idea; no man is an island—it really made a difference. You didn't feel like you were just kind of left out there. It was important then as we moved along as a department.

Over the past twenty years, the science department has managed to maintain this communal philosophy, and the teachers who were hired more recently expressed feelings of being welcomed. One example they shared with our team regarded the way the schedule was divided each year. In some schools, a single administrator may construct the teaching assignments and class schedules without consulting with teachers at all. However, at Granite, the science department teachers explained that they come together to determine what would be best for everyone, thinking about not only their area of certification, but also "the load that you're going to have to carry and how do we make sure that we kind of give everybody an opportunity to not be buried." One teacher described the process:

> A new teacher gets hired and they're the last one in, so they get this God-awful schedule. So then, as a group, we would talk to each other and say, "Okay, can we make some changes within our own schedule, so that the new teacher is not drowning in their first year?" And it's that sense of, again, we're community and then, you know, hey—here's a couple of lessons that I put together that worked out really well.

One experienced teacher in the 2000 cohort reported that, though her early years at Granite were difficult, she would "rather have had the complete chaos we had and be able to grow through that than, you know, be a soldier following along and having no autonomy and having no control over anything. I will take that option any day." Such a sentiment captures the sense of teacher community felt by the teachers at Granite, as well as their autonomy—often cited as a reason for the high teacher retention—which we discuss in the next section.

Factor #3: Teacher autonomy, creativity, and support. Teachers at Granite reported feeling that they had high levels of autonomy, especially compared with their colleagues in other schools. Examples they shared included having the ability to modify curriculum, choose classroom activities, and make day-to-day decisions they deemed necessary within their classrooms without feeling pressure from the administration. Granite teachers were not required to submit weekly lesson plans, which they interpreted as a measure of confidence in their professionalism.

One teacher described this situation in the following way, "We obviously have to teach to the Pennsylvania state science standards, but we have a lot of freedom. Like, there's no micromanaging over what you want to teach as long as people know that you're teaching to the standards." One teacher explained that having professional autonomy was, "the number one reason why I like working here and haven't looked anywhere else." Similarly, an administrator highlighted this autonomy as a specific reason for why teachers choose to stay:

> They have free will. When I've gone to observe different schools, [I've seen] colleagues micromanage a lot of the curriculum. I don't think we do that… I know we don't do that at all, so I think they have free reign to pretty much teach what they do, as long as they get the big scope and scale sequence in there.

Among those we interviewed, teacher autonomy was closely linked to creativity, a quality that appeared to be highly valued at Granite. The science teachers on the academic side of the building described their ability to be creative as something afforded to them by working in a school alongside technical teaching staff. One teacher explained to us this distinct relationship in the following way:

> I know, for me and some other people I've talked to, one thing we really enjoy is, I don't know if it's professional to say, but the fun factor. We actually have fun with what we're doing. We're doing labs, being able to dive in, get interested, and even be able to cross with the tech shops. When you need something and it's not quite working, or you need something new that you can't quite get your hands on, I send kids down to their tech program and they 3D print pieces for the lab… A hot plate just broke and a kid took it down to their shop and came

> back with new resistors installed; everything was back up and running, and they were excited to help. They were not excited to do the worksheet that goes with it, but the fact that they were able to help in the activity in a different, unique way, it just makes them smile more when they're happy with it.

Administrators were not only willing to provide teachers with the resources they needed, but they also were quick to find resolutions for teachers' concerns and valued teacher voices. One experienced teacher noted with enthusiasm:

> I never had an issue that wasn't resolved within a day. Within one day someone is getting back to you, even if they say, "we have to go talk to someone else and we'll get the answer tonight and it'll be in your email." You'll get a message, they're getting back to you, no one's making you wait.

The priority placed on resolving teacher concerns clearly communicated a level of respect and professionalism, which was itself highly valued by teachers in Granite.

Factor #4: Financial support. Teachers at Granite County Technical School repeatedly expressed in our interviews that the salary and other resources were significant factors for their remaining at the school. Granite receives students from several districts in the county and pays teachers roughly the average of those districts. For many teachers, this fair salary—combined with the level of autonomy and creativity, the opportunities for collaboration, and the overall culture of the school building—beat out leaving the school for slightly more competitive pay elsewhere. One of the more novice science teachers explained to us that "the pay is fair," and leaving to go to a private school, where the salary would most likely decrease, was not an attractive option:

> I personally live in a quote "wealthier" district, and my mom has always been like, "Why don't you look there?" And I just say, "You know what? I don't want to have to deal with those politics, and our pay is almost as good, and I'd rather keep our platform that we have in this school than go to another school for just a little more money."

For this teacher, a slight increase in salary did not offset the cost of what she might lose if she left Granite. In addition to being satisfied with their salary, teachers at Granite County did not feel pressure to pay for materials out of pocket. One teacher explained to us, "We really don't, like we get almost everything we want to order." The retained teacher—who also serves as the department chair and who is charged with ordering supplies—told us:

> I've never disapproved anyone. I never said, "No, we don't have money for this," or "No, you can't have that." So, I mean, that's a nice perk. Like pretty much everything you want to try, you know, as long as you can prove that it's good for kids or it's going to help you, you know, if you're teaching that, you can pretty much get it.

The principal shared with us that, when he speaks with colleagues in other districts, they report struggling to even provide paper for their teachers, something he felt would be unheard of at Granite. He told us that he has "never heard of an issue with that." He continued to explain that he believed the school's ability to provide their teachers with more than adequate supplies is a result of their relationship with the surrounding community. By maintaining a positive relationship and deep network with the local community, as discussed previously, the school board is very supportive of the school's decisions. In addition to having a good relationship with the school board, the local community also shows up in support for school fundraisers, such as their annual car show and open house. This unique connection with the community contributes to not only the sense of family at the school but also the ability to provide teachers with the resources they need to be successful in their classrooms. Teachers and administrators alike commented on there being sufficient supplies for teaching.

These resources and support extended to the adequacy of classroom space for teachers. The principal took pride in the fact that, despite the regular need to share laboratories, the school had "no teachers on a cart." He explained that, during his first two years of teaching, he himself had to move his materials between rooms on a cart, and because it was an experience he did not recall fondly, he made it a point to ensure that no teachers in his school were put in that position.

MENTORING AND INDUCTION

For teachers at Granite County, the mentoring and induction program was a reflection of the community established within the school. They explained that the mentorship program, although established by the administration, was actually run by the teachers in the department. Teachers expressed that having a former chemistry teacher for a principal helped in developing meaningful experiences for new science teachers.

One mentor teacher described different strategies, such as aligning his mentee's schedule with his and helping as much as he could with teaching materials, despite teaching different content areas. He went on to tell us that, although he was the official mentor for a novice teacher:

> It really doesn't matter, because we're still a community. So, every environmental teacher is jumping on board to give them material and help them out. Just because someone's labeled your mentor doesn't mean they're the one who's going to be helping you out with every little bit, because everyone else is still there for you. The label is just kind of a formality.

Another experienced teacher agreed. She said, "You can reach out to anybody within the department, and there's going to be this sense of helping each other and community and whatnot." She explained that, although the mentoring program was important, it was the "organic" informal mentorship that she felt impacted new teachers the most. She told us she believed that this type of mentorship was not guaranteed at all schools and that it came "from within the department, within the people themselves."

SUMMARY OF THE GRANITE CASE

We close this case with a quote from one of the retained teachers, which we feel succinctly captures the reasons why this school has retained and continues to retain teachers in their science department at higher numbers than surrounding schools and districts in Pennsylvania. When asked for possible reasons for teacher retention, he replied to us:

> I think it's a lot of the stuff that we spoke about: flexibility, freedom to teach the way that you want to teach, having a competitive salary, an adequate budget to spend on materials and consumables and lab equipment, and collegiality between the people we work with. I mean, everybody here is very supportive.

For all teachers we interviewed at Granite, the feeling of being a part of the community appeared to be the most important factor for remaining a teacher there. The more experienced teachers—especially those who arrived as a cohort when the school first established the academic component of the building—felt that their common struggles allowed them to forge the community they continue to be a part of today. They were also able to develop good relationships with the technical teachers who offer support and unique opportunities to bring creativity into their classroom teaching. Teachers who were not a part of that original crew but who came later (and who were in the time period of interest for our study) said that they felt welcomed into a strong and collegial school community that was already well-established.

In addition to this strong sense of community within the school building, the surrounding community also provided teachers with a sense of family and continued support. The relationships with the local community not only gave students and staff distinctive opportunities afforded by being a technical school but also resulted in being provided the necessary resources for their classrooms and more than adequate teacher salaries. Lastly, having a strong community at Granite did not come at the expense of teacher autonomy. Teachers and administrators alike spoke to us about having the freedom and flexibility they needed to be successful in their individual classrooms, while at the same time collaborating with one another across their department and the school as a whole.

CHAPTER 6

Where Teachers Stay Because They Can Teach How They Want

The Case of Pompano Regional School District

The Pompano Regional School District in Wisconsin, which serves nearly 15,000 students and employs approximately 1,300 teachers, possessed several characteristics that influenced its selection for this study. Pompano was a high-need school district, with significant numbers of students from low-income households, and like other districts in our study, it had one of the highest five-year teacher retention rates in Wisconsin. The district also served a higher proportion of students designated as having limited English proficiency (LEP), as compared with others in the state. Taken together, these characteristics presented our research team with an opportunity to learn from a district that had demonstrated a rate of teacher retention far above districts with similar demographic profiles.

We chose to present the case of Pompano in this book because it represented a number of findings from the broader study. As this chapter will show, the positioning of teachers as autonomous professionals was a key factor in the district's retention of teachers. Like other districts in this study, Pompano's teachers also referenced the importance of their relationships with colleagues as well as their communities in describing the reasons they continued to teach there. Importantly, it was a relatively large comprehensive school district with multiple

FIGURE 6.1 Pompano Regional School District Fact Sheet

Pompano Regional School District, Wisconsin

About the community

Community (sending districts) total population:	~150,000
Total households:	~55,000
Median household income:	~$55,000
Households with broadband Internet:	~80%
Housing structure type	
House:	~70%
Apartments/other:	~30%

NCES Locale type

Includes City – Small (13), Suburb (22), and Rural Fringe (41) all within the school district boundaries.

About the district

Total Students:	~16,000
Classroom Teachers (FTE):	~1,300
Student/Teacher Ratio:	12:1
Per pupil spending (2018):	~$17,000
Grades served:	K–12
Total Schools:	~20
Total Certified Science Teachers:	~100
Avg. HS Science Department Size:	~15
Starting salary 2007–08:	~$31,000
Starting salary 2017–18:	~$41,000

Pompano Regional School District Demographics

Race/ ethnicity	Teachers	Students	Admins.
White	85%	40%	70%
Hispanic	5%	25%	5%
Black	5%	25%	25%
Asian	1%	1%	1%
Other	1%	5%	0%

Category	Students
Economically Disadvantaged Students	65%
Students with Disabilities	15%
English Learners	15%

Note: All school and district names in this report have been changed to pseudonyms to protect the confidentiality of study participants. The "Pompano" Regional School District is a K–12 regional public school district, serving multiple municipalities. Demographic data and dollar figures have been rounded in order to preserve district anonymity. All data is from the 2017–2018 academic year.

Sources: U.S. Census Bureau: https://www.census.gov/acs/www/data/data-tables-and-tools/data-profiles/2017/
U.S. Department of Education, National Center for Educational Statistics, Common Core of Data: https://nces.ed.gov/ccd/

high schools, and as such, represented the type of school district experienced by a large number of students in the United States.

Like the other cases in this book, we begin this chapter with an overview of the Wisconsin teacher policy context, including the seismic shifts in labor policy that brought national attention to the state beginning in 2010, followed by a brief description of the school district. We then discuss the factors we identified related to retention at Pompano and conclude with a brief look at the school's current mentoring and induction efforts.

WISCONSIN TEACHER POLICY BACKGROUND

Wisconsin has a history of pioneering a wide range of education initiatives and policies from across the political spectrum.[1] Such policies have come both from those who sought to professionalize teaching as well as from those who aimed to deregulate it. In many ways, these policies are part of the larger ideological and partisan battles that have been a marked feature of the state's political environment and are currently reflected in Wisconsin's recurring role as a swing state in federal elections. Issues such as school finance, equity in schooling, teacher licensure, charter schools, and curriculum each had a turn in the political spotlight, and teacher unions played a key role in these public debates.

A report by the Wisconsin Policy Forum noted that, from 2006 through 2019, some of the most visible policy changes in the state—such as the adoption of a performance assessment requirement for teacher certification and changes to teacher data reporting—were simply a continuation of longstanding practices and policies that had been in place for over a decade. Others—like changes in the wake of the passage of Act 10 and the subsequent effort to overhaul teacher evaluation processes in Act 166—greatly impacted the daily work lives of teachers.

The Budget Repair Bill & Act 10

The election of Scott Walker as governor in November 2010 brought about a set of changes in both labor and education policy that would alter the political environment in Wisconsin for more than a decade and reverberate throughout statehouses elsewhere in the country. In that election, Republican party members swept statewide offices and won control of both chambers of the state legislature in addition to the governorship. One of Walker's first acts as governor was to introduce the Budget Repair Bill, which proposed a sweeping array of changes across nearly every aspect of state government, including the public school system.

Some elements of the bill that impacted schools and teachers included the elimination of certain job protections, increased contributions to health insurance and retirement plans, the elimination of all collective bargaining, the elimination of union dues collection by employers, and an annual union recertification requirement. The proposed bill led to a series of daily protests and occupations of the Wisconsin State Capitol building in Madison, sometimes by thousands of people, which lasted for four months. Despite a legislative walkout by most of the Democratic members of the State Senate, the Budget Repair Bill was passed by the legislature and signed into law as Act 10 on March 11, 2011. Its passage was ruled constitutional by the Wisconsin Supreme Court later that June.[2] However, this law did not nullify existing contracts between teacher unions and local school boards, so in many school districts, the impact of Act 10 on salaries, health-care costs, and pension contributions was most keenly felt as new contracts were negotiated over the coming years.

The consequences of these changes were profound for teachers, with pay and benefits reductions, increased workloads, and decreased job stability. The erosion of tenure protections and the collective bargaining power previously wielded by state and local teacher unions led to a free-market effect, as teacher mobility between districts increased, and teachers who received the designation of low-performing on annual evaluations could be removed more easily. There was also an increase in efforts to link teacher pay to performance. Notably, prior to Act 10, there was no gender pay gap in the state's teacher workforce. However, after the implementation of "flexible pay" salary schemes following the elimination of collective bargaining agreements, an identifiable wage gap emerged between women and men.[3]

Between 2012 and 2018, student enrollment in Wisconsin teacher preparation programs dropped by more than a third. In 2016, the State Superintendent of Schools Dr. Tony Evers—who would go on to defeat Walker in the 2018 Wisconsin governor's race—led the writing of a report that pointed to Act 10 as a driver in the state's teacher shortage. Subsequent analyses of the impact of Act 10 on teachers found that teacher attrition did indeed rise in the years following the law's passage.[4]

Teacher Licensing

Like nearly all states in the US, Wisconsin began re-examining its approach to education in the wake of national reports in the 1980s, leading to the strengthening of license requirements for teachers. One of the first teacher policies to emerge in Wisconsin was the culmination of years of advocacy by leaders from the state's tribal population. By the end of the 1980s, these efforts led to legislation— known as Act 31—requiring instruction in the history, culture, and tribal sovereignty of the eleven federally recognized American Indian nations and tribal communities in Wisconsin public school districts. One component of this legislation placed specific requirements on teacher certification and licenses, including: "the study of minority group relations, including instruction in the history, culture and tribal sovereignty of the federally recognized American Indian tribes and bands located in this state."[5] It is notable that, despite all of the changes in teacher policy following the passage of Act 10, these Act 31 requirements have endured without major challenges and currently remain an integral component of both K–12 schooling and teacher preparation in Wisconsin.

The Minority Teacher Loan program, also created by Act 31 in 1989, primarily supported the preparation of teachers for school districts with significant populations of students of color. With this program, teachers meeting the eligibility criteria could borrow up to $30,000, and each year that they taught in a qualifying school district, 25 percent of the original loan would be forgiven. Between 2006–2019, the percentage of students of color in Wisconsin schools increased from 24 percent to 31 percent, while during this same time, less than 5 percent of the teachers in the state were teachers of color.[6]

The four broad categories of teacher licenses in Wisconsin have remained relatively stable, even as the requirements to achieve them have changed. The first level of certification was reserved only for temporary, emergency, or other short-term licenses, while the second was for the more common initial educator license, which included a general requirement for mentoring. Though the state made changes over time to specific licenses since 2004, the meeting of specific academic requirements for initial licensure has remained a mainstay of teacher credentialing and includes subject matter preparation, a grade-point-average threshold, and tests of subject matter knowledge. Teachers at the initial educator stage are required to successfully teach for three to five years and complete a professional development plan. The third-level license of a professional educator had a duration of five years, and teachers had to complete a new professional development plan in order to be eligible for renewal. Though well-intended, evidence began to accumulate that the bureaucratic demands of these and other licensing requirements were contributing to the state's teacher shortage.[7] Consequently, in 2018 the renewal requirement for the professional educator license and the master educator level above it was lifted and was retitled as a lifetime license.[8]

Teacher Preparation

There are few distinctions between traditional and alternate route preparation in Wisconsin state policy. Wisconsin has numerous university-based educator preparation programs offering a traditional path to certification, where teacher candidates are required to complete coursework and participate in supervised clinical experiences in schools. Other pathways into teaching do not require the completion of an educator preparation program as a prerequisite to being hired as a teacher of record. In Wisconsin, the term "alternate route" is reserved for teachers who meet initial requirements, are hired by a school district, and then enroll in a state-approved alternate route educator preparation program. Like many states, Wisconsin has a provision for issuing licenses based on previous teaching experience in other states and currently includes an equivalency pathway to include teaching experience in PK–12, private/charter schools, post-secondary, or industry as well. In 2018, the state also approved an additional pathway for initial certification, that of the American Board for the Certification of Teacher Excellence (ABCTE), which is an online-only certification program that does not require a classroom placement process.

Teacher Evaluation

Throughout most of Wisconsin's public schools' history, teacher evaluation had been largely carried out as a function of each individual district. By the start of 2007, state regulations required each school board in the state to "establish specific criteria and a systematic procedure to measure the performance of licensed school personnel."[9] During this period, data concerning teacher performance was retained by each individual district and not reported to the state. In 2009, Wisconsin Act 60 was passed to permit the use of student standardized test scores as a component of teacher evaluation and also set qualification criteria for evaluators, though this was never made an explicit part of teacher evaluation in state. In 2012, the Wisconsin Legislature passed Act 166, which set the stage for a new teacher evaluation system in an era without teacher tenure. The act established a common statewide teacher evaluation system, based on the Danielson

Framework for Teaching model, and was fully implemented at the start of the 2014–15 school year.[10]

THE CITY OF POMPANO AND POMPANO REGIONAL SCHOOL DISTRICT

Located alongside one of the Great Lakes bordering the state of Wisconsin, the area surrounding the modern-day city of Pompano has been called home by the Menominee, Ojibwe, Potawatomi, and Ho-Chunk people. Prior to the US Civil War, Pompano was a vital hub through which hundreds of enslaved people escaped to freedom. Since that time, the area has helped to settle multiple waves of immigrants. Between 1920 and 1980, the area's population grew alongside its industrial base, attracting large numbers of Black Americans from the southern US, who sought both jobs and relief from terror.[11] In recent years, immigration from Spanish-speaking countries has increased, and the number of residents identifying as Hispanic has risen to equal that of Pompano's African American population. Pompano regularly appears on lists of most affordable places to live and remains known for its wide range of manufacturing businesses. The town is also well-known for its diverse architecture, including the modest brick homes built over the years to accommodate the expanding work force.

In the years following World War II, there was a concerted effort by federal and state governments across the US to consolidate small school districts in order to take advantage of efficiencies made possible by advances in transportation and communication. In Wisconsin, this led to a reduction in the total number of school districts in the state from 7,777 in 1938 to less than 500 only 30 years later. Pompano Regional School District was formed as one of these district consolidations in the early 1960s and today operates dozens of schools serving tens of thousands of students from the city of Pompano and its surrounding suburban and rural fringe communities. The district rose to national attention after leading a successful school desegregation campaign in the 1970s that served as a model for similar efforts across the country. Over the past two decades, the district's fortunes have been moored to Wisconsin's very public battles over school funding, labor rights, and the role of state government in education.

Today, the district publicizes its commitment to serving its diverse community with the breadth and kinds of programming that are only feasible in large comprehensive school districts. Offerings include early childhood schools, dual immersion language elementary schools, as well as middle and secondary magnet schools for fine arts, STEM, and International Baccalaureate (IB) programs. The district runs career and technical education programs throughout its high schools and operates a district-wide virtual school and an alternative school. And yet, as our case below will demonstrate, Pompano Regional School District remained small enough that people across the district knew one another, and district administrators were accessible partners rather than a distant bureaucracy.

Findings

In this section, we discuss four factors that appeared to influence the high teacher retention rate we observed in Pompano Regional School District. These are (1) a high level of teacher autonomy, (2) strong relationships and support from coworkers, (3) the benefits of being from the community, and (4) personal rewards from their teaching assignments.

Factor #1: A high level of teacher autonomy. Of the teachers we interviewed in Pompano, many identified their freedom to make instructional decisions in their own classrooms as a reason to stay. One teacher likened their autonomy to that of a small-business owner and appreciated that administrators were not "on our butts about a bunch of different little picky things." One such example came from a teacher in a Pompano school where they were not expected to submit weekly lesson plans. This teacher told us, "We don't have to submit them. So, it feels like the administration trusts us here, at least that's the feeling I've gotten. There's a level of trust." Another teacher told us he felt the autonomy in his school was especially helpful for new teachers, "because you can kind of try a lot of stuff there." We also heard from a teacher who reported that the administration was "not coming in and trying to micromanage our classrooms, and they never have." She added that she had the freedom to select what happened in her classroom and provided an example specific to what content she would teach and how she would teach it: "If I feel like teaching about an oil spill that happened, then I'm going to bring it up. I'm going to show news clips and teach about it." Multiple teachers connected this sense of professional autonomy in the classroom to their ability to be creative and respond to the needs of their students, and one in particular gave a clear example:

> So, I am teaching an ecology class. I love being outside, I'm a big outdoorsman. So, we have a pond by our school, so I asked one of our principals if we could get a bunch of fishing poles and stuff. We just went fishing for like a week and

> a half. We collected some data on the fish and put it all together to try to determine if the pond was healthy or not. But after I planned on being done, the kids were like "Can we just keep going fishing?" and I was like, "Sure, let's spend another day fishing."

Autonomy was also described by a teacher as an intentional feature of the school district organization:

> A big part of why I stay where I am and enjoy what I'm doing is because you know, I do have this little kind of fiefdom carved out for myself. My administrators don't necessarily fully understand the content of my classes and the pathway, and you know, they are confident to just let me do things the way I see fit. And you know, that's quite nice. I think everyone would appreciate being an employee within an organization that allows them that level of freedom and sort of self-direction.

This teacher drew upon his earlier career in a STEM field to highlight how much he valued this autonomy and appreciated that his current role as a teacher allowed for less insistence upon "formalities and doing things for the sake of doing things."

One teacher felt that it was because of her training in science that she was able to navigate the difficulties of the classroom without a large amount of supervision from her administration. "I don't know, I just went off of whatever seemed right and seemed to work best... It was definitely very hectic, but at the same time, you know, I actually did enjoy it."

However, this degree of teacher autonomy did have a downside. Some teachers reported that the vast amounts of freedom they enjoyed was sometimes accompanied by a lack of feedback and accountability. However, for the majority of teachers that we interviewed, this tradeoff was a reasonable one, because it meant they were in control of their own teaching. The combination of autonomy and trust from the district administration—which was notably *not* framed as neglect by the teachers that we interviewed—appeared to foster a culture of professionalism among teachers.

Factor #2: Strong relationships and support from coworkers. Many of the teachers that we interviewed in the Pompano Regional School District made it evident that the relationships they built with their science department colleagues played a significant role in their decision to stay. This sentiment was echoed across schools in the district among retained and novice teachers alike. One teacher noted that, in the beginning of his career, he chose to remain in Pompano because he was "fully vested in the loan forgiveness program."[12] And though he cited this financial benefit as an initial reason for staying, he continued: "the longer I'm here, the more I like our science group, it's really, really good." For many science teachers in Pompano, the relationships they formed with their colleagues was the basis of support they received from individuals in their department:

> Whenever I needed help, I knew I could go to people who are either teaching the same curriculum as me at the same time or have taught it, and they would give me whatever they had and help me in any way I needed. It's a very nice feeling when you know you have your department people who do this, who have done this for years, to rely on for resources and material.

One science teacher summed up the importance of supportive colleagues: The extent to which that department is willing to step into that role and offer that support to help somebody figure out the ropes and learn how to do things… doing all that stuff goes quite a long way. You know, a department that is supportive and you know, that is able to help you deal with any situation, ease your anxiety, and otherwise make that kind of job easier for you goes quite a long way.

Each school had local subject department heads who also contributed to these networks of support for teachers. One retained teacher explained that she could always choose to "go to the department head, but because I have so many people to ask, he wasn't overburdened."

Similarly, another retained teacher shared with us that his colleagues were the main reason he stays where he is:

> The other science teachers that I work with have been, like, some of my favorite people I've ever worked with. So just my colleagues, especially directly there in the science department, are a big reason for me staying. I just really enjoy hanging out with them. There's some really, really good teachers there that I'm learning a lot from, and I don't really want to leave them.

This same teacher appreciated the wide range of personalities among his colleagues and noted that most of the science teachers in his department did not originally intend to become teachers:

> They're super welcoming. There's a bunch of different personalities in there, which was nice. A lot of them came from the field, which I think is interesting. Most of them weren't planning on being science teachers and were working in the field and didn't like it. One of the guys I came in with was subbing, and he fell in love with teaching, so he came in. One is an art major, which is kind of funny. But they all have their different styles, and we get along really, really well.

Although Pompano had a formal mentorship program, most teachers felt the majority of the support they received in their initial years of teaching came from informal mentorship. One retained teacher explained that, although the district did provide various organized supports, she received much of her teaching knowledge from her methods teacher and student teaching supervisor prior to becoming a teacher of record. Another teacher discussed how they took it upon themselves to shadow two of the experienced teachers in their department:

> I found two teachers that I really respected and appreciated the way that they taught... I just kind of sat in their pockets and was in their rooms. Like, every day at the end of class or at the end of the day, I would ask, "This happened today, what would you have done? Or this happened today, this is what I did. Is that something that makes sense? Or just like, helping with planning, helping like, "Okay, I have this group of kids that are doing this. What are some strategies I could do to kind of help me with that?" So, just a lot of picking certain teachers' brains.

This same teacher put forward the idea that his informal mentors took on motherly roles for him, not only due to the difference in age but also because he valued the knowledge they held and their willingness to share that with him. He went on to explain that although there was a district-wide induction program, he did not have a specific mentor or induction coach working with him during his first year teaching.

We found more than one teacher in the district who mentioned that they began teaching as a second—or sometimes even third—career. To many of them, teaching was a career where the demands of the job matched their affinity for the subject matter. One teacher described how her love of "the idea of the medical field" led her first to work hospitals, and then at a lab job. Eventually, she came across an opportunity to use her science degree in the field of teaching and was now in her sixth year as a teacher.

We interviewed one retained teacher who suggested that science teachers in the Pompano School District had high rates of retention because teaching was not their first experience in a work environment:

> I think having that experience goes a long way towards making your peace with a lot of the issues that end up driving novice teachers out of teaching… As someone who had this experience within the private sector, there are things that you would not expect someone to complain about as a professional. Like, there's this notion that perhaps the grass is greener elsewhere. And having been elsewhere, I know quite well the grass is, in fact, not greener. So, you know, there isn't this notion of I was sold on education being something that it wasn't, now I'm stuck dealing with these kids, and I thought I was going to come change kids' lives, none of them even care. You know, it's more, so I knew what this job was and I chose to do it because I wanted to do that sort of thing, and I'm content… and it's easier for me to see the positives instead of just focus on the negatives.

Although this idea of switching into the career of teaching came up a few times, we felt that, rather than standing alone as its own factor for retention in this case study, these experiences tended to contribute to a shared understanding teachers had with one another in their departments. Sharing the experience of being career switchers allowed them to develop stronger links with their fellow teachers. These links also appeared to be strengthened when teachers were placed in close proximity within their building. One teacher who had recently become a building department head noted, "Part of it is being in the same hallway, building relationships by talking between classes. That builds camaraderie." One teacher remarked on the very clear social benefits from sharing hallways and classrooms:

> So, our science department is kind of cool. All the rooms are connected to each other through doors. There are more science teachers than there are rooms, so we have to share rooms with other teachers. So, you're constantly talking to them like, "Hey I need to set up a lab, is that all right?" So, like, as you're walking through, you'll say hi to all the teachers and see how their day is doing. And because we have more teachers in rooms, we share offices. So, like, every single one of my preps, I have at least two other teachers in my office that we can kind of just talk and hang out with.

Some teachers recognized the tradeoffs of sharing spaces with other teachers. One teacher noted that, prior to having her own room, she was "forced basically to interact with the other teachers." However, now that she has a room of her own, she also enjoys staying in her classroom all day and having more control about when she interacts with other teachers. "I can organize my space the way I want it," she noted, and not feel as if she is intruding into other teachers' classes.

Factor #3: Roots in the community. A recurring theme in our interviews was that teachers in Pompano both initially applied to teach and stayed in the district because they themselves were from the community. Indeed, many of the teaching staff we interviewed grew up in Pompano and were even alumni of the schools in which they worked. Such an outcome is well-documented in the teacher workforce literature.[13]

One of the department chairs we interviewed attributed teacher retention to the teachers having a greater understanding of the community, a result of being part of it prior to becoming a teacher. She said, "A lot of the learning about the community, like, you've kind of already checked that box, you know, because you grew up here you have a family here, so you have experience here." In a different interview, one of the retained teachers said, "I suspect more of them are people from the area who have a more developed sense of what the areas are like, what the community is like, what the characteristics of the students are like, and are going back into education." Another teacher plainly stated, "Let's see, what else made me stay? Well, I graduated from here, and now I work here, so that's pretty cool." One teacher we interviewed had not grown up in Pompano but had attended college in the area, which offered her "a lot of that experience in and knowledge of the community." This idea was echoed by one of the retained teachers, who otherwise struggled to identify reasons for his district's high retention rates. He said, "it might be just that they want to teach where they grew up."

Other benefits related to the surrounding community surfaced in our interviews in Pompano. One of the teachers explained the benefit of working in the same district that her children attended, including sharing the same days off. Another teacher, who grew up nearby, recently decided to purchase a home in Pompano. She found the city of Pompano "nice because it's a lot cheaper to live here," but noted that the cost of living did not particularly impact her decision to remain teaching in the district.

Another community-related factor—brought to our attention by a district administrator—was that the community was given the opportunity to be part of developing curriculum goals within the district of Pompano. About six years prior, the district moved towards an academy model within its larger comprehensive schools. The district administrator described the implementation of the academy model at one particular high school:

> We really did a lot of background in terms of—in the community—what kinds of skills, what kinds of jobs are needed and in demand, and what are serving as barriers to our students to entering the workforce or, you know, college and then the workforce after. So, we did a lot of work in terms of aligning what we offer to students to an academy or pathway. So, for example, one of the pathways there at the time that I worked there was health sciences and education. So, if a student was to enter the health sciences pathway, they were part of a group of students of that same focus, there was a series of classes in health sciences that they would take. There were conversations around, you know, if you desire a career in health sciences. What does that look like in terms of what we offer that would prepare you for college postsecondary or a career in the medical field postsecondary. A lot of that work was really focused on getting kids engaged and getting them to see that what they're doing now has meaning and has impact postsecondary. So that was really exciting work.

This same administrator later told us that, in addition to the academy models, the surrounding community is also influential in the types of professional development offered to Pompano teachers, as well as the opportunities made available to students. This administrator explained that the district has made an effort to "build up connections with community partners, whether that be the universities that are close to us but also businesses that are around us, too." Examples of these opportunities included externships for both teachers and students, which provided further opportunities for teachers to interact with community partners. Notably, multiple people commented on the difficulty of keeping these partnerships sustained during the COVID-19 pandemic.

Factor #4: District support for individual teacher needs and personal rewards from their teaching assignments. We propose one remaining factor—more tentative in nature—that we believe affected teacher retention in Pompano. Many of the teachers and administrators we interviewed made mention of individualized reasons for remaining within the district of Pompano. However, the exact reason was not always shared amongst them or across the different school buildings in which they taught. In an effort to capture each of these important reasons into this case, we began to realize that, although the reasons may not have been the same, they most likely resulted from the agency the district gave teachers over their own teaching careers. We use the term *agency* to refer to teachers' control over the direction of their careers, as distinct from teacher autonomy over their own classroom teaching discussed above. The difference appears to have been a consequence of the ways in which the district supported individual teachers' own visions for their teaching career—including which students they were to teach. For some, their preference was with high-achieving students, while others found teaching students with the highest needs fulfilling.

For example, two of the teachers we interviewed cited the higher level of student performance that kept them in Pompano. For these teachers, it seemed to be the anticipated perks associated with longevity, or holding out for the favorable teaching assignment, that bolstered their capacity to remain in their school. One teacher, who had been in the district for over ten years, discussed her early years teaching a particular group of ninth-graders, purportedly the most difficult grade to teach at the school. She told us that the freshman classes were routinely given to "the newest teachers." However, over her time in the district, she received training to teach one of the specialized pathways in the school and went from teaching "people who hate science, to people who absolutely love it, and it's been awesome." She explained that having the opportunity to teach a course to students who were more inclined to learning science allowed her "to be more creative" in her teaching.

Another teacher specifically cited the ability grouping of students as a factor in his retention:

> The pathway I teach is one that tends to attract the higher achievers within the school. It's a college prep pathway; it offers college accreditation for doing well enough in the classes. And, as a result of that, I tend to attract students who are a little bit more academically inclined, and as well, tend to be more mature, I suppose, for the lack of better descriptor, and as a result of that, I really don't get the worst of it. I have kids who are not causing me a lot of emotional turmoil, challenging my authority, or otherwise burning up willpower.

This same teacher compared his retention with the attrition of others: Realistically speaking, I think a large part of it does boil down to the fact that I have students who are better than the average student within the building, and to play devil's advocate, you could make a very strong argument that many of the things that I've said would ring hollow if I had very difficult students who were particularly rowdy and left me emotionally drained at the end of every day. I see that in some colleagues, where they deal with rough classes, all day in and day out, and I don't think it's hard to see why [they leave] at that point.

By moving teachers away from classes of students they felt were more difficult and into placements that met their own expectations of what teaching should look like, the district helped to keep these teachers within the schools they were teaching. This, of course, raises questions about both equity in classrooms related to tracking and the overall impact of such a strategy on the school and district as a whole. Yet, we include this example here because the teacher cited his pairing with a particular group of students as a reason for staying.

Others we interviewed spoke more plainly about how the district moves teachers between schools or between subject areas within a school as a way of reducing teacher attrition. Our tentative claim is that Pompano supports teacher retention by being attentive to the needs of its teachers. One of the administrators told us that, during her time teaching in Pompano, the school underwent a significant drop in enrollment. Rather than reduce the size of the district's teacher workforce (i.e., lay off teachers), the district restructured in order to keep its teachers. This administrator noted that the district gave particular attention to new teachers during this restructure: "We were able to keep folks that came on board simply because, you know, as the school shrunk and folks retired, we just didn't fill those positions. We were able to structure the schedule in a way that we kept people." This idea was echoed by one of the teachers we interviewed. They told us, "They're very good with moving people around, so like, if you're struggling or just disliking something, they're good at, you know, placing you somewhere else." However, both the administrator and the teacher explained that this type of restructuring becomes more difficult when a teacher holds a specialized or less flexible teaching license.

We also included in this factor the personal rewards that teachers may have experienced from their particular teaching placement. One such example was the feeling of helping students in need, what some teachers described in one way or another as playing a part in providing an equitable teaching experience for students. According to one teacher, to those outside the district, Pompano often gets a "bad rap," and expressed that one of their main reasons for staying is because they want to continue to support their students. One teacher explained to us:

> One thing that I think a lot of us can relate to is that our school is pretty low in the district, we have very low reading and math [scores] and, in general, I think a lot of us feel, not guilty or responsible, I don't know what the correct word for this is, but a lot of us really just want to help them. Like with my seniors I'm

> teaching, some of them don't know how to do percentages... And we, I think, as a science department, we understand that it's not them, they've just been wronged somewhere along the line. Like, if you're a senior in high school and you don't know how to do fractions, it's not your fault. So, I think a lot of us just get really connected to the kids and don't want to leave them and just be like, "you're somebody else's problem now."

Another teacher said, "To be completely honest, when I'm thinking of teaching, I want to teach more at-risk students. I want to be involved in the experience of students who don't get the resources that every other student gets." She continued by saying that for her, one of the "big things that's kind of kept me around" was her ability to "teach a diverse set of students that aren't as privileged as other students in the surrounding areas." For this teacher, not only was teaching the high-need population of students at her school important but coaching them even more so. She explained that the families of her players were unable to pay for their children to participate in club sports in the city, a major avenue for other players in the districts to gain advanced skills and experiences. She told us:

> I think that's another reason why I've stuck here as well, because I just feel like my players deserve a quality coach, not just anyone they can find that can act like they know what they're doing. Regardless of the fact that they don't have money or experience, I feel like they deserve someone to teach them the game properly. So that's honestly, probably, the biggest reason why I'm still at [school name].

Teachers reported an appreciation for the diverse group of students they taught in Pompano. For some, this may not have been the reason they initially chose to work in the district, but it eventually became one of their main reasons for staying. One teacher said, "Well, the students are pretty cool. You get some rough classes; it's the typical mix of kids from wildly different backgrounds. I mean, you got kids that live out in the richest place in the city next to kids who live in apartment complexes in very poor areas. So, you get a wide variety of personalities."

One teacher noted the importance of student diversity in their retention. After a brief discussion about district demographics, this teacher said, "Very diverse cultures are awesome for me, I really appreciate that."

MENTORING AND INDUCTION

In Pompano, teachers participate in a new-educator orientation, which takes place in August, prior to the start of the school year. Similar to other districts across the country, this consists of technology training, along with meeting various district personnel. Additionally, teachers are provided what was described as necessary professional development, such as workshops on the district's Individual Education Plan (IEP) process, social emotional learning, and general classroom management strategies. During the orientation, new teachers also have the opportunity to meet their induction coaches.

Previously in Pompano, individual mentors from the same department were assigned to teachers new to the profession and to the district and paid a stipend from the district. In 2017, Pompano moved to a model of full-time induction coaches, funded through federal Title II funds, who are solely focused on mentoring and do not have their own teaching load. The individual overseeing instructional coaches in the district explained that induction coaches serve in a nonevaluative capacity, with their biggest role in helping teachers with their "instructional cycles." Consistent with the teacher autonomy and agency described above, teachers we interviewed appreciated the latitude they were given in choosing the components of their induction and professional development.

SUMMARY OF THE POMPANO CASE

From our interviews, it was clear that teachers in the Pompano Regional School District valued their autonomy, particularly the ability to teach with little micromanaging from administration. Additionally, although the district provided a structured mentoring and induction program for the teachers in Pompano, it was the informal relationships they developed with their colleagues that many cited as a primary reason to stay teaching in the district. In addition to their relationships with each other, several teachers reported connections to the community, including their own personal histories and partnerships fostered by the district in developing curriculum and professional development opportunities. Lastly, teachers in Pompano seemed to benefit from the district's attentiveness to their individual needs and desires as teachers, offering a sense of agency in their careers that allowed them to flourish and remain teaching in the district.

CHAPTER 7

Where Teachers Stay for Kinship and Community

The Case of Kingfisher School District

The schools in the Kingfisher County Public School District serve over 20,000 students and are spread over a wide geographic area among the county's many farms and wetlands. We selected the Kingfisher School District for closer study because it had one of the highest retention rates for novice science teachers in the state, including a larger than average number of novice teachers who were designated as non-White and non-Hispanic in state staffing files. Only after identifying the district as high-retention and selecting it for a case study did we learn that Kingfisher County has been and remains home to a large Native American population. As will be demonstrated, this fact proved salient to teacher retention in the district.

Out of the North Carolina districts we studied, we present Kingfisher here because we feel it provides unique and informative insights about teacher retention while echoing themes we found elsewhere. As this chapter will show, we identified the role of kinship and community as key factors in the retention of teachers in this district; our use of the term *kinship* is drawn from the work of Native and Indigenous education researchers that we describe in greater detail below.

We begin this chapter with an overview of the North Carolina teacher policy context, followed by a brief description of Kingfisher County and its school district. We then review each of the retention factors we identified at Kingfisher and conclude with a brief look at the school's current mentoring and induction efforts.

NORTH CAROLINA TEACHER POLICY BACKGROUND

North Carolina's educational policy between 2007–2018 has been one of tension between the forces of professionalization on one hand and of deregulation on the other.[1] North Carolina's contemporary educational system was shaped in large measure by policies championed by Republican Governor James B. Hunt, who served a total of four terms between 1977 and 2001. Hunt was credited with a number of targeted changes in North Carolina's schools that impacted the work of teachers, including the provision of teacher assistants to every early-elementary-grade classroom, substantially increasing teacher salaries and incentivizing teachers' professional development, and the and the incentivizing of National Board Certification for North Carolina's teachers.[2]

In the 2012 election, Republicans gained control of the governor's office and won veto-proof supermajorities in both legislative houses of the General Assembly, leading to a number of subsequent changes in educational policy, including the abolition of teacher tenure—referred to in the state as *career status*—for any new hires.[3] North Carolina has historically been a "right-to-work" state, in which union membership cannot be compelled as a condition of work, and contracts between units of government and labor organizations concerning public employees have been illegal for over seventy years.[4] With such limits on the power of labor unions to shape educational policy and practice in North Carolina, teacher associations continue to remain engaged on issues such as teacher working conditions.[5]

North Carolina teachers are employed by their local educational authorities, but educator salaries in North Carolina are determined and financed by the state legislature, which distributes funding directly to districts for educator salaries and benefits.[6] Between 2008 and 2014, the state-established salary schedule was increased by the legislature only 1.6 percent, lagging behind inflation (which was about 10 percent over the same period), thus erasing prior gains that North Carolina had made in bringing teacher salaries in line with that of other states.[7]

Individual districts may elect to pay salary supplements to schoolteachers and staff to offset the higher cost of living in certain districts, or even as incentives. These funds are raised through local tax levies, and studies have shown their impact on school funding equity across districts in the state.[8] Prior to 2013, teachers with a master's degree or other advanced degree received a salary supplement from the state, but this was rescinded by the North Carolina legislature for all educators except administrators, child study specialists, school counselors, or other employees whose credential required the degree.[9]

Teacher bonuses, first implemented in North Carolina in 1996, have served to both recruit and reward teachers. Districts may offer signing bonuses to attract teachers to high-need schools or positions. Such bonuses may range from an unconditional $1500 upon signing an employment contract to $10,000 or more when certain conditions are met.[10] In some cases, bonuses have been used to incentivize teacher performance, either directly in relation to student achievement or collectively, by rewarding bonuses to school faculty and staff for student outcomes.[11]

In 2013, when the state moved away from degree-based upward mobility on the salary scale, earning a National Board Certification became one of the only ways for teachers to gain an increase in their monthly pay.[12] Currently, North Carolina has the greatest number of National-Board-Certified teachers in the country, with nearly 25 percent of all teaching staff having received certification from the National Board of Professional Teaching Standards.[13] In order to prepare for certification, teachers are allotted up to three days of paid leave, and teachers who complete the certification receive credits towards renewal of their Continuing Professional License.

Teachers in North Carolina are required to complete a two-step licensing process and an evaluation of teacher effectiveness that includes student outcomes. Teachers must first obtain their Initial Professional License by completing an approved educator preparation program, either through a traditional university pathway or through the state's Lateral Entry (i.e., alternate route) program. After at least three years of teaching, teachers can apply for their Continuing Professional License, which must be renewed every five years. Teachers in North Carolina with less than three years of teaching experience are considered *beginning* or *new*, and those with three or more are referred to as *experienced*. This nomenclature is used for both licensing and for teacher evaluation.

In North Carolina, all licensed teachers have long been required to receive an annual evaluation, but the determinants of that evaluation have shifted significantly over the years. In 1986, North Carolina took steps to develop an evaluation tool based on both the literature surrounding effective teaching practices and the input of North Carolina classroom teachers. The result was the Teacher Performance Appraisal Instrument (TPAI), which included key standards for teacher performance.[14] These standards were later revised under the Excellent Schools Act of 1997 to include a greater focus on teachers as leaders, content proficiency, and the ability to develop respectful classroom communities with a diverse student population. This gave North Carolina a head start in meeting some of the highly qualified teacher requirements that would be a feature of subsequent federal legislation. In 2007, and again in 2011, teacher evaluations were revised to include a focus on the Framework for 21st Century Learning and the newly approved North Carolina Professional Teaching Standards. This was accompanied by the North Carolina Teacher Evaluation Process (NCTEP) as a method for evaluating teachers on their implementation of the standards. Like many states in this study, the incentives offered by the federal government during the Obama administration led to an intertwining of teacher evaluation and measures of student outcomes in North Carolina, driven by the development of statewide data systems.

In 1992, North Carolina was one of the first in the nation to develop a longitudinal educational data system. Within the next decade, a partnership between Duke University and the North Carolina Department of Public Instruction led to the creation of the North Carolina Education Research Data Center. As detailed in appendix B, the state continued to receive federal funding to refine its state educational data systems, including a $400 million Race to the Top grant in 2010. This funding led to the development of NC SchoolWorks, which expanded the current data system to track educational data from prekindergarten through postsecondary education.[15] In 2013, the inclusion of value-added models incorporating student achievement outcomes into teacher evaluation resulted in the creation and adoption of the North Carolina Educator Value-Added Assessment System (EVAAS).

One other outcome of the state's Race to the Top award was increased support for new teachers. A state survey in 2010 showed that over half of new teachers with three or less years of experience were not provided with an opportunity to observe other teachers and almost half did not meet formally with their mentor teachers. As a result of these survey results, the state created the Beginning Teacher Support Program, with specific requirements for districts and teachers in the first three years of their career.[16] This program was developed in collaboration with the University of North Carolina System of Colleges of Education and serves all new teachers in the state. One tangible outcome relevant to the present study, noted in the case below, is that each district was required to have a Beginning Teacher Coordinator who had access to state materials and guidance for the support of new teachers.[17]

KINGFISHER COUNTY AND KINGFISHER COUNTY SCHOOL DISTRICT

The state of North Carolina can be divided geographically into a mountainous western region, the central Piedmont foothills, and an eastern low and flat coastal plain—where Kingfisher County is located. Over the past century, the area has slowly transitioned away from tobacco and cotton agriculture toward growing its manufacturing base. The county remains mostly rural, with plenty of land between the towns and townships where many schools are located. [18] There is one main city where a community college, a branch of the state university, and the county's only hospital are all situated. Kingfisher often ranks low on statewide social and economic indicators, including those connected to educational outcomes. Kingfisher County has never been heavily populated, and today draws few visitors except for those passing through. Yet historically, it has served as a refuge for those escaping enslavement and ethnic persecution whose adversaries did not wish to follow them into the wetlands.

The area is home to a significant American Indian population, who are predominantly from one state-recognized tribe.[19] The fact that many of the students, teachers, administrators, and support staff were of Native descent was frequently referenced by those we met and interviewed in Kingfisher in the course of our research there.

The Kingfisher County School District operates over thirty elementary, middle, and high schools throughout the county. Most of these schools are comparatively small, with the exception of three large high schools that serve over a thousand students each. Nearly 30 percent of the students are categorized as economically disadvantaged. In some documents, we saw Kingfisher referred to as a "majority-minority" school district because White students made up less than 10 percent of the population. Indeed, as shown in Figure 7.1, 60 percent of the teachers and 80 percent of the administrators in the district were also

FIGURE 7.1

Kingfisher School District, North Carolina

About the community

Community (sending districts) total population:	~150,000
Total households:	~55,000
Median household income:	~$55,000
Households with broadband Internet:	~80%
Housing structure type	
House:	~70%
Apartments/other:	~30%

NCES Locale type

Rural – Fringe (41): Census-defined rural territory that is ≤ 5 miles from an Urbanized Area, as well as rural territory that is ≤ 2.5 miles from an Urban Cluster.

About the district

Total Students:	~21,000
Classroom Teachers (FTE):	~1,00
Student/Teacher Ratio:	16:1
Per pupil spending (2018):	~$11,000
Grades served:	K–12
Total Schools:	~35
Total Certified Science Teachers:	~70
Avg. HS Science Department Size:	~10
Starting salary 2007–08:	~$34,000
Starting salary 2017–18:	~$38,000

Kingfisher Regional School District Demographics

Race/ Ethnicity	Teachers	Students	Admins.
White	35%	10%	20%
Hispanic	–	–	–
Black	20%	20%	20%
Asian	–	<1%	–
Native American	–	40%	–
Other	40%	10%	50%

Category	Students
Economically Disadvantaged Students	30%
Students with Disabilities	5%
English Learners	<5%

Note: All school and district names in this report have been changed to pseudonyms to protect the confidentiality of study participants. The "Kingfisher" School District is a county-level K–12 public school district. Demographic data and dollar figures have been rounded in order to preserve district anonymity. All data is from the 2017–2018 academic year. Teacher and Administrator race/ethnicity in North Carolina was only reported as "White," "Black," and "Other." Includes local salary supplement ($2000 in 2008–9, $3000 in 2017–18) added to the state base pay determined by the North Carolina Legislature.

Sources: U.S. Census Bureau: https://www.census.gov/acs/www/data/data-tables-and-tools/data-profiles/2017/
U.S. Department of Education, National Center for Educational Statistics, Common Core of Data: https://nces.ed.gov/ccd/

non-White. However, in our conversations with people in Kingfisher, we also found that racial and ethnic categorizations were invoked less often than those of family and tribal identity.

Findings

As a result of our site visit to Kingfisher and subsequent data analysis, we posit three factors that likely influenced the high novice-science-teacher retention rate observed in the Kingfisher School District. These are 1) teaching as a good and available job, 2) the pull of home and the local community, and 3) opportunities for professional growth and development. This section is followed by a brief description of current mentoring and induction efforts at Kingfisher School District.

Factor #1: Teaching as a good and available job. The literature on teacher attrition is replete with stories of disillusionment leading to teachers leaving their positions or the profession altogether.[20] What was notable about the teachers our team interviewed in Kingfisher was that nearly all described their reasons for staying in the profession as being the same as the reasons that they initially entered. In our Kingfisher interviews, conducted in the spring of 2022, we were surprised to encounter little to no sense of disillusionment; this conveyed the impression that teachers entered the profession possessing a realistic awareness of the work of teaching. This perspective was most evident in teachers who switched into teaching from a previous career, and many highlighted the fact that teaching was an available option to them because of their prior work and college degrees.

Most of the science teachers we interviewed in Kingfisher obtained degrees in science or science-adjacent fields and only later made the decision to pursue teaching by entering the profession through North Carolina's lateral entry pathway into teaching.[21] One of the lead science teachers at Kingfisher Central High School highlighted this fact for us: "I think right now we only have three [science teachers] who are not lateral entry." Most of the Kingfisher science teachers in this second-career category noted that they happened to have enough credits to apply for a science teacher certification because their original career goals required the majority of their coursework to be in the sciences. One teacher told us: "I knew I wanted to teach, but at the time when I was in college, I was unsure about what I wanted to teach. I was qualified for science, so I started lateral entry."

A number of Kingfisher teachers reported they did not originally intend to enter teaching, but teaching was one of the few jobs available in the county for science majors. One of the retained teachers explained that local "job options are farming, retail, or teaching. [With] not a lot of job opportunities, teaching is a good option." This was echoed by another retained teacher, who said that the two biggest professional opportunities for individuals with a science degree in the area were in health fields and teaching. Another retained science teacher, who had lived outside of the county for several years, made the decision to return home due to a family member's illness. Despite having no plans to teach, people in her life suggested she look into becoming a teacher. She resisted the idea initially, responding to the suggestion of teaching with "It ain't gonna happen!" However, over time, teaching emerged as a reasonable option for her to pursue with her background in science.

A few teachers shared that their main reason for going into—and remaining—in teaching was so they could also take on coaching positions at their schools. One teacher explained their experience of becoming a science teacher in order to coach at Kingfisher South: "I ended up doing the science route, and I had been trying to get to PE (physical education), but I got used to being in the science classroom." Another teacher told us:

> The reason why I started teaching is because I actually started coaching here. This is my fifth year coaching, and then there was a science position opening that came available, and it kind of drove me into the classroom. So, I figured I'd have more availability as far as coaching and teaching at the same time.

Despite having undergraduate degrees in fields outside of education, many of the lateral entry teachers we interviewed described finding a new role as teachers in or near the schools they had attended in their youth. Some never left the area—while others made the decision to return home—and now saw teaching as a mechanism for giving back to the community in which they were raised. When asked about the pathway to teaching in Kingfisher, one teacher replied:

> Why did I become a teacher? I wanted to give back to my community. I work at the same place I was born and raised; I mean, in the same area. I had some really awesome teachers during my school years who really encouraged me and pushed me, and I wanted to do the same for students here in Kingfisher County. It's home to me.

As will be discussed in the next section, many of the teachers had personal ties to the area, but here, we highlight the pattern of these decisions to enter teaching being driven by teaching as a well-paying professional job that allowed them to stay in the area.

Teachers also described to us certain benefits of the teaching profession more broadly. One example given to us by a science teacher related to the way a teacher's schedule aligns with goals of raising a family. "It's easy to drop your kids off and come here to work." Other teachers expressed how the teacher schedule "provides time to raise a family." One teacher—in her second career and having a child later in life—felt that teaching aligned well with the needs of being a parent, noting, "I would have the same schedule that [my child] had." She contrasted teaching with working in a hospital, where she would most likely have had to work weekends and holidays.

Other teachers agreed that, although teaching was not easy, the hours made the teaching profession worth it for them. "If I left teaching here, it would be for community college or university to increase my salary, but who wants to work those hours?" Others explained that, although teacher pay was not necessarily good compared to jobs outside of Kingfisher County, it was better than most other local options. "For this area," one teacher told us, "it is hard to match the salary with another job." In addition to salary, teachers valued the health insurance and retirement benefits that the job provided. All of these factors attracted teachers into the profession in the first place, and continued to be good reasons for them to stay in the district.

Factor #2: The pull of home and the local community. For the majority of the science teachers and administrators that we interviewed in Kingfisher, the choice to teach was often tied to decisions about where to live. In response to the question of why science teacher retention was so high in Kingfisher, one teacher responded, "Well, I mean... because everybody's also from here and then stays here." Many of the teachers we interviewed were teaching in the very same schools they had attended as students. One of the novice teachers at Kingfisher Central observed, "I think the outlier is *not being* from here." One retained teacher told us, "That's very important. Kingfisher County is where I was born and raised, and I have no intention to ever leave them. So, going to another school district has never been an option for me or has never been a perceived thought. I like working here in my hometown."

Unlike many of her colleagues, one teacher always knew she wanted to teach and described the pull to return home to become a teacher:

> I went to NC State, graduated from NC State in 1996. I'm originally from the county. Went off to school, came back, decided to give back because we are a rural county, we're highly poverty at risk county. I got a teaching-fellow scholarship and decided to come back to where I'm from... Probably half of the teachers, there's three or four on our hallway that I actually taught. So, I have a vested interest in this school and the kids.

Others expressed the choice to teach locally in terms of a sense of responsibility to their community:

> I have nieces and nephews coming through, family members coming through, church members' children coming through. So, it's just, I don't want to say I feel obligated, but I almost feel like I need to stay here for all these kids. It's also rewarding because a lot of our kids go to our local university and graduate and then they work in our community.

This notion of teaching as a "familial duty" was more clearly stated by one of the novice teachers, who noted, "You want to take care of your parents, your siblings, you want to be a pillar in that sense, you have church connections."

Being from the area also meant that individuals in the school established particularly close ties with their fellow teachers and staff in the building. It was common for individuals to identify their school community as close-knit, but that description falls short in describing the relationships we observed in Kingfisher. When someone in a Kingfisher school says their teaching community is like family, it is not always metaphorical. Many teachers are, in fact, related to the people they work with. Others are friends and neighbors who have known each other and each other's families for generations. An example of this generational presence within the school district occurred when one science teacher's father entered the library while the interview was taking place on the other side of the room:

> Well, I do know a lot of people here, like my dad just walked in [nods head in direction of the door], he's been here thirty years. The head principal here, he taught me. He was actually a history teacher when I was in high school here, 2007 through 2011, and now he's the boss.

Although the teacher retention literature speaks to the phenomenon of teachers returning to teach in their hometowns, there seemed to be additional influences at play in Kingfisher County.[22] The character of the district's Native American culture was often invoked as a reason for the closeness experienced by their school community.

> Well, that has to do with who we are, our culture. First, foremost, who we are, what type of people we are. Most of the people around here, I don't know if you know it, but we're Native American, so that has a lot to do [with it]. We also live within smaller communities, and the people there know each other, they're family, they're friends. That's how we are around here. We're community based. If you live in a community, more than likely you are living around your family, you're living around family, friends, people you've known, your family's known for years, so decades. So that's how it works. And that fosters the environment here, the school culture, how we do things.

For this local Native community, the closeness and the familial ties described by the individuals in Kingfisher central closely resembles the concept of *kinship*, often referred to by Native cultures throughout the United States and elsewhere. Many Native cultures live within networks that cannot be easily described through the western concept of the nuclear family unit.[23] Such family networks serve several functions outside of childrearing, including maintaining autonomy from colonial ways of living, and includes a sense of belonging with both the people and places from which they come.

And yet, there is a long history of public schooling being used as a mechanism to destroy kinship systems among Native American communities.[24] As noted professor of American Indian Studies Leo Kevin Killsback (Northern Cheyenne) described, such efforts have served to privilege and reinforce "white male patriarchal kinship and family systems."[25] In a broader discussion about Indigenous education, Cornel Pewewardy (Comanche-Kiowa), Anna Lees (Waganakasing Odawa, descendant), and Hyuny Clark-Shim highlighted the fact that, "while there is no single epistemology connected across tribal nations, Indigenous education traditionally occurred holistically and in social settings that emphasized the individual's responsibilities and contributions to the larger community."[26] As we demonstrate below, these responsibilities and contributions were clearly evident in our visit to the Kingfisher School District, and it does appear that indigenous kinship systems are recognized—and even flourish—in schools there.

For example, the sense of kinship was exemplified when speaking with one of the high school science department chairs:

> You have to understand, everyone you've seen today, they've known each other or their family. The girl, the young lady next door, I taught her in school. But I have known her since she was a little thing. I know her mother, she teaches English... Her sister works here in another department. Her sons come through here, know her family, even the principal. I knew him, I taught his son. So, you know everybody, and it's just family, and that means a lot. I think it means a lot that we know each other, or we church together, or we ball together, or we just hang out, or we have mutual friends, that just means a lot.

He then wove this idea of sustained individual relationships into a description of the community:

> I knew my neighbors. Me and my neighbors were cousins. If we weren't cousins, the neighbors, we knew the neighbors because my grandparents knew their parents, their grandparents, you know what I'm saying? So it was that. We worked together. We farm—you got to realize that too. You won't have nobody old enough to talk about it, but farming was a big thing around here and when I was younger. They farmed together during the summertime; they picked cucumbers during the summertime together. They did tobacco in the summertime together. That's how you get or foster the community aspect, how people... We just know each other. We relate, so that makes a difference. It makes a big difference.

It was impressed upon us by multiple interviewees that their Native American culture influences school dynamics, as part of the broader community in which the school is situated. Our research team received multiple invitations to return later in the year for the annual Powwow. "You'll be able to see what I mean by what family is," one teacher told us. "You'll see what family really does look like, what a community looks like." We were also encouraged by multiple people to visit a nearby museum that featured the history of the local tribe, which we did, in order to better understand the familial relationships within Kingfisher schools that were identified by participants as important to the issue of teacher retention.

It is this kinship that appeared to ground the relationships teachers had with their coworkers and sustain the support they received in Kingfisher. The science department chair recounted his first years at the school in this way:

> At the time when I started teaching, I knew basically the whole entire staff, and they knew me, so it's not like I didn't know who they were, and I didn't... and I knew I could approach them.

He explained that he struggled a lot in his first five years of teaching and often wanted to leave the profession. However, one of the reasons he attributed to his decision to remain teaching was his relationships with his coworkers. He continued by telling us, "The ladies that were here actually were former teachers of mine... So, when I come in, they gave me material. They gave me everything I really needed." One of the novice teachers echoed this sentiment:

> Graduating from here, I know, like, a good portion of the teachers out here. Some of them were my teachers when I was in school. So, that's kind of nice. I have that comfort and that relationship already with them... And then that just kind of makes you feel like you're already home or part of the family. So, I think you have that sense of comfort.

Another teacher at Kingfisher expressed the idea that, because his coworkers were former teachers of his, "It made me more at ease with that person." He told us they were able to joke about his years as a student, while at the same time giving him a sense that he was now a colleague: "He didn't make me feel he's up here [hand up high], and I'm down here [hand lowered]. He didn't do that."

At Kingfisher South, one teacher noted a type of support that occurred because it was "just passed down from our generations, our family works here." He continued:

> A lot of my coworkers, we all... I don't know, it's like birds of a feather flock together. All of my guys that I grew up with, we all came back here, and now we're all teaching, literally. I don't know, I can't speak for others... I just know, personally, that we stay around here because we, of course, are going to have support—for two, we know people care about us, and then we can reach the kids because they know us personally.

Teachers in Kingfisher felt strongly that being from the community and even more specifically, working at the school they graduated from, allowed them to offer and receive more support from their colleagues. They noted that community ties helped them deepen their relationships with students in their classrooms:

> Well, I love the kids, of course, and once again, I'm from here. The kids, they know of me. A lot of kids know me, their parents went to school with me or was a little bit older than me, and so, it's kind of easier because I can reach them, and then I understand their background, the reason why they behave the way they do or the reasons for their actions.

Others added to this belief that being from the area allowed them to have stronger connections with one another, fostering a much deeper sense of care for the people they were working with, which led to higher rates of retention. One teacher described the connection this way:

> You work a little bit better and you work a little bit harder when you have ties to something. Whereas, if you can cut something loose with the quickness, you're like, I don't care. I don't care I don't have any ties, when you don't have ties there. And see, we all are from here. We have ties here.

For the overwhelming majority of teachers in this district that we interviewed, being in their home community was a driving factor for choosing to live and teach in Kingfisher County. One of the retained teachers in the district described succinctly, "It's because we are from Kingfisher County and we see the need. We are just from this area."

Factor #3: Opportunities for professional growth and development. When asked about professional development, almost every teacher we interviewed mentioned different opportunities that were available to them at the district or school level. One of the opportunities that stood out were the district-funded retreats that took place within the time frame of our study's retention data (2007–2018) but were no longer offered by the time we visited.[27] Teachers who had worked in the district for ten years or more looked back on these retreats as highlights in their teaching careers. One long-time teacher noted, "We would actually go on retreats. We would have teacher retreats. And it's kind of like, it would just give us a boost." These retreats would take place over a weekend, at places such as Myrtle Beach, where teachers would engage in professional development similar to what they would receive on a typical professional development day in their school building. One teacher said, "When we do our retreats, we get caught up. We have fun. We are there to do our job and learn, but at the same token, we're there to learn from each other and build relationships." Another teacher noted that the retreats "rejuvenated" teachers. Although the novice teachers we spoke with did not have the opportunity to attend these retreats, it was clear that it was foundational in supporting many of the retained teachers, as well as giving them something to look forward to during the year.

Teachers also referenced opportunities that were specific to the science department. Many were focused on biology teachers, given that biology is a tested subject on the North Carolina standardized tests. Other opportunities that were mentioned were those used to meet the state's teaching license renewal requirements. One recent professional development that was not mandatory—but did count towards license renewal—took place in the summer of 2019 and was centered around the Next Generation Science Standards.[28] One of the retained science teachers at Kingfisher Central told us that she "learned a lot about it, and [she] brought that knowledge back." Other science-specific professional development came in the form of teacher work days, (i.e., in-service days), where students would stay home and teachers would take part in professional development. One teacher told us that these days would look differently over the years depending on the administration, and teachers would be encouraged to work collaboratively with their colleagues or be left to work individually.

Teachers mentioned that different science content areas had the opportunity to have day-long planning sessions. These sessions typically took place twice a year and occurred away from their buildings so that teachers would not be disturbed while they were working. One teacher described what occurred during these planning sessions:

> Gathered our supplies, our pacing guide, standards, all that, and we went to the middle school... We planned our semester. We planned all of our tests. We worked on lesson plans, a skeleton. Standards that we struggle with, our students struggle with, we focused on those, gathering resources. It was almost like a brainstorming.

Whether outside-of-district or school-sponsored professional development, teachers reported being supported in attending a variety of outside opportunities. One retained teacher told us, "Our principal is really good about leading. If we want to go to a workshop, I mean, I've never known him to say no." Examples of such professional development opportunities included the Bertino Forensics Summer Institute for teachers in New York and the annual National Science Teachers Association (NSTA) conference. Registration, travel, and accommodation were covered by the Kingfisher School Board. One teacher reported, "I've never been turned down for anything that I've ever needed." Prior to the COVID-19 pandemic, many teachers took advantage of these types of professional development opportunities, and there was hope that they would be reinstated in the coming years.

Another opportunity for professional development was through the local universities. One district administrator explained that they "have a good relationship" with one local university in particular.[29] One teacher recalled a professional development session at the university that had been specifically devoted to the issue of teacher challenges over the course of a career, which he connected directly to his retention:

> When I first started teaching—so again, maybe about, let's say, 2008, 2009—I had a professional development that the university set up, and we did it through them. It talked about the yo-yo effect of teachers, the highs and the lows. The first five years you're going uphill, it's going to be a struggle, and then you hit year seven and you're sort of, kind of getting under grips on things. And then you might drop off. You might get a little complacent. So, you drop back down in the valley, but it's not as far down as you would have been in your first year.

This affiliation with the local university was only one of a number of offerings for teachers through higher education institutions. Another teacher told us about training offered at North Carolina State University:

> If you go through NC State, they have all kind of stuff for agricultural uses. There's all kind of things for professional development in your content area that's available. You might have to pay for some of it if you don't want to reach out to your district, but there's things available.

One final professional opportunity mentioned by teachers was a joint program funded by grants and run by the local university in partnership with the local Native American tribe. One teacher said, "They have a lot of programs… and they push STEM. They have a lot of science camps during the summer and events during the year." Teachers noted that the university "looks to our science teachers to run the camps." These STEM camps provided students and teachers alike with the opportunity to travel to different out of state locations, such as the Kennedy Space Center in Florida or to Washington, DC.

Not only were teachers supported in their professional growth through different professional development opportunities, but it became apparent that the district also supported teachers in obtaining advanced degrees. A large majority of the teachers we spoke with obtained their Master's Degree in Education during their time in the district. This support for degree advancement suggests that district administration was in support of teachers furthering themselves professionally and that doing so was a net benefit to the district.

MENTORING AND INDUCTION

In Kingfisher County, all new teachers, including those new to the district, are assigned a mentor teacher for three years in the district's state-required Beginning Teacher program. Although this program experienced changes during our study period, the district had consistently worked to provide beginning teachers with support. Although some teachers referred to the support of their official mentor as meaningful to their continued retention, others felt that the informal mentorship they received from colleagues held greater value as one of their reasons to continue teaching in the district.

In the recent past, new teachers were paired with one of only four mentors assigned by the district. These four district mentors provided the support to all new teachers in the district (referred to locally as "Beginner 1s" or "B-1s") and were overseen by a district administrator. One teacher who had been through the program explained how the mentors were distributed: "They worked with the B-1s, 2s and 3s. And, of course, by the time you were a B-3, you didn't see that person very often." According to one of the retained teachers, meetings with mentors were scheduled and would typically take place every other week, with additional meetings in between if teachers felt they needed extra support. The retained teacher told us that for her, much of the mentorship centered around "classroom management," where the mentor teacher would observe her in the classroom and provide feedback. For this teacher, her mentor was essential to her first-year retention: "Two things that helped me survive my first year... One was the mentor teacher." She elaborated:

> She had been in a classroom for a long time before becoming a mentor teacher. And she had such a presence and just really would sit down. She'd come before school started at eight o'clock, and we'd go through and talk stuff. She was real good about if I had a question to help me work through some of those, for example, classroom management and give me ideas. I loved her to death.

In addition to individual mentorship, all new K–12 teachers of all subjects would meet once a month for new-teacher training sessions, where there would be speakers, activities, and opportunities to ask questions of district staff.

With the arrival of the statewide Beginning Teacher Support Program, the mentor program for the secondary schools transitioned to having individual on-site mentors that received a stipend of $100 per month.[30] This stipend is paid by the district. The Beginning Teacher coordinator, who oversees the mentoring program in the district, explained that mentees are encouraged to meet with their mentor teachers weekly in their first year, biweekly in their second year, and as needed in their third year. Mentors were informed of selection via email and prepared with district checklists to help structure meetings with their mentees, review weekly lesson plans, and conduct classroom walkthroughs.

Additionally, mentors are required to complete two, fifteen-hour online modules as their mentor training at the beginning of the school year.[31] Although mentors and mentees are typically paired by their content, science teachers may be paired with mentors from a different science discipline. In one of the Kingfisher schools we visited, those that taught the same discipline shared a common planning period, which allowed for meeting times to be more easily arranged. In the elementary and middle schools, the district maintained but modified this model of mentorship. Mentors were given the designation of academic coach and no longer held teaching positions in the district. The Beginning Teacher coordinator noted that she would like to see this model of mentorship implemented at the secondary level.

Currently, the Beginning Teacher coordinator surveys and meets with all new teachers to address topics of interest, such as classroom management. These meetings take place after school for approximately two hours every quarter, with secondary teachers meeting on one day and the elementary and middle school teachers on another. One of the main purposes of these Beginning Teacher meetings is to address issues around the monitoring tool used by principals to evaluate teachers' effectiveness, in which teachers are required to conduct a self-assessment of their own teaching practices, and then produce a professional development plan. Prior to a summative evaluation by their principals, teachers also have at least one nonsummative evaluation by their principal as well as a peer teacher observation.

In addition to the meetings, the coordinator explained that she also holds a "summer boot camp." This boot camp primarily functions to introduce novice teachers to district expectations, including the evaluation process, issues of licensure, and as she explained, "the rules that we expect of them coming in." Typically, supervisors from all content areas are in attendance, as well as the district superintendent. Kingfisher teachers frequently spoke about the formal mentoring and induction processes as factors they felt impacted their retention in Kingfisher County.

Kingfisher was one of the last schools to be visited by our research team, and the theme that *the department is the mentor*, which we had encountered in so many other high-retention schools, was quite recognizable to us by this point. Many of the teachers we spoke with highlighted experiences of informal mentorship they had received during their time in their schools. One such example of informal mentorship came from one of the retained science teachers who had never been an official mentor but felt as though they unofficially acted as one. This teacher described emulating the different support approaches that had been given by two informal mentors when he was a novice teacher. The mentoring he saw as important was, "simple stuff that kind of gets overlooked, like how to get supplies or what to do when you need to call out or take a sick day."

SUMMARY OF THE KINGFISHER CASE

In this case study, we identified three primary factors that appeared to influence the high rates of teacher retention in the Kingfisher School District. The first was that teaching was seen as both a good and available job, for which the Kingfisher teachers were well-qualified, in a place where good jobs were not always easy to come by. Second, having a career in their home community appeared to be important to many teachers and administrators in Kingfisher. This was strongly related to teachers' identification and sense of belonging with the local Native American tribe. There was ample evidence to suggest that teachers saw their work in schools as an extension of kinship and community ties, and that schooling in Kingfisher was not antithetical to sustaining Indigenous culture, as might be the case in other public school districts with Indigenous populations. Finally, teachers uniformly noted they were provided opportunities to grow and advance through professional development. Teachers directly referenced such opportunities as factors in which they believed teachers chose to remain in the Kingfisher School District.

CHAPTER 8

The Reasons Teachers Stayed

In this chapter, we discuss the findings that emerged from our cross-case analysis of the thirteen districts in this study, including the four shared in the previous chapters. Table 8.1 offers a brief description of each of these cases. By using teacher embeddedness as a lens through which to conduct this investigation, our research attention was drawn to the ways in which teachers seemed to fit into their organizations and communities, the ways in which they formed relationships with others, and the tangible and intangible assets from their work lives that they marked as valuable.

In chapter one, we shared the results of the cross-case analysis detailed in the present chapter, which yielded ten distinct categories of factors that appeared to influence teacher retention across the case study districts.[1] Each of these factors was evident in one or more of the four cases shared in the previous chapters, and many of them were present in some way within each of the other cases as well. For convenience, we list the ten factors again, presented in the order with which they appeared most frequently as major themes across the thirteen participating study districts:

1. Supportive relationships with colleagues
2. School- and district-level systems and culture of support
3. Compensation
4. Teacher autonomy
5. Specialness of place
6. Availability of resources for teaching
7. Opportunity and agency for professional growth

TABLE 8.1 Case study sites for the IMPREST project

District / LEA (State)	*Description*	*Enrollment (Approx.)*	*% Low-income*	*% Limited English*
Aspen School District (NJ)	Regional secondary school district with 1 high school. Non-high–need LEA. High retention.	3,000	10%	2%
Birch Charter School (NJ)	Urban charter school affiliated with a local university. High-need LEA.	500	75%	0%
Chestnut School District (NJ)	Large suburban district with 2 high schools. Non-high–need LEA. Very high teacher retention.	11,000	20%	<5%
Hickory Island School District (NJ)	Small district with 1 high school, seasonal population. High-need LEA.	1,000	70%	20%
Mulberry School District (NJ)	Urban school district with 3 high schools. High-need LEA. Success in retaining teachers of color.	9,000	60%	5%
Granite County School District (PA)	Regional vocational school district with 1 high school. Non-high–need LEA.	1,500	5%	<5%
Sandstone School District (PA)	Regional suburban school district with 1 high school. High-need LEA. Large English learner student population.	13,000	40%	15%
Wallago Area School District (WI)	Rural regional school district with 1 high school. High-need LEA.	3,000	40%	5%
Rivuline Regional School District (WI)	Very large urban district with 25+ high schools. High-need LEA.	70,000	85%	10%
Pompano School District (WI)	Large urban district with 5 high schools. High-need LEA.	16,000	66%	10%
Egret School District (NC)	Large regional district with 15+ high schools. High-need LEA.	70,000	25%	5%
Linnet School District (NC)	Medium-sized municipal district with 2 high schools. Non-high–need LEA.	12,000	12%	<5%
Kingfisher School District (NC)	Large regional district with 5+ high schools. High-need LEA. Success in retaining teachers of color.	20,000	40%	<5%

Source: Data for the 2017–2018 school year. Common Core of Data. US Department of Education, National Center for Educational Statistics. https://nces.ed.gov/ccd/.

8. District- and school-level race consciousness
9. Affordances related to school size
10. Personal satisfaction and the rewards of being a teacher

We discuss each of these ten factors in turn, drawing from the cases to illustrate with examples.[2]

1. Supportive relationships with colleagues

Over and over, teachers in these high-retention districts told us that one of the most important reasons they remained was their colleagues. Teachers described their colleagues as helpful, open, and cooperative, and many reported a strong sense of camaraderie in their departments and with others in their schools. We heard many stories about new hires being welcomed into the faculty by their colleagues as novice teachers and the transformation of working relationships into long-lasting friendships.

The willingness to share resources was often at the core of this support. In the previous chapters, we offered examples of individual approaches to this collaborative collegiality, such as the novice teacher in Pompano who spoke of asking for and receiving resources from more senior colleagues and the experienced Granite County teacher who saw sharing resources as an essential element of his department's ethos. In a more systemic example, we saw how newly hired teachers in Aspen and Chestnut were given immediate access to a shared drive full of unit plans, lessons, slide presentations, and activities. In Sandstone, where the experiences of virtual teaching during the pandemic were still fresh in teachers' minds, this sharing went both ways as noted by the district science supervisor:

> As far as sharing materials and ideas, we have had a couple new teachers, and I think we have a good group of experienced teachers that are willing to share ideas and even learn from those who are younger. We've been getting a lot of great ideas, you know, obviously, from those newer teachers who are fresh out of school and you know, exposed to some newer ideas and technology, especially helping some of the more veteran teachers who might not be as experienced with the technology. But they really do come together, even, you know, through our virtual meetings... We have a department group text where people share ideas.

Teachers told us that, in addition to sharing resources and materials, they received informal mentorship from the individuals within their department and school. Many explained that, although they were assigned a school or district mentor, their departmental colleagues provided the most meaningful support. While there were certainly instances of teachers naming a particular person as meaningful to their retention, it was far more common to hear stories of collective support. Within our research team, we started using the phrase "the department is the mentor" to characterize this phenomenon in the science departments we studied.

It was also common in our interviews to hear about collegial support that arose from teachers' daily interactions with one another. Shared lunches, hallway duty, and preparation periods all offered teachers space and time to discuss their struggles and triumphs in the classroom with one another (as well as what they did for fun over the weekend). From our interviews, we saw evidence of individuals and collective groups of experienced teachers serving as mentors for novice teachers. One science teacher in Rivuline described it to us in this way:

> I will just say one thing that's so impactful is having other science teachers mentor me and collaborate with me, because you can have that generic mentor be helpful in some part, but just having someone in the science department mentor and really take you under their wing, it was so much more impactful for me and gave me more confidence in what I could do.

While many of the new teachers we encountered in our case study sites were assigned "official" mentors by their school or district, they often made distinctions between these formal mentors and the informal mentors they found among their colleagues. We will develop this theme further in the mentoring and induction section of chapter 9.

The absence of teacher isolation across all of our case study districts was striking. Though we keep open the possibility that this finding was an artifact of our methodology, the teachers we interviewed all showed evidence of close ties with colleagues. In some cases, teachers appeared to develop close ties out of shared challenges, as was the case for the cohort in Granite who collectively figured out how to start and maintain an academic program in a vocational school. Another example included having coworkers as family members and neighbors for generations, like in Kingfisher. Departmental support also came in the form of professional learning communities, which were described by one teacher in Wallago as "sacred time" for collegial collaboration intentionally structured into their schedules. In the larger districts, we heard an appreciation for the fact that there was "always someone who could answer your question," while in the smaller ones, teachers and administrators alike reported the faculty as "close-knit." Whatever their challenges, the teachers in these schools clearly felt that, because of the links they developed, they were not alone.

2. School- and district-level systems and culture of support

A common feature of the districts in our study was the existence of what we came to recognize as a systemic organizational culture of teacher support. This culture was evident in the ways that schools and districts intentionally provided support for new teachers through regular organizational operations. This larger system of support was cited by teachers as important for teacher retention, in addition to the particular benefits derived from such support that we will discuss later in the "Opportunity and agency for professional growth" section.

Systemic cultures of teacher support can be characterized by the time, work, and monetary expenses invested in teachers to help them grow professionally, work in adequate conditions, and meet their professional needs. School leaders in these districts commonly expressed care and appreciation for their teachers, provided socioemotional support, solved problems, and gave personalized assistance when it was needed. Teacher appreciation efforts in the Aspen, Birch, and Chestnut school districts reflected the priority these districts placed on making teachers feel valued and cared for. In Aspen, the district supported new teachers through an induction program they called the Teacher Academy, which provided novice teachers with pedagogical support and opportunities to connect with the community. Aspen also supported their experienced teachers by offering reimbursement for external professional development and graduate-level coursework. Teachers noted that being encouraged to participate in the hiring process of new teachers was itself an expression of the district's appreciation of their value.

In Birch, teachers mentioned their district's partnership with a local university, which permitted both teachers and students alike to use the university facilities. This partnership was considered by Birch teachers as evidence of their value to the district. Birch teachers also mentioned that their supervisor was very supportive in building relationships with teachers. One experienced teacher noted, "Thankfully our supervisor is very supportive that way, and tells us, 'If you need something, please come to me.'"

Teachers at Chestnut mentioned feeling valued, cared for, and supported in their school district because of their school's clear priorities. "Here, it's academics before athletics," one teacher noted, "which helps us as teachers." One teacher framed this support as a "push for education":

> You have great kids. You have great families. You get tons of support from the families for education. There's a push for education. Having gone here and having friends through here and my family, it makes it easy to come to work and teach.[3]

In Egret County Public Schools, teachers suggested that their retention was influenced by the district's personalized assistance with pedagogy and consistent attention to their individual needs. Teachers there noted that their schools provided social-emotional support, and genuinely cared about teachers' personal lives and professional growth:

> I can look up a lesson, but you can't look up how to manage. Well, you can, right? But when you're a first-year teacher, you're not thinking about doing personal development. You're thinking about, "I'm trying to survive." I guess maybe it's a top-down thing, where you feel supported, and so you're able to work with your colleagues and support them. Those things, I think, keep the science teachers here.

While the specifics varied across study sites, we often heard teachers link a district's culture of teacher support to decisions to stay. This is shown in the case of Mulberry's systematic support for mentors and induction coaches in schools and Pompano's overt restructuring of schools in order to prevent teacher layoffs. In Rivuline, where there was perhaps less evidence for a systemic culture of support, there was still an appreciation for what teachers termed the "benign neglect" of administrators. In some districts, teachers cited support from the teachers' union, including coaching and concrete suggestions for improvement, as part of the system of support.

There was one district in one of the larger Pennsylvania cities that had far and away the best teacher retention for any district in our entire study—nowhere else came anywhere close to this district's five-year teacher retention rate. Despite our team's sustained efforts over the better part of two years to accommodate the requests of the district's external research approval process, the district ultimately declined to participate in our study, stating, "While the study has great interest to us, the district does not feel it can devote the staff time required to participate fully in this study." They also cited the ongoing disruptions due to the pandemic, as well as administrative personnel changes, as reasons for the denial. One lesson that our team took away from this failed recruitment effort was the seriousness with which the district protected its teachers from outside interference. In a roundabout way, this district provided evidence of the culture of support it had for its teachers by keeping us out.[4]

3. Compensation

In our conversations with teachers, compensation was a frequently cited reason for retention. Here, compensation refers primarily to salary and employee benefits but may also include items such as extra-duty pay for coaching or club advising, professional development reimbursement, and in some places, performance or hiring incentives. For the sake of comparison, the starting salaries (rounded, for anonymity) for each of the thirteen districts, including how far above or below they are from the state median starting salary, are shown in table 8.2 for the 2007–2008 school year, the first hiring year that we tracked in our study.

TABLE 8.2 Starting teacher salaries in the high-retention districts we studied.

Starting salaries in case study districts (2007–2008)	*Bachelor's degree (with % difference from median)*	*Master's degree (with % difference from median)*
Median NJ starting salary	**$43,749**	**$47,979**
Aspen School District (NJ)	$46,000 (+4%)	$50,000 (+4%)
Birch Charter School (NJ)	$40,000 (-9%)	$42,000 (-12%)
Chestnut School District (NJ)	$44,000 (+1%)	$48,000 (+0%)
Hickory Island School District (NJ)	$49,000 (+11%)	$53,000 (+11%)
Mulberry School District (NJ)	$48,000 (+9%)	$54,000 (+13%)
Median PA starting salary	**$40,000**	**$42,000**
Granite County School District (PA)	$46,000 (+15%)	$54,000 (+29%)
Sandstone School District (PA)	$35,000 (-12%)	$36,000 (-15%)
Median WI starting salary	**$32,938**	**$41,843**
Wallago Area School District (WI)	$33,000 (+0%)	$36,000 (-14%)
Rivuline Regional School District (WI)	$35,000 (+6%)	$41,000 (-3%)
Pompano School District (WI)	$38,000 (+14%)	$43,000 (+2%)
NC base salary	**$29,750 (level A00)**	**$32,730 (level M01)**
NC base salary + local supplement		
Egret School District (NC)	$32,000 (+8%)	$35,000 (+7%)
Linnet School District (NC)	$36,000 (+22%)	$39,000 (+20%)
Kingfisher School District (NC)	$32,000 (+7%)	$35,000 (+6%)

During the time period of consideration in our study, nearly all public school districts in the states of New Jersey and Pennsylvania determined teacher compensation through negotiations between individual school boards and local teacher unions, with new contracts bargained every few years. In Wisconsin, where severe limits were placed on collective bargaining in 2011, individual school districts still established rates of teacher compensation. All three of these states had very wide ranges in the salaries they paid to teachers. Salary differences across districts in these states could differ in four main ways: the base salary for a starting teacher, the possible maximum salary, the time or steps needed to advance to that maximum salary, and compensation for graduate coursework. And from year to year, even without a new contract, the median salary in a district was apt to change depending on the experience levels of those teachers who were retiring or leaving.

In North Carolina, however, the state legislature was responsible for setting pay rates for teachers, and districts were permitted to raise funds for salary supplements, which could be used to offset the higher cost of living in certain areas or fund teacher incentives. Consequently, there was very little variation across school districts in North Carolina with regard to teacher pay.

Clearly, the absolute starting-salary level differed tremendously both across states and within them, as did the median district salaries. In chapter 9, we will offer further discussion about salaries and retention, but in this section, we convey how teachers characterized the role that compensation played in their decisions to stay.

In relation to retention, the teachers we interviewed characterized their compensation in one of two ways: retention in the school/district or retention in the profession. When making comparisons to other districts—as the New Jersey, Pennsylvania, and Wisconsin teachers frequently did—such comparisons referenced retention in the school or district. In places outside of urban or suburban areas, like Wallago and Sandstone, teaching was referenced in terms of being a good job in places where opportunities for similar-paying employment were less available. However, in North Carolina, compensation was typically only discussed in terms of retention in the teaching profession.

Looking across all of the cases, the fairest way to characterize the relationship between compensation and retention is probably that the teachers we interviewed felt that their pay was essentially adequate. However, teachers discussed compensation very differently from the way those same teachers referenced support from their colleagues and workplaces. The teachers we interviewed rarely described compensation attracting them into or keeping them working in a particular school or district, though Mulberry teachers were an exception, because many of them had specifically been recruited from low-paying districts. General levels of salary and benefits were mentioned as important for keeping teachers in the profession, though we heard this less in North Carolina.

Teachers often compared their district's salaries to that of other school districts or the state median. It was common for teachers interviewed in our study to claim that their district's salary levels were either slightly higher or slightly lower than neighboring school districts and interpret this fact as meaningful. When teachers claimed that their district's salary was higher than neighboring districts, they frequently took this to mean that their district placed greater value on compensating teachers appropriately, as was the case in Mulberry and Linnet.

When we actually looked into salary differences across districts, there were rarely clear-cut conclusions to be drawn. Certainly, teachers in Chestnut, Mulberry, and Rivuline drew clear connections between the competitive salaries in their district, teacher retention, and contract negotiations by their local teacher unions. In the districts where salary advancement occurred, either through new contracts or advancement up the salary guide over time, teachers took notice. It was also true, however, that teachers were often incorrect in their assessments that their salaries were higher or lower than surrounding districts or the state as a whole. To us this suggested, in addition to the compensation itself, teachers' beliefs about their salaries—correct or not—also played a role in retention.

Interestingly, in districts where compensation was not invoked as a reason for retention, some teachers saw their perceived lower compensation to be a tradeoff. For example, a Granite teacher shared that a higher salary would not be worth losing access to material support and supplies from their department chair, noting that their requests are hardly ever rejected. In Aspen, teachers considered their perceived lower salary as a similar tradeoff for the additional resources that were available for students and teachers alike. One teacher stated, "When I first got hired here, the pay was terrible, but when I looked at it compared to the resources we had, it was immeasurable. That was very important to me. The fact that my pay wasn't that high, I could rationalize it. The draw for me here was because of all the opportunities for teachers and students, plus it's a beautiful school." In chapter 9, we will consider the idea that the socioeconomic and demographic profile of the students themselves was considered an asset by some teachers.

Compensation that was not linked to salary or benefits was also highlighted by our study participants. Though it is likely that such practices were not unique to the districts we studied, teachers cited this compensation as meaningful and connected to their retention. For instance, in Egret, Kingfisher, and Sandstone, mentors for new teachers received stipends from the district, which they reported as leading to better-structured mentoring and induction programs that helped retain teachers. In Linnet, teachers received extra pay for giving up planning periods to assist elsewhere in the school and valued this opportunity. Notably in Aspen, the teacher who served as the induction coordinator received both a stipend and a reduced course load, a form of compensation that was directly related to an effort to retain teachers in the district.

4. Teacher autonomy and professional agency

In selecting a categorical label for this theme, we wished to capture two related but distinct concepts—teacher autonomy and agency—each pertaining to the power teachers are able to exert over the decisions they make in the course of doing their jobs. We introduced teacher autonomy with Richard Ingersoll's definition in chapter 4, which relates to teachers' pedagogical choices within the classroom.[5] We use the term *professional agency* here to refer to matters of professional identity, career trajectory, and the ability to shape work environments.[6] Clearly, both teacher autonomy and professional agency are rooted in the concept of self-efficacy and have significant overlap with one another.[7] Yet, both were needed thematically in order to capture the range of responses as they related to teacher retention in this study.

A key feature of teacher autonomy is being able to exert professional judgment about how to teach within the established curricular and structural constraints of the organization. In accounts of the teachers we interviewed, most reported being able to make their own decisions about their teaching practice. Many were clear about the value they placed on the absence of any pressure by their administration to compromise their professional judgement in working with students or their colleagues.[8]

Across multiple sites, teachers reported that their administrators did not micromanage them, but rather treated teachers like professional and knowledgeable collaborators. Evidence from the Mulberry, Granite, and Pompano cases to this effect was presented in prior chapters, but we also heard versions of this sentiment elsewhere. In Birch, one teacher said, "I feel like I can be myself without someone controlling me... Yes, there's always feedback and keeping me on track, but at the same time, I have a lot of freedom." In Egret, one teacher mentioned that when his new science supervisor and principal did not understand how the science teachers handled their department and curriculum, they responded, "Okay, we don't understand it, but we'll just let you do this." Teachers in Rivuline viewed their own use of professional autonomy as a means to create and implement engaging learning experiences for their students.

It is important to note that, in most places, teacher autonomy was an intentional feature of the system and was supported by administrators. Teachers valued the ability to be creative in the classroom and enact their own personal style when teaching but were also mindful that such freedom was preconditioned on their expertise as professionals. An administrator in Egret mentioned that giving input to teachers in their school resulted in hard-working teachers who go above and beyond for their students and pointed to workshops and curricula that were developed by such teachers. In Hickory, one teacher referenced the way that classroom observations were not stressful or intimidating, that feedback was typically positive and constructive, and that these evaluations—mandated by state law—were largely collaborative.

An illuminating counterexample of this intentional autonomy could be seen in Rivuline, where multiple teachers saw their freedoms as a consequence of what one teacher called the district's "benign neglect." The teachers we interviewed felt their autonomy in what and how to teach was not necessarily because they were trusted professionals, but rather because it was a large district with many moving parts. One teacher said:

> It's such a big district that, you know, they have so many problems that they have to deal with. The things I do are small-scale compared to that. As long as I don't make the news, I feel like I can do what I want, and the kids really appreciate that.

This sentiment was echoed in almost every interview in Rivuline. Another teacher said to us, "I would say it's the autonomy. You can really kind of get away with doing what you have to do to teach what you think is right." One Rivuline teacher reported feeling that he had more freedom in the classroom than a teacher in the suburbs would, because those districts have "administration and helicopter parents breathing down your neck."[9]

In terms of professional agency, teachers in our case study districts reported that having voice in the operation of their school was something they valued highly. This professional agency was characterized by the ability to communicate concerns, share ideas, and even offer critique without fear of repercussions. This was especially strong in Egret, where multiple teachers stated that one of the main reasons they remained in the district was because they had a voice in how the school and the classrooms are run.

Teachers in Egret, as well as in Granite and Aspen, noted that it was not just having a voice that made the difference but being heard. In these districts, teachers reported being part of the hiring interviews, participating in school-level deliberations, and making impactful decisions in their professional learning communities—which included the shaping of mentoring practices for new teachers. In this way, the building blocks of supporting teacher self-efficacy through teacher autonomy and professional agency ended up supporting teacher leadership practices. One district subject supervisor in Egret described how the superintendent made such an outcome her aim:

> [She] has tapped, empowered, trained, and grown the capacity through us of teacher leadership. And so, she now has empowered teachers to take that role as leaders in professional development and curriculum development and curriculum writing. We still supervise the efforts with them, but they are the [right] people, because who better to know what the classroom should need than those who are in the classroom.

We wish to note that the presence of this sort of teacher autonomy and professional agency, coupled with a supportive and collegial environment for collaboration, appeared to be a potent safeguard against teacher isolation.

5. Specialness of place

In 1978, environmental psychologist Harold Proshansky coined an academic label for an idea that has likely been around as long as humans have found and connected with special places in the world. Proshansky defined *place-identity* as: "those dimensions of self that define the individual's personal identity in relation to the physical environment by means of a complex pattern of conscious and unconscious ideas, feelings, values, goals, preferences, skills, and behavioral tendencies relevant to a specific environment."[10] With respect to our aim of understanding why teachers were more likely to be retained in the districts we identified, we recognized that place-identity played a key role. Sometimes we heard about the geography of a place, and sometimes we heard about the people, but more often, we heard about both.

For so-called hometown teachers who returned to teach at (or near) the schools they attended as students themselves, the physical geography of a place constituted only one aspect of the sense of belonging that they reported as related to their reasons for staying. The presence of family members, church connections, and a sense of familial duty were also mentioned as reasons for teachers to remain in their hometowns and contribute to their communities as teachers. For example, one teacher in Egret was very clear in making exactly that connection:

> Why did I become a teacher? I wanted to give back to my community. I work at the same place I was born and raised, I mean, in the same area, and I had some really awesome teachers during my school years who really encouraged me and pushed me. And I wanted to do the same for students here.

In our discussions with teachers and administrators in Hickory, it was clear that the island setting of the school and community comprised an important aspect of individuals' attachment to their work. It was a district of contrasts, with residents that included both year-round low-income families in public housing as well as a more affluent population of seasonal tourists and second-home owners. Despite being a crowded beach town in the summer, Hickory Island was noted by all of the interviewees as a great place to live and work.

We learned that quite a few teachers in the district grew up or vacationed in Hickory, and administrators we talked with felt these teachers wanted to give back to a community that shaped them. One teacher noted, "I think we all get into education because you want to give back, right? And who better to give back than the people who took care of you?"

References to the layout of the island community, the locations of housing and schools, and the natural and human-made features of the area all conveyed a sense of place that was woven into teachers' reasons for staying. The size and tight-knit nature of the community was such that teachers frequently encountered students and their families in town, and some noted that they regularly joined students on the walk to school. The proximity of the schools to the beach and the ability to take advantage of the island's amenities were highly valued by the teachers. This physical environment—and the place-identity it created and fostered for those who lived or worked on Hickory Island—loomed large in our conversations with teachers there and were cited as significant factors in their decisions to stay. One teacher who grew up on the island elaborated on how an understanding of the place impacted their own classroom teaching:

> I have a connection to the area. I think that also helps with having a connection with the students. I'm understanding where they come from, even if they're from a completely different background than myself, I know what it's like to live here where it's crazy in the summer and you have to work a bunch of jobs and then it's completely dead in the wintertime.

In the foothills of North Carolina, the specialness of the Egret School District lay as much in the community's history and culture as it did in the landscape. Significant events in both the Revolutionary War and the Civil Rights Movement occurred within the school district's present boundaries, and there was a discernible through-line between the local activism for justice in the 1950s and 1960s and the ways in which contemporary educators in Egret County Public Schools went about their current work. This point is discussed more in the section below on district- and school-level race consciousness, but we note here that many Egret teachers described the area as a special place for these reasons.

Similarly, the teachers and administrators we interviewed in Kingfisher clearly connected teaching to living in a community among the particular people there. The farms, marshes, and rivers in the area may have played a role in the specialness of place for Kingfisher teachers, but certainly, place-identity was also driven by the people who lived there. "Kingfisher County is where I was born and raised and I have no intention to ever leave them," said one teacher. Not leaving *there* but leaving *them.* Teacher retention was surely a natural consequence in a place where networks of friends, family relations, tribal culture, and a unique history all came together. Recall that in both the Kingfisher and Mulberry cases, teachers and administrators pointed to parents who also worked in the district.

A number of teachers across our high-retention sites discussed the importance of living in the community in which they worked for a variety of reasons. For some, this meant coming back to their hometown, and for others, it meant moving to and becoming a part of the community in which they now worked. In Sandstone for example, one administrator discussed the importance of ties between teachers and the community to retention:

> Many of them [teachers] are tied to the community, many of them have been born and raised here, and you know, I don't think they would leave to go to another school that they're going to drive a half an hour every day. They can stay in their hometown school... Our teachers are living here in the community, and this is part of their community. I think that's a big part of sticking around.

Certainly, we saw such hometown teachers in Sandstone, Pompano, Kingfisher, and elsewhere, so we cannot overlook the possibility that, for someone with the requisite education and skill level, teaching may have been a good and available job in the particular place they wanted to live.[11] By working in the community they were already a part of, teachers came to their teaching practice with a greater understanding of how the school functioned and the ability to develop relationships with their students.

Other teachers who were from outside of their school's local area also reported feeling connections to the community and experiencing a hometown feeling. One of the retained teachers in Wallago told us, "I mean the community has been great. I've made a lot of connections, a lot of friends, and so that keeps me here as well." One administrator in Hickory emphasized how important it was for teachers to feel they were part of the larger community: "If you're going to be a part of this school," he said, "you're going to be a part of this community, there's no choice about that."

A number of the teachers in certain districts mentioned connections to local higher education institutions, yet the robust connections described by Linnet teachers was geographic in nature enough to warrant inclusion under this category. The district was located in what one teacher called a "college town," and teachers we talked with spoke about the advantages of living and working in such an area.[12] Many of their students' parents worked for one of the local universities and were strong advocates on behalf of the school system. As will be discussed in the next section, this had implications for the resources available to the Linnet teachers.

6. Resources for teaching from the school and community

Another theme that arose from our conversations with retained teachers was the importance of having adequate resources for teaching. For most, this meant having the necessary supplies to teach students without having to reach into their own pockets. One novice teacher from Wallago told us that, during her interview process, "it seemed like there was good funding, that I would have support," and that was what convinced her to accept the position. As noted earlier in the section on compensation, the school finance research is very clear about the fact that money matters in education, and this is just as true for supplies and teaching resources as it is for salary and benefits.[13] One resource that teachers in Birch and Mulberry cited as critical was the physical space of the school itself, which permitted nearly all teachers to have their own classroom rather than having to share.

Sometimes, resources came in the form of partnerships with local universities, as was true in the cases of Birch, Linnet, Kingfisher, and Rivuline. By having relationships with universities, teachers had access to university spaces, materials, professional development opportunities, and in the case of Birch, a source of qualified interns and student teachers.

In addition to having connections with the local universities, some of the educators we spoke with cited community members and parents as a source of providing classroom supplies and other school-related resources. Relationships with community organizations in Granite and Pompano not only supplied the school with materials for teaching but also served as internship locations for students. In Wallago, local businesses provided the school with specialty manufacturing equipment that students could use, and community members were regularly welcomed into the school as guest speakers. Teachers also expressed an appreciation for efforts to foster community engagement. In the city of Mulberry, this was evidenced in the city's planned events, such as planting community gardens or community-wide reading events, where the school and city worked together to involve teachers, students, and students' families.

In Linnet, parents who worked in the science industry or in university science labs often served as a source for providing laboratory materials that teachers may not have otherwise had access to. One of the science teachers at Linnet commented:

> My first year there I said, "Oh, I really wanted a skeleton, but I forgot to order one." And I just sort of mentioned that to the kids like, "Oh, I would love to show this to you on a skeleton, but I don't have one." And two days later, a parent dropped off a skeleton like, "Oh I got it for you." "Cool, thank you." We've got parents that work in laboratories, and we've had a lot of science equipment donated to us a bunch of years ago. We had about $200,000 worth of science equipment donated from a lab that shut down. So, we don't really want anything as a science department.

Two of the districts we studied, Aspen and Linnet, seemed particularly well-resourced. One effect of sufficient funding identified in the school finance research is the reduction of certain types of scarcity-related stressors that impact student outcomes and make teachers' jobs more difficult in less well-off schools.[14] This fact may itself be a reason for increased teacher retention. An administrator in Linnet described the issue in this way:

> The counselor ratio has always been good. To have a social worker at all the schools to deal with other student issues —I think that plays a big part in the retention just to make sure the students are happy, and then all you have to do as a teacher is the content, knowing that the students are supported.

We will return to this idea at the end of the chapter, when we look at the differences in retention factors between districts that were labeled as high-need and those that were not.

In Wallago, the district had arranged the weekly school schedule in such a way that all students—elementary, middle, and high school alike—were dismissed an hour early on Wednesdays so that teachers could meet in professional learning communities (PLCs).[15] The administration and teachers of the district considered this an in-kind contribution of time by the families of the students. One Wallago teacher noted the depth of this community support:

> Parents were very supportive of allowing the school to provide teachers with the Wednesday afternoon PLCs, even though that meant their children would be leaving school early one day each week. They also recently passed a multi-million-dollar referendum to build a new elementary school.

Such professional growth had implications for teachers' own professional agency, a thread we continue to follow in the next section.

7. Opportunities for professional growth

In some districts, teachers pointed to opportunities for professional growth as contributing reasons for their retention. Teachers cited having access to financial support for professional development and advanced degrees as particularly important. Teachers also cited opportunities to participate in leadership activities beyond the classroom that supported their professional growth, such as writing school curriculum, leading professional development sessions, mentoring novice teachers, and participating in the leadership of teacher unions.

In a number of the cases, teachers mentioned compensation for professional development and continuing education as a benefit. In Rivuline, teachers received financial assistance for college courses, which they claimed also fostered connections among colleagues across the large district. In Wallago, teachers reported being paid to attend professional development, with the district covering registration costs and providing substitute teachers.

In the districts with university partnerships, teachers sometimes had access to special offerings, such as the programs described in the Kingfisher case at three different university settings. One unique feature of Birch's university partnership was that teachers could take a total of six graduate credits each semester without cost. According to the curriculum supervisor, teachers valued the convenience and advantage of engaging in professional development opportunities with adequate financial support, which often led to further opportunities:

> Having relatively easy access to graduate work opens the doors to getting your Supervisor Certification and things like that. Because we're such a small school, leadership positions open up pretty quickly. So, it's like where me or someone else have found themselves being the department lead after being here for two or three years. So, I think, because there is sort of the ability to move up to some extent and take on leadership roles.

Teachers directly mentioned opportunities for professional growth as a factor in their decision to stay in their school district. Teachers in Aspen noted they also greatly appreciated the district's willingness to provide necessary substitute coverage of their classes so they could attend professional development during the school day.[16]

8. District and school-level race consciousness

Although race holds little meaning as a modern *scientific* idea, it retains power as a *social construction* that has social, political, and legal dimensions.[17] Discrimination based on race—i.e., racism—has been a permanent feature of life in the Americas for over 400 years and in many ways, remains deeply entrenched in the educational institutions and processes within the United States.[18] Karen Manheim Teel and Jennifer E. Obidah have studied how race operates in the teaching and learning process; in classroom, school, and district-level decision-making; as well as in their work with educators and school leaders. They use the term *race consciousness* to indicate the possession of an "awareness of race, of the possibility of their own racism and the racism of others, and the significance of these perceptions."[19]

In certain districts, we found a deep appreciation by teachers and administrators (who mostly, but not all, identified as teachers of color) for when the existence of race and the impacts of racism were acknowledged, recognized, and acted upon by school and district leaders. In these places, it is fair to say that race consciousness was part of the operating system of the school. As examples accumulated of this responsiveness to race and racism, we chose to characterize teacher retention in these places with the label of *district- and school-level race consciousness.*

Some of the schools in the case studies exhibited evidence of significant race consciousness among educators, where teachers and school administrators not only acknowledged race but intentionally implemented policies and practices to support both students and teachers of color. Numerous examples of this were presented in the Mulberry chapter, such as the district's high schools emulating the environments of Historically Black Colleges and Universities (HBCUs). In the Kingfisher chapter, we showed what district race consciousness looked like in the cultural context of a district with a majority-Native–American population. Yet probably the best example of race consciousness comes from Egret, where the district's clear commitment to its students of color could be seen as a historical reverberation of the national movement for civil rights. One administrator in Egret noted that district initiatives relating to diversity and equity often reflected and honored this effort:

> [Egret County] is the home of the city and movement that swept the nation. The students that went to this school, my father and three other individuals, sat at the lunch counter and refused to leave until they were served and began a sit-in movement all over the southeast—and then it moved throughout the United States at historical black colleges and universities.

Administrators in Egret made great efforts to hire local teachers of color and to develop and promote school leaders and district administrators who they felt could understand the struggles of the community. One retained teacher discussed how these efforts were expressed in hiring committees:

> They're big on how you make things equitable, because they want everybody to be successful. There's a big difference between equality and equity, and they really are pushing that... They want people who already have a social justice mindset. We all have our implicit bias, but just who already have the mindset of helping everybody versus just a few people.

A retained teacher in Egret, who left teaching and came back, emphasized the importance of having such a diverse community in the school:

> The core to diversity is different, but here's the catch here. I feel supported here, and I feel like the teacher collaboration is strong, okay? So that makes me feel like, "Okay. I made the right decision to come back." Because at first, I was worried that when I first came back that the atmosphere wasn't conducive for me. I think the first thing you get to feel like is the people who you come back to are welcoming. They accept you as a part of their structure or what you're going to do. I immediately felt that when I came here. I was a part of the structure, not just another person that came to work, but I was structurally a part of what they were trying to do. So, I felt that was key.

Though it is difficult to make any claims about race and hiring practices, we can say with certainty that administrators in some districts, like Birch and Hickory, spoke openly about aspiring to have the demographic profile of their students be reflected in their teacher workforce, which it currently did not. In comparison, administrators in Egret and Mulberry made no secret of recruiting teachers of color from surrounding districts, with the promise of a more welcoming and emotionally healthy environment. They also hired and developed administrators of color—a fact not lost on the teachers of color there.

Birch, Hickory, Egret, and Mulberry also offer examples of working with newly hired teachers in mentoring and induction programs to understand the pedagogical implications of equity and student diversity. In Hickory, where the teachers were mostly White and the students were mostly Black and Latina/o, this meant giving explicit attention to equity practices during the initial orientation to the district. Recall from the cases that both Egret and Mulberry quietly ensured that novice teachers of color were mentored and coached by experienced teachers of color.

Some of the other schools and districts we visited struggled to separate the operation of race from other socioeconomic categorical markers. Phrases such as *high-need*, *inner-city*, or *urban* regularly served as proxy labels for race in professional discourse and were connected to the degree of personal satisfaction teachers felt in supporting the students in classrooms. For example, one teacher in Rivuline expressed:

> I think I [became] good at teaching here. I think it's a high-need area, and it needs good teachers. I have a sense of pride teaching here, knowing that I'm teaching in a high-need school, an inner-city school, something that a lot of people couldn't handle and couldn't do. So, I am proud of that.

Teachers in Aspen and Linnet, two districts with large majorities of White students, spoke about how many of the factors that often lead to teacher burnout and attrition were simply not as present in their work lives; the reason for this was directly related to the fact that they did not have to deal with the difficulties that came with teaching students from certain backgrounds as much. Consequently, teacher burnout in these districts was lower and retention was higher. One teacher in Linnet—when talking about English language learners, students experiencing homelessness, and students struggling with drug abuse—phrased the issue this way, "When you just have a couple of students who are dealing with those issues… you don't burn out." Similarly, one teacher in Aspen explained:

> We don't have the same student population as perhaps an inner-city school does, where perhaps the burnout rate is a bit higher. So in general… I don't feel tremendously threatened when I walk into one of our classrooms.

Some of the districts with majority-White student populations that we studied demonstrated little evidence of school and district race consciousness. One could be forgiven for concluding that a *lack* of race consciousness was also correlated with teacher retention in these school districts. Scholars have noted that in such settings, teachers may view students of color as liabilities.[20] On the surface, the two examples provided may not appear to be related to a limited level of race consciousness, however, by using language such as *inner-city* and *threatened*, which fail to explicitly acknowledge student race, teachers may be drawing upon harmful stereotypes and color-evasive ideologies in education.[21] Similarly, by associating burnout with the number of students of color a teacher has in the classroom, White teachers in these districts may have viewed students of color as liabilities, which is the exact type of endemic racism that districts like Mulberry and Egret seek to surmount.

It would indeed be troubling if some teachers felt a better sense of fit from working in a district where race or racism was seldom discussed or because they did not have to teach many students of color. Those who study racism and the social operation of race may be unsurprised by this possible finding, given the long-lasting resistance to school equity and residential desegregation in the United States. It is also disconcerting to think about the implications for students of color—not to mention everyone else—in these classrooms and schools. In the next chapter, we will situate and discuss this possible finding among other problematic reasons for teacher retention and show that such circumstances need not simply be accepted.

9. Affordances related to size

The size of a district, school, or department did not appear to have much of an influence on whether people stayed. Yet, for the teachers we interviewed, those working in small schools or districts cited the benefits of that smallness in their reasons for staying. Correspondingly, teachers in larger schools and districts also pointed to the affordances of those schools, as related to its size, as a factor in their retention. One explanation for this finding may be that teachers seek and find jobs in the types of schools that fit their preferences, but the unpredictability of the labor market makes this seem unlikely. More plausible is the idea that, as teachers continue in their careers, they gain an appreciation for what their workplaces have to offer, which is likely a function of how big the organization is and how many students it serves.

During our interviews with the teachers at Birch and Hickory, teachers said that working in a small school was one of the reasons they decided to remain in the district. These teachers frequently used the term *tight knit* to refer to the relationships that colleagues had with one another when there were comparatively few of them. They explained that the small size of the school increased their ability to form closer relationships with colleagues, students, and members of the community. One of the retained teachers in Birch told us, "They don't pay much, but I love the small size schools. It's like a family school. You get to love others because you get to know them more—students, teachers, administration, and parents." These teachers also told us that administrators in their schools offered personal support and were attentive to teachers' needs, factors they attributed to the size of the school.

Teachers in smaller districts explained that their schools also had smaller class sizes. This was evidenced in our interviews with teachers in Hickory, where the student-to-teacher ratio was far below the state average and was even lower in the advanced science courses. One science teacher conveyed to us what this kind of classroom was like for him:

> My biggest class has fifteen kids, and that's probably an overload. In most cases, I get six to nine kids per class. So, my ability to kind of focus, get to know where they're at, and then kind of take them along as a herd and get to know them personally, get to know them as a student and kind of figure out what their aspirations are and build on those, is a lot easier here than it is [in other districts].

In larger districts, teachers who wanted a change could remain in the district by moving to another school within the district, a practice we documented in Rivuline. Another affordance of a large school was the variety and larger number of colleagues. When there are others in a school or district who teach the same subject area or grade level, then there are potentially more people with whom to collaborate. One teacher in Chestnut, who had previously worked in a smaller district, noted, "That was probably the biggest difference when I came here. All of a sudden, I'm not the only physics teacher, and there's people that I can work with and share ideas with."

10. Personal satisfaction and rewards

The former catch-all explanation of job satisfaction as a reason for teacher retention still makes our list, though now as one factor among many. Across our case studies, the unique features of each individual's assignment, school, and district certainly influenced teacher retention. However, in identifying this theme in the data, which occurred at every site, we could not help but notice that some of these reasons were more properly attributed to the profession of teaching rather than to a particular school.

For example, many teachers talked about reasons that are often considered hallmarks of the teaching profession, such as impacting someone's life and giving back to the community. Others noted that the job was suitable for having time to raise a family. Teachers talked about the rewards of teaching in challenging schools that needed "good" teachers and in the feeling of success from learning to become such a teacher. For teachers in Rivuline, this satisfaction was connected to a sense of efficacy in being able to teach their particular students. One teacher explained the connection between helping students in need and the personal satisfaction of working in a high-need district:

> I think, deep down, it's because I want to teach the kids that deserve it. I mean, I could do this anywhere, but I feel like these kids are the kids that are really getting what they should get. They know that they're getting top notch education, and they end up going to college prepared, and I feel like they deserve that. They're not getting that in every classroom and every discipline area, but I feel like I send them off to college ready to go. I've got a ton of kids that end up being engineers and chemists, and you know, I feel good about that. I feel like I'm doing a better job here than most of the suburban students are getting.

Many teachers also described the personal satisfaction of working with young people and being a trusted adult in students' lives. One Linnet teacher found great satisfaction in teaching students who they identified as "interesting and invested":

> I think that I've had, over the years, a number of students that just come to hang out during lunch chat about, "Hey, I read this article," or "I watched this movie and this thing happened, do you think something like that could really... " The kids think about stuff. They don't just allow things to wash over them. They bring a lot to the classroom. I get interesting questions every single day. I get questions where I go, "You know what? I don't know." And there's a little place I have carved out on my board where I write their questions. I'm like, "I don't know. I'm going to look that up, find that, let's learn something new."

In Sandstone, one teacher mentioned the rewarding feeling of being able to impact someone's life. She described teaching as a fulfilling vocation from which she had been personally able to grow but mostly valued the way her work kept her life interesting:

> I like a lot of things about it. I also enjoy teaching and meeting people, and I like that it's different every day. You definitely do not get bored, its different every year. And you know, on those occasions where a kid will tell you that you've made a difference, or something like that, sometimes it's enough to get you through the hard days, you know?

SPECIFIC FACTORS FOR THE RETENTION OF TEACHERS OF COLOR AND TEACHERS IN HIGH-NEED SCHOOLS

Many of the retention factors specific to retaining teachers of color and for teachers in high-need schools have been discussed above, but here we wish to highlight the specific factors that were important to each group.

Teachers of Color

Three districts we examined had exemplary rates for retaining teachers of color. Our findings attributed retention in these districts to the ways they centered the importance of equity in their goals and actions. The commitment of the district to the education of children of color was cited by participants as a significant factor in retaining teachers of color. Black teachers in particular described the ways in which the values of the school and the district were clearly evident and matched their own.

For many teachers of color, supportive working conditions were a primary reason for their recruitment and retention. Mulberry district offered a degree of refuge and a supportive environment for teachers of color. The schools operated with a well-defined purpose for African American uplift, shared by teachers, principals, and community members. Teachers in Mulberry felt comfortable and supported due to the distinctive culture of the school district and community. The commitment of teachers of color to an equitable education for children of color also overlapped with having a supportive professional environment. For example, teachers in Egret emphasized that, because they had professional input, they felt like they were making a difference in the classroom. Similarly, the Native American culture in the district of Kingfisher influenced school dynamics and contributed to the close-knit broader community.

What these three sites had in common was a school organization and community where teachers felt they belonged, were supported, and could do their jobs. Such could be said about the other districts in this study, but there was something else going on as well. In a report published for the Portland School District in Maine—which documented the experiences of teachers of color there—Doris Santoro, Julia Hazel, and Alberto Morales presented two main findings, which they expressed as metaphors. The first was that the structural policies and practices of the district created what the district's teachers of color called "an impenetrable wall of Whiteness." Teachers of color in Portland public schools described the multiple ways in which the district erected barriers around issues of hiring, equity, support, and access to professional development. The second finding was that the problematic interpersonal relations and lack of cultural awareness among many staff had led to teachers of color to feel dismissed, devalued, isolated, and criticized for who they were. The authors termed this the "smog of cultural racism."[22]

In the three districts with exemplary rates of retention for teachers of color, we saw little evidence for an "impenetrable wall of Whiteness" or a "smog of cultural racism." In fact, we found the complete opposite conditions, which we posit influenced teachers to stay. Instead of barriers to hiring and equity, we saw outreach to teachers of color. Teachers felt supported in their teaching and in their professional growth. Rather than finding teachers who felt isolated, devalued, and subject to microaggressions, we saw teachers who were flourishing in communities of shared values. Of course, these are broad strokes, but the findings are clear.

Teachers in High-Need Districts

Given that nine of the thirteen cases in our study met the federal definition of a high-need school or district, the majority of the ten factors described in this chapter were common in many, if not all, of the high-need schools and districts we investigated. However, there were some interesting commonalities and contrasts between the retained teachers in high-need schools and those in the non-high-need schools. Teachers at both types of schools greatly valued their collaborative colleagues, supportive school and district environments, adequate compensation, and autonomy.

The hometown teachers who returned to give back to their communities were almost exclusively at high-need schools, though not all of the high-need schools we investigated had such hometown teachers. All of the teachers in high-need schools reported that having a well-paying job in their community was a key factor in their retention. It is also notable that the three districts with high rates of teacher-of-color retention were located in high-need districts.

A theme in common among all four non-high-need districts was that they were fairly well-resourced, at least according to the teachers and administrators we interviewed, and was cited in each of those districts as a factor related to retention. Teachers in these districts could teach how they wanted and with the materials they needed. In contrast, only one of the nine high-need districts mentioned the adequacy of resources as a factor in retention. Though teachers talked about resources at nearly every school, in the high-need schools, this was just one of many concerns. At the non-high-need schools, resources often seemed the primary concern. Recall the example shared above of an Aspen teacher's acceptance of the apparent tradeoff between salary levels and student resources. Casting an eye toward our teacher embeddedness framework, it may have been the case that the available assets in these schools—along with the low probability of finding similar levels of resources elsewhere—exerted a powerful influence on the retention of teachers in these districts.

WHY THEY STAYED

When we look back on the theory of teacher embeddedness to make sense of these findings, we find a satisfying alignment to the categories of fit, links, and assets in each of our cases across the domains of the school organization, the profession, and the community. Correspondingly, each of the ten retention factors identified from our cross-case analysis hangs within the teacher embeddedness framework rather well. Collegial support draws upon the relationships within the school, and the fit between the values of a teacher and their colleagues are likely to grow closer over time if values are shared. Teacher autonomy is an asset that teachers value, which communicates values of trust in professionalism. This, in turn, likely increases the fit of a person to their organization. Knowledge of their community is a valuable asset for hometown teachers, and the existing links they have with their communities serves as a strong pull to stay. This was true particularly for retained teachers of color who spoke of the alignment of values between them, their school leaders, and the community.

We pause here momentarily to point out that, in the recent past, many efforts to increase teacher quality and reduce unwanted attrition have been driven by practices rooted in behaviorist ideas.[23] Over the past three decades, the teacher policy landscape has been dominated by incentive- and sanction-driven processes, such as summative teaching evaluations, value-added measures of teacher effectiveness, scripted curriculum, and merit pay.[24] Yet, when we examine the factors identified in this study as salient to retention, it is clear that professionalism, collegiality, respect, and self-efficacy were common threads. Teachers in the districts we studied did not stay because they were incentivized to do so. They stayed because they felt supported and trusted in their work. They stayed because they had the resources and autonomy to feel effective and important. They stayed because the organizations and communities where they worked were like a healthy ecosystem, and they were not isolated from one another. The new teachers stayed because the people that they worked with took collective responsibility for their success. And of course, they stayed because their job included the opportunity to build relationships with colleagues and students that sustained them over time.

CHAPTER 9

Conclusion

Helping Teachers Stay

In this final chapter, we take stock of the lessons learned from our research and offer recommendations for what school leaders, policymakers, and teachers themselves can do to try to ensure good teachers do not leave for the wrong reasons. First, we briefly discuss retention across the four states in our study. Next, we see what can be learned specifically about new-teacher support from the mentoring and induction efforts in our case study districts. We then examine the difficult but real issue of retention for questionable reasons and close by sharing what we see as the main implications of this study's findings.

LOOKING AT RETENTION ACROSS THE STATES IN OUR STUDY

It was evident throughout our study that state policies played a critical role in determining teachers' classroom experiences and their professional trajectories. Here we examine the broad retention trends across each of the four states, and share a few key findings from that analysis. A more detailed description and quantitative analysis of the role of this state context on the retention of all novice science teachers in each state may be found in appendix C.

In looking across teacher retention rates of the six cohorts from all four states, we found that New Jersey, Pennsylvania, and North Carolina all had five-year novice-teacher retention rates in the 40–50 percent range, confirming once again the statistic that roughly half of all new teachers leave within their first five years of teaching. Our data only looked at retention in district, so it is quite likely that the retention-in-profession rate for the teachers in our four states was substantially higher. In contrast, Wisconsin's five-year rate of retention in district was 68 percent. This rate was not only higher than the other three states, but it was consistent across all six of the Wisconsin cohorts hired between 2007–2012.[1] Although this finding seems puzzling, we see a possible explanation offered by teacher embeddedness.

As noted in the Pompano case, the introduction and passage of Act 10 in early 2011 galvanized thousands of labor union members—which included many teachers—to organize and protest in an attempt to defeat the legislation. Large-scale demonstrations and a sustained occupation of the Wisconsin State Capitol in Madison lasted four months, until the affirmation of Act 10 by the Wisconsin Supreme Court later that June. The protest transformed over the rest of 2011 and 2012 into a state-wide movement to recall Governor Walker and other state legislators.

Though ultimately unsuccessful in its aim to remove elected officials from office and undo legislation, this effort did inspire many teachers and other public employees to become more involved in state and local politics.[2] Over time, Act 10 increased teachers' workloads, decreased pay and benefits, and made school jobs less stable.[3] All of the Wisconsin cohorts we studied experienced these events at some point during their first five years. Over this tumultuous period of time, the apparent hostility of the Wisconsin State Government towards organized labor was paired with an unmistakable outpouring of public support for teachers. Certainly, the degree of organizing and action within groups of teachers varied a great deal across the districts and schools of Wisconsin. However, we suggest the possibility that amid this activity, teachers' links were strengthened with one another, buffering the shock of the uncertainty and instability created by the passage of Act 10.

A comparison against the shock of COVID-19 in 2020–2021 on the careers of teachers is instructive. Rather than strengthening links, one of the first-order effects of the pandemic was the reduction of interpersonal contact between teachers. Links were weakened, and teacher retention suffered as more teachers—especially new teachers—left their jobs.[4]

State policy certainly set the boundaries for what was possible in the school districts within the four states we studied and mattered a great deal to teachers, schools, and districts. Issues like teacher certification, collective bargaining, tenure, curriculum, and regional structures of professional support all impacted the working lives of teachers in our study. Noting the exceptions above, state policies themselves paradoxically often had quite limited effects on novice teacher retention, even as these policies shaped the conditions under which they worked. At least according to the teachers and administrators we interviewed, the reasons they stayed were much more related to teachers' colleagues, organizational conditions, and communities.

THE ROLE OF MENTORING AND INDUCTION PRACTICES IN TEACHER RETENTION

The distinction between mentoring and induction is often defined by the degree of individualized attention received by participants. In this study, we defined *mentoring* as a one-to-one relationship between one less-experienced teacher and one with more experience.[5] We defined *induction* as more programmatic and group based, often (but not always) with an established curriculum.[6]

Within these definitions, there were a wide range of approaches and models for how, how often, and where mentoring could take place. When looking across these induction and mentoring programs, it was evident that some districts generally followed their state guidelines, none of which were particularly prescriptive, while others greatly exceeded what was required. We saw a range of designs in this study, including direct personal mentoring by experienced teachers, less-intensive coaching and support models, and district-wide induction programs. All of these were designed to support new teachers during their first years of teaching and perhaps experienced teachers new to the district or building as well.

In a number of districts, mentoring and induction programs were run by the principal, an administrator, or the human resources department, but in certain districts, there was an individual assigned with a specific role related to mentoring and induction. In North Carolina, this individual was often given the title Beginning Teacher (BT) Coordinator, a reflection of the language used at the state level, where new teachers are referred to as beginning teachers (BTs). In Granite County Technical School, although the mentorship program was technically overseen by administrators, we were told that it was actually run by the teachers in the departments.

Mentoring Programs

Depending on the state, mentors were generally tasked with supporting new teachers for a period of one to three years. Many were also required to complete a certain amount of mentor-specific training, either online or in person, ranging from fifteen hours to two days. Additionally, many of the districts we studied required mentor teachers to complete a certain number of teaching years in order to become an official mentor. For example, In Egret, mentor teachers needed at least four years of teaching experience.

In Sandstone and Wallago, however, where mentor teachers did not receive specific training, the principals in each district took careful consideration to select mentors they felt would be best suited for the position. The principal of Sandstone School District explained, "We do pick our mentor teachers, you know, we don't give it to everybody. They are purposely chosen and matched up with people as best you can." In Wallago, the principal told us that when choosing a mentor, he looked for someone who was collaborative, open-minded, willing to learn, had good/constant communication with mentee, was positive, and "understanding of the direction that we need to go to increase student achievement, based on our kids."

Often, mentors were matched in one-to-one relationships (one mentor to one new teacher) and often according to grade level, content area, or both. In one of the Kingfisher schools we visited, individuals teaching the same discipline shared a common planning period, which made mentor/mentee meetings more feasible. In Wallago, however, new teachers were intentionally paired with a mentor outside of their department. It was taken as a given that science teachers would already support one another, and the administration felt it was important for new teachers to get a perspective from those outside of their department. Another unique example of mentoring was in the Egret School District, where new teachers of color were mentored by experienced teachers of color, a feature only possible due to the large number of teachers of color in the district.

In some districts, additional positions were developed specifically for the purpose of working with novice teachers and providing additional support. In a few of the districts, we saw unique positions. In Linnet, the district provided teachers with "advocates" in addition to mentors and induction coaches. One administrator had been assigned an advocate role in the past, which she explained in this way:

> Once a month, we are to give them ten dollars or something and touch base with them. So, whether I bought them lottery tickets or breakfast, or whatever it was, to touch base. How are things going? Let me just give you a little something. "I'm thinking about you" note or something.

Aspen had a similar "buddy system" to support experienced teachers who were new to the district. Mulberry School District also provided additional support to their new and experienced teachers by assigning district-level trainers—provided with cell phones purchased by the district for that very purpose—who worked with teachers across grade levels and subject areas.

Induction Programs

It is common for teacher induction to be used as a shorthand for the process of human resource onboarding of new teachers upon first arriving to a school or district. However, in the districts we visited, this was rarely the case. Induction activities may have included some onboarding at the start, but in most of our case study districts, induction was a long-term and sustained activity that continued throughout the academic year, and activities were as varied as the districts. In Hickory, one of the induction sessions was a bus tour throughout the town that ended at the public housing projects, where community members met the new teachers for a picnic. New teachers in Aspen attended a New Teacher Academy for an intensive summer week, with monthly follow-up sessions throughout the year.

Typically, induction programs began in summer and continued monthly throughout the school year. Meetings covered a variety of topics related to new-teacher support, from traditional onboarding procedures to more focused attention on supporting new teachers' acclimation to the culture and community of the school. In Kingfisher, the BT coordinator surveyed teachers regularly to make sure that the meeting topics would be timely and helpful. In Hickory, due to the lack of diversity of the teaching staff in comparison to the student population, induction included attention to raising awareness among their new staff on issues related to equity in education.

The relationship of mentoring and induction programs to teacher retention. Even though many of the teachers we interviewed said they appreciated their district's mentoring and induction programs, very few people made any explicit connections between these programs and their decisions to stay.

Teachers saw them both as part of their district's network of support (discussed in the previous chapter) and an obligation that added one more thing to their already long to-do lists. Some of teachers we interviewed felt their programs were not particularly helpful, and that the material conveyed in the meetings could just as easily have been communicated via email. For others, however, induction programs offered valuable information and support for them as new teachers.

Most frequently, we heard that it was the informal mentoring they received that influenced their decision to stay.[7] Even more specifically, in five of the districts we visited, teachers reported that it was the science department as a whole that provided this informal mentorship. As noted earlier, our research team began referencing this finding as "the department is the mentor" whenever we noticed it.

RETENTION FOR QUESTIONABLE REASONS

Our study was designed to identify the reasons teachers stayed in their schools and districts. Yet, suppose the reasons that some teachers stayed was not the sort of thing that one might wish to replicate. Throughout our research, we were in contact with a large number of school districts who ultimately were not a part of our study for one reason or another. In our travels, we came across some examples of retention that did not provide the same sense of enthusiasm in our research team as the factors listed in chapter 8 did. We wish to briefly share some of these examples, without naming names.

The Retention of Ineffective Teachers

One valid critique of our study is that we did not—nor did we intend to—connect teacher retention to student outcomes. It would be fully justified to argue that our recommendations could be followed faithfully by individuals who were unsuited to remain in the classroom, and therefore, their retention would hardly benefit students. What if a collegial community of teachers in a school exists but is not oriented toward student academic outcomes? One can imagine a scenario where teachers' daily efforts are organized around priorities other than teaching and learning.[8] If ineffective or incompetent teachers are retained for whatever reason, such an argument would conclude that their retention is undesirable.

Our colleague Julie Luft, who has researched new science-teacher supports throughout her long and distinguished career, served on our project's advisory board and reminded us in our first meeting that retention itself is not an unqualified good, and that not every teacher ought to be retained.[9] There are many reasons why an ineffective teacher might end up being retained by a school or district, and though a comprehensive examination of the topic is beyond our purposes here, we cannot deny that it happens.

We do know, however, that an incredible amount of effort across the US has been put forth in the past two decades to strengthen teacher preparation and teacher evaluation systems. More importantly, these efforts have also sought to provide teachers with useful feedback to help them improve. Our own view about teacher development is that effectiveness is predicated on professional growth over time, something that can only happen if someone stays.

Patronage

Political patronage in public-sector employment has a long and well-documented history in the United States and throughout the world.[10] Over the past century, the growth of unions, civil service protections, and civil rights legislation have all had an impact by increasing job protections, improving workplace safety, and ensuring due process in hiring and employment. Within education, the days of experienced and committed teachers being dismissed to make room for someone's less qualified relative or friend would seem to be behind us.[11] Certification requirements alone have done a great deal to professionalize the teaching workforce, and all fifty states and District of Columbia have minimum standards that must be met in order to be employed as a teacher in a public school.[12]

And yet, there was one district where we kept hearing a particular story. This was a place where people wanted to live because it was home, but the economy was nothing like it was in the past. High-paying work was hard to come by, but employment as a teacher was a good and available job. The teacher retention rate in the area school district was very high, but we found potential participants much less willing to talk with us. Eventually, we received information via multiple back-channels that this district had a bit of a corruption problem, and that employment there operated as a "pay-to-play" bribery system, with the general understanding that if a person left, they could not return. Somewhat bewildered, we set all of this information aside and continued with our research.

A chance encounter with a local elected official—who had lots of time to chat—surfaced the issue for our team once again. When the official mentioned the area he represented, the conversation turned to the schools and the high rate of teacher retention evident from the public staffing data. This got a knowing laugh, and he said, "You know why, right? It costs $10,000 to get a job there. You actually have to go see a guy. Everybody knows how corrupt it is there, and it's quite the old boys' network." It is possible that patronage in public-sector jobs may not be that far in the past after all.

Race, Segregation, and Teacher-Student Match

Another issue that emerged in our study concerned schools in which the population of both teachers and students was predominantly White. Quite simply, we wondered if the racial match between White teachers and their students could be a factor in the high teacher retention rates in certain schools and districts. And yet, there were plenty of other districts in each state with a similar demographic profile of White teachers and students that had lower teacher retention. Perhaps in combination with other factors, however, such as the availability of resources for teaching, such teacher-student match across race, culture, and social class could in fact exert influence over the retention of certain White teachers. In this way, the Whiteness of the student body may have be considered by some teachers as an asset, and therefore part of their embeddedness.[13]

A 2022 report by the US General Accounting Office to the US Congress found that as the K–12 student population becomes more diverse over time, many schools continue to be divided over racial, ethnic, and economic lines. The introduction to the report states:

> Students who are poor, Black, or Hispanic generally attend schools with fewer resources and worse outcomes (about 80 percent of students attending low-income schools are Black or Hispanic). They are also more likely to be referred to alternative schools for disciplinary reasons, and Black students experience disproportionate and more severe discipline, which can remove them from classroom learning. These inequities can have serious life-long implications, including lower earnings and less access to post-secondary education and skill building… More than a third of students (about 18.5 million) attended a predominantly same-race/ethnicity school—where 75 percent or more of the student population is of a single race/ethnicity.[14]

The *Brown v. Board of Education* decision of 1953 overturned legal *de jure* racial segregation in the United States, but clearly, modern forms of de facto segregation still exist.[15]

A wide body of research has investigated the impact of racial/ethnic matching between teachers and students across a range of educational practices and outcomes.[16] Much of this research demonstrates the largest effects are on Black students and Black boys in particular. For example, one recent study showed that Black students assigned to a Black teacher have higher scores on certain achievement tests.[17]

Our suggestion is that this race/ethnic match could reasonably extend into White teacher retention in such segregated schools. We noted certain words and phrases in language that certain interviewees used to describe the children in their schools, such as "good," "interested," and "engaged" students. They also used different words, like "low-income students," or kids with "home problems" to describe students in other schools. While respondents did not invoke race during these comments, we are aware that the opposites of these descriptors *are* used more often to describe students of color.[18] Still, it is not provocative to suggest that many White teachers are more comfortable teaching students who look like themselves. Indeed, this finding has been demonstrated repeatedly.[19] Our proposition, extending these findings, is that perhaps the comfort afforded by White racial teacher-student match can be considered an asset that positively influences White teacher retention.

The lesson for policymakers is the same one that desegregation efforts have sought to hammer home since the start of the Civil Rights Movement in the early twentieth century: the illusory gains of segregation come at the price of justice. As Martin Luther King said in his letter from the Birmingham City Jail, "Injustice anywhere is a threat to justice everywhere. We are caught in an inescapable network of mutuality, tied in a single garment of destiny. Whatever affects one directly, affects all indirectly."[20]

IMPLICATIONS AND RECOMMENDATIONS

In this final section, we consider the implications of our findings across this six-year research study and make some specific recommendations for administrators, policymakers, and teachers themselves.

Rethinking Mentoring and Induction

New employees in any organization need support, and clearly, mentoring and induction programs have a key part to play in retaining teachers. Mentoring programs for teachers are often designed in such a way to minimize power relationships and maximize access, done so by assigning experienced colleagues who teach similar subject areas or grade levels as mentors. Having an assigned mentor who is a peer and not an immediate supervisor (such as a vice principal or a department head) makes it possible for beginner teachers to have their questions answered by someone who is not also evaluating them, which hopefully creates more trust and openness in the mentoring relationship. Yet, as necessary as mentoring and induction programs are, they are likely not to be the proximal cause of a teacher's retention in a school or in the profession.

One of our main findings concerned the power that collegial relationships, opportunities for collaboration, and informal mentoring had on teacher retention. School leaders might think about increasing opportunities for teachers to interact with one another, even in unstructured ways, that serve to strengthen their ties and personal relationships. Within corporate environments, team building efforts and social activities are not only sanctioned but often considered to be an essential part of smooth operations. Schools may have their own versions of these—such as professional-learning committee meetings, back-to-school nights, and varsity basketball games—but unless there is a concerted effort to help novice teachers connect with others who share their values when they participate in such events, the chance to forge stronger links and fit may be lost. The district bus tour and community picnic we heard about in Hickory is a good example of the kind of effort that serves to connect new teachers with students' families and other members of their community.

School leaders can be deliberate in how they design such opportunities and intentionally create openings for novice teachers to connect. In this study, we saw department chairs who made sure that new teachers had access to the resources they needed as soon as they were hired and were deeply invested in their success. We also encountered neighborhood gatherings meet-and-greets with students' families, and community-run garden projects, all of which to connect new teachers to the area. The resources that teachers value are often very modest—a staple remover and construction paper for bulletin boards, wipes to clean off sticky desks, or a bag of corn starch for a science lab. Making sure teachers have what they need to do their jobs is an investment that pays dividends.

Rethinking Mentoring and Induction Recommendations:

For Teachers

- Develop and sustain collaborative and cooperative relationships with one another, and be willing to share resources, especially with new teachers.
- The department is the mentor. Recognize the power of informal mentoring, and check in on new teachers to see how they are doing. Offer help in learning the culture of the school.
- Teacher learning is reciprocal, so model professional learning for new teachers by inviting them to offer solutions to your own problems of practice.

For Administrators

- Make time and space for teachers to build their networks of informal relationship during the school day, and invest in strengthening teachers' relationships with one another.
- Closely attend to issues among teachers that have the potential to erode trust, and make an effort to address them.
- Check in on new teachers regularly to see if they have any pressing needs or questions, and make sure that they can ask without fear of embarrassment.
- Support school and district mentoring efforts by ensuring that mentors are appropriately selected and well-prepared for the role. Learning to mentor takes time, and just because someone is a great teacher does not mean that they know how to be a good mentor. At the same time, recognize the limits of one-on-one mentoring relationships.
- Induction programs are a form of sustained professional development and work well when tailored to the values and expressed needs of teachers. Human resource onboarding ought to be considered a separate process from induction.
- Create opportunities for new teachers to connect with the community, both inside and outside the school (e.g., family literacy nights, bus tours, community picnics).

For Policymakers

- Both formal and informal mentors value resources that help them become better colleagues to novice teachers, but if they are overly prescriptive, these resources are less likely to be seen as useful. Consider ways that states can support districts with specific resources for mentor training and new-teacher support.

- Teachers and administrators value their time. Finding creative solutions for professional learning during the school day—such as the example of the Wallago district that had one early release day per week—will pay dividends. Consider advocating for such policies that do not simply squeeze professional learning into already crowded school days.
- Teachers found dedicated mentors and instructional coaches valuable, and those we encountered in this study were often focused solely on that work. They were not—as we have encountered elsewhere—seen as surplus teachers who could be slotted in to perform other roles around the building, such as substitutes, test preparation coordinators, etc. Specific state policy concerning such positions, such as including them in school funding formulas, would likely strengthen these efforts.
- New teachers who have difficulty finding and affording housing near their job may be less likely to be retained. Enact policies that take teacher housing shortage issues seriously.

Teacher Autonomy, Agency, and Protection

Throughout this study, we saw teachers value their autonomy in the classroom and the agency they had related to their career trajectories. We saw administrators who trusted teachers to make curricular and pedagogical decisions instead of micromanaging them, and who provided resources whenever possible for both teaching and professional development. We saw opportunities for teachers to give input into the important matters that affected them and participate collectively in supporting their colleagues. Perhaps most of all, we saw healthy professional communities of educators engaged in shared goals around ensuring students were well-served by their schools. For example, in Granite, we saw a supportive and responsive administration, who did not leave teachers' problems or questions unaddressed for more than a day. In Mulberry, we saw how much teachers valued being able to exert an influence over their own professional development.

Since the early days of public education in the United States, the work of teachers has been pulled in tension between two poles.[21] The first views teachers as faithful and competent enactors of the educational agenda of their superiors, while the other sees teachers and administrators as knowledgeable professionals and coequal partners working with their own responsibilities in different parts of the educational system. In the schools and districts that we visited for this study, the latter was a more accurate description.

We suggest that teacher retention in our study was driven by administrative protection of teachers' professionalism as much as anything else. Supportive school leaders who fostered a culture protecting teacher autonomy and agency in their schools—which sometimes included keeping researchers like us at bay—served to strengthen teacher embeddedness in their organizations.

Teacher Autonomy, Agency, and Protection Recommendations

For Teachers

- Teachers are professionals, so it is reasonable to claim the autonomy that is needed to do the job well as a professional. Unrealistic demands to quickly cover curriculum may be resisted, especially when at odds with contemporary understandings about teaching and learning.
- New teachers know that they have responsibilities but are often less well-versed on their rights. In this study, teacher unions and teacher associations played a key role in teacher retention, so connecting teachers to these organizations is important.
- Like in many professions, learning to say no to administrative requests can feel daunting, however, protecting one's time is critical to retention. We recommend the phrase, "No, but thank you for asking," as a helpful response.

For Administrators

- Teachers will typically want to be good and effective teachers. If they feel micromanaged or excessively constrained, they will have difficulty acting on their ideas. If they are given no curricular guidance at all, then they may feel overwhelmed. Finding the balance to meet each teacher where they are in terms of the instructional support they require is a central intellectual task for administrators.
- New teachers may still be mapping out the boundaries of their autonomy and the processes of collegial collaboration and often appreciate support that helps them think about these areas of teaching, instead of simply being told what to do.

- Trust teachers and invite them to be part of solving problems. If they decline opportunities, respecting that decision can go a long way. If they accept, be prepared to listen to their ideas and collaborate with them on solutions.
- Some experienced teachers have not had trusting experiences with administrators and may be overwhelmed by an offer of more autonomy. It is okay to take things slow, but a good first step is teacher-directed professional development.
- Involve teachers in hiring decisions whenever possible. Share hiring criteria and application evaluation tools and incorporate teachers' input into the hiring process.
- Administrators can also benefit from professional development around ways to support teachers as professionals.

For Policymakers

- Ensure that teacher pay is on parity with other professions that require a similar degree or credential, and keep pace with the cost of living in a given area.
- Consider enacting policies that support the professional growth of teachers. Financial support for advance course completion and professional development was particularly valued by teachers in the high-retention districts we studied.
- Create career pathways for teachers that do not remove them from the classroom, such as instructional coaching or teacher leadership positions. Recognize that many teachers seek opportunities for personal and professional growth.
- Attend to issues that impact autonomy and agency, such as patronage hiring, discrimination, and scarcity of resources.

Specific Supports for Teachers of Color

Such a culture of protection was even more important to novice teachers of color, who shouldered the additional burden of navigating through the smog of racism while getting through their first years of teaching. Prior studies and our own research both showed that teachers of color valued connections to the community and being able to give back in some way, and this in and of itself was an important reason for retention. Teachers of color also valued having administrators and mentors of color, as well as opportunities to pursue leadership themselves.

And yet, teachers of color can only be retained if they are hired in the first place. It is well-known that the demographics of the US teacher workforce do not reflect that of the student population, and as noted above, this fact was laid starkly in front of us as we conducted this study. We note that one hiring strategy in Mulberry was to identify teachers of color from surrounding districts and encourage them to apply for a job in their district, where the salary was comparable, but the climate was much more welcoming.

Specific Supports for Teachers of Color Recommendations

For Teachers

- Teachers who do not identify as teachers of color need to recognize that teachers of color—and new teachers of color in particular—have qualitatively different experiences as teachers. The friendly experienced teacher who may have helped one teacher may not be so helpful to another, and ongoing microaggressions and the smog of racism can take a toll.
- Be an empathetic listener, and be sure to talk through and consider actions that have the potential to address problems—or make them worse.
- Be a connector, and help new teachers of color build their organizational and community networks, especially if they are new to the area.

For Administrators

- Hire teachers of color, and make sure that they have the same opportunity to be placed on the salary guide at a level commensurate with their experience and expertise.
- Consider the ways in which organizational fit for teachers of color may be different than for others in the district. Seek opportunities for the values that bring teachers of color into teaching to be affirmed without adding obligations or time burdens.
- Be alert for the emergence of racism-related issues, particularly from other teachers or administrators, that could potentially impact the decision to stay by a teacher of color. Make it a point to discuss any barriers that a teacher of color may be facing in their daily work, take any necessary administrative actions, and follow up with teachers to see if problems have been satisfactorily addressed.

For Policymakers

- Attend to the hiring of teachers of color in state and local contexts. If data suggests that teachers of color leave certain districts at higher rates, then ignoring the issue is likely to sustain segregation. The commitment to live and work in a multiracial, pluralistic, democratic society means that students require the opportunity to encounter teachers from diverse backgrounds, as well as their own.
- Consider policies that support individuals in their effort to earn a four-year college degree, which is necessary for teachers in nearly all certifications across the United States.
- Incentivize the selection of teaching as a career by continuing to support teacher loan forgiveness programs and grants to pursue teacher certification.
- Support efforts to adequately fund schools so that all students have the opportunity for a high-quality education.

Homegrown Teacher Cultivation and Support

Although we expected to encounter teachers with pre-existing ties to their schools from their days as students, the number of hometown teachers we encountered was still surprising. In our account here, we are indebted to others who have researched this phenomenon more in-depth, and note that the topic still seems like an area ripe for future research.

What is clear is that teachers return to their communities to teach for a number of reasons. For some, like the teachers in Kingfisher, the ties of kinship and culture were strong and exerted a powerful pull home. Many saw teaching as a good and available job in the place where they wanted to live. Others felt a moral obligation to give back to the communities that nurtured them, a sentiment that was more often heard from the teachers of color we interviewed.

This raises the question about what districts might do to encourage people who grew up in a particular community and understand it deeply to return as teachers. Over the past decade, there has been a great deal of attention paid to so-called grow-your-own programs, which explicitly seek to support the preparation of teachers from local students, paraprofessionals, and community members.[22] Such programs appear to produce teachers who are more likely to stay, especially if they are the products of collaborations between districts and teacher preparation programs. And yet, in places like Pompano, Sandstone, and Hickory, we also saw large numbers of hometown teachers who returned with only the slightest of nudges.

Homegrown Teacher Cultivation and Support Recommendations

For Teachers

- Talk to K–12 students about the career of teaching and the process of becoming a teacher.
- Invite former students to come visit your classroom as a guest speaker, so that they have the feeling of being in a classroom situation in which they are not a student.
- Stay in touch with former students, and nurture the interests of those who may have an interest in teaching. Become familiar with the different pathways to teacher certification available in your state, so that you can make useful recommendations.

For Administrators

- Support a future teachers' club, and sustain connections with graduates. Connect with local teacher preparation programs to develop ways that schools can be used as field sites for teacher preparation.
- Work with the local teachers union or association to sponsor one or more students to substitute in the district or work as club advisors. Offer financial support for the costs of fingerprinting, background checks, and credentialing.
- Make as many opportunities for students to see themselves in a teaching career as possible. Support district efforts for older students to work with younger ones, so that they might start to develop an identity as a potential teacher.
- Make a sustained effort to recruit second-career teachers who live in the area and who may be graduates of the school or district. Hold information sessions about employment in the district, and reach out to local employers, who may be quite willing to connect with schools.

For Policymakers

- Offer support for grow-your-own programs, which may produce more teachers possessing a familiarity with the district and a disposition towards giving back to a community that supported them. Such programs have been particularly successful in recruiting and preparing teachers of color.

- Support centralized job search resources that make it easy to find and apply for teaching jobs.

The Role of Teacher Preparation Programs

Obviously, teacher education programs are likely to strengthen teacher retention when they prepare teachers well for the students they will teach and the classrooms where they will work. It may seem at first glance that teacher preparation programs would have little else to do with teacher retention, but we have noted a few possibilities in the course of our research.

Most teacher preparation programs are run by universities, and the resulting connections between school districts, teachers, universities, and the communities in which they are situated serve to strengthen supportive ties. Time and again throughout this study—in Birch, Egret, Kingfisher, Rivuline, and elsewhere—we have seen local universities play a role in the professional lives of teachers. Links between universities and districts supported professional development, supplied resources, offered spaces for activities, and provided other opportunities for teachers and students.

Teacher preparation programs often straddle the two worlds of K–12 schools and universities. Sending prospective teachers into classrooms to learn how to teach is a type of apprenticeship, and modern programs view cooperating teachers as knowledgeable professionals who have much to contribute by passing along their hard-won knowledge. Teacher education programs support the retention of K–12 teachers by affirming their expertise. They also provide a model for prospective teachers, so that they know how they ought to expect to be treated as professionals in the future.

Similarly, there has been a recent effort by specific teacher education programs to continue to support their graduates in their teaching.[23] For example, the teacher residency program that both of us were involved in at Montclair State University offered three years of coaching and induction support for teachers hired into Newark Public Schools. While such support for novice teachers is typically welcomed by school districts, care must also be taken to coordinate with existing mentoring and induction programs in order to ensure that novice teachers are not overwhelmed by multiple and overlapping well-intentioned efforts.

Teacher Preparation Program Recommendations

For Teachers

- Working as a cooperating teacher can be a rewarding avenue for professional growth. If you are ready to do so, make it known to your administrator that you are interested in taking on an intern or student teacher.
- Prospective teachers may benefit from early exposure to observations of collegial collaboration, which may counter some of the negative messages they hear about the teaching profession.

For Administrators

- Sometimes there are overlapping efforts by teacher education induction programs and district support programs for new teachers. Have a frank conversation with novice teachers to gauge their needs for support and adjust as needed.
- Encourage connections between teachers and Universities. Such connections may sustain teachers is various ways and can include supporting those learning to teach in multiple ways.
- Work closely with teacher education programs to ensure that any placement of teacher candidates is accomplished thoughtfully. No teacher should be assigned to be a cooperating teacher against their will.

For Policymakers

- Support high-quality teacher preparation efforts in multiple modalities. Traditional teacher preparation, alternate route programs, and teacher residency programs each serve prospective teachers in different situations. All need support.
- Consider enhancing structural supports for learning to teach. Many current teacher preparation programs in the United States place financial strains on prospective teachers and time burdens on cooperating teachers.
- Fund collaborations between universities and districts in order to relieve the financial burden of trying to develop, implement, and sustain university-school partnerships.

Data Systems and Future Research on Teacher Retention

Using state-level school staffing data to research teacher retention, as we have done in our study, offers promising avenues of research on pressing questions concerning the education workforce. Such research includes examining factors related to teacher retention, such as the presence of additional certifications (e.g., teaching students with disabilities, subject area, bilingual/bicultural certifications), salary, demographic matches between teachers and the district, and the effects of various state-level policies. This data could also be used to examine equity issues, such as gendered salary gaps resulting from mobility or discrimination during the hiring process, or whether second-career teachers are retained at comparable rates to their younger counterparts. These findings would have implications for teacher recruitment, preparation, and retention, and would be valuable for teacher educators, administrators, and policymakers alike.

And yet, the accuracy, quality, and other purposes of that data remain a barrier to its expanded use. Time and again, we found errors and omissions in data that impacted the questions we could ask, the ideas we could pursue, and the claims we could make. Structurally, the incongruence of data structures from year to year impacted the ability to make comparisons and draw conclusions. It would be enormously instructive to have certification information in staffing data, but instead, states regularly reported what teachers were *assigned* to teach, making it almost impossible to tell if a teacher was being asked to teach outside of their certification.

Another example concerns the relationship of teacher salary to retention, one of the top priorities conveyed to us by the National Science Foundation in funding this study. In our analyses, we used the base salary provided in the state data; however, there was little guarantee that this number was accurate, even if it reflected the negotiated contract or legislatively mandated amount. For one thing, compensation often includes medical benefits, pension plans, and other assets. As we saw in a number of districts in the study, teachers often considered their resources for teaching as a benefit as well. Additionally, teachers may or may not have the opportunity to earn more money from additional assignments, such as coaching, advising clubs, or taking on extra teaching assignments, and these were rarely reported in the data we used. With respect to retention, these additional assignments can serve to embed teachers more firmly in their schools and their communities, a finding we saw in districts we visited. However, if teachers feel pressured to take on extra assignments when they would otherwise prefer to say no, their sense of fit may weaken within their organization as a consequence of this additional work.

Data Systems and Future Research on Teacher Retention Recommendations

For Teachers

- Teachers have the right to ensure that the data kept by their employer is accurate and private.

For Administrators

- Share teacher data with teachers themselves, so that they can verify that it is correct (including race, ethnicity, and gender designations).
- Data concerning school and district employment trends should be available to teachers and part of a broader discussion about working conditions and school culture.
- Investigate the reasons for teacher retention locally by talking with retained teachers about why they stay. Use this information to help support new teachers.

For Policymakers

- Standardize longitudinal data collection and make staffing data public. Include accurate salary and certification in these data sets.
- Continue local and national efforts to ensure data quality and accuracy.
- Collect and produce longitudinal (five-year, ten-year) retention data reports on schools, districts, and subject areas to identify where policy pressure might be exerted to grow the teacher pool as needed.

CONCLUSION: USING EMBEDDEDNESS THEORIES TO GUIDE ADMINISTRATIVE DECISIONS

The framework of teacher embeddedness—with links, fit, and assets on one axis and the domains of the organization, profession, and community on the other—offer a few final suggestions for teacher retention efforts. As administrators, policymakers, and teachers themselves make decisions about how to increase the likelihood of retention, it is worth thinking about the possibilities within each square of this matrix.

We also take note of the importance that teachers in our study attached to simple acts of kindness, such as administrators or colleagues checking in to see how things are going. New teachers have the combined task of learning the demands of the job of teaching while also learning to understand the organizational culture of the school, all of which can be confusing, even to the most well-prepared teachers. Therefore, even just saying "good morning" to a novice teacher at the start of the day can have an impact. Similarly, simple offers to chat over lunch, help put up a bulletin board after school, or cover a class in an emergency have the power to change the way a novice teacher thinks about their whole career.

Not everyone will stay, and that is understandable. Each strand of this metaphorical web—the links to others, the comfort of fit and shared values, and the assets to do the work well and enjoy life outside of school—embeds teachers more within their school and community, increasing the chances for their retention in their job and sustaining them in their profession. That is why teachers stay.

APPENDIX A

Methodology

In this appendix, we describe the data sources and methods used at each phase of our study for those interested in understanding more about how we conducted this research. As noted in the introduction, we remind readers that although we present this book as generalizable across a wide group of teachers, our data collection was limited to that of secondary science teachers, as this was the target population of interest, and the problem of secondary science teacher retention was the initial problem our study sought to investigate.

This study, which began in August 2018, was funded with a five-year Track 4 Noyce Research Grant from the National Science Foundation and was extended an additional year due to pandemic-related delays. An advisory board consisting of experts in the field of teacher preparation and retention met with our research team at regular intervals over the duration of the grant. The project culminated with a conference on teacher retention at Montclair State University in June 2023, which brought together many of the participants from our case study districts and other teacher-retention researchers from across the country.

What follows is a detailed description of the four distinct methodological phases of our study. In the first phase, we used publicly available data to track the retention of individual secondary science teachers in four states (New Jersey, North Carolina, Pennsylvania, and Wisconsin) over a ten year period. Using this data, we then completed the second phase, which included identifying candidate school districts for further case study based on their record of retention in the focus areas and then recruiting selected districts with a high rate of novice-science-teacher retention to participate in a site visit and qualitative data collection.[1] In phase three, the data from this visit was then analyzed to construct a written case study to describe the factors influencing teacher retention in each locational education authority (LEA). The fourth phase was a multiple-case analysis of the thirteen complete LEA-level case studies, which was then conducted with the goal of identifying common themes across the cases. This ultimately led to the ten factors introduced in chapter 1 and described in detail in chapter 8.

PHASE ONE: ANALYSIS OF STATE-LEVEL DISTRICT STAFFING DATA

Our goal was to identify factors related to teacher retention by talking with the people in districts where teacher retention was high. In particular, we sought to learn how they explained their own high rates of retention. This was not just a theoretical commitment but a premise that guided the entire structure of our study. Thus, the first step required identifying which districts those would be. In order to do so, we needed to obtain access to teacher data from each of the four states in the study. As described below, we used individual state staffing datasets from the 2007-2008 through the 2017-2018 school years.

In this study we joined a growing number of researchers who have turned to a relatively new kind of dataset: state-level school staffing reports.[2] While in certain states these reports have been available for decades, the US Department of Education's Race to the Top grant proposal process, as described in appendix B, brought new attention to the pressing issue of the development of comprehensible and reliable longitudinal data systems.[3] As a consequence, many state-level education data systems now have unique teacher identifiers that allow for education researchers to examine questions about teacher retention at a scope and level of detail that was previously available only to state departments of education.

Data contained in state staffing reports typically includes certain common fields, such as first, middle, and last name, salary, and year of birth. The reporting of race and ethnicity has changed over the past decade; given that states must report race and ethnicity data to the federal government, many state data systems have adopted federal guidelines that present ethnicity as a separate category and allow respondents to choose more than one race.[4]

Sex data was also included in this dataset, and the teacher-level data examined for this study included only male and female response options. By the final data year of this project (2017–2018), all of the states in this study no longer published race/ethnicity or year of birth in their publicly available staffing data, though the Pennsylvania Department of Education provided our team with this data upon request. Salary data was reported differently in nearly each state, but it was possible to determine the yearly annual base salary of each science teacher with up to five years of experience. The starting salary in a district was determined by taking the base salary of a new full-time employee, but in many cases, it was unclear as to whether the salary included supplements, extra-duty pay, or other adjustments. In cases where there were two identically credentialed full-time employees with different salaries, the lower of the two salaries for a new employee was considered the starting salary. However, sometimes public contracts had to be consulted to determine the starting salary if other discrepancies remained.

The professional data in these reports typically included educational-attainment level, teaching assignments (used as a proxy for certification area), full- or part-time status, years of experience in the district, and years of total teaching experience. The school assignment, location, and district were always included. Many also provided the grade level or grade band taught (e.g., elementary, middle, high school). Some states included a field for the preparation pathway (e.g., the New Jersey data provides the option for the selection of a traditional or alternate route). Used in combination with other district and school data made publicly available by state departments of education, it was possible to link other contextual factors such as district size, school size, and student demographics to the data on individual teachers.

The four states in this study, as shown in table A.1—New Jersey, North Carolina, Pennsylvania, and Wisconsin—were chosen because they were high-population states with diverse populations, had a mix of rural, suburban, and

TABLE A.1 Population and district data for selected states in 2017

	NJ	*NC*	*PA*	*WI*
Total state population	8,900,000	10,400,000	12,800,000	5,800,000
Number of teachers	116,351	98,590	120,681	60,649
Number of secondary science teachers	~7,000	~8,000	~9,000	~5,000
Total regular local public school districts	562	121	500	420
Number of districts with at least one novice high school science teacher between 2007–2018	242 (43%)	85 (70%)	353 (71%)	182 (43%)

Source: US Census Bureau. Data Profiles database. https://www.census.gov/acs/www/data/data-tables-and-tools/data-profiles/2017/;

US Department of Education, National Center for Educational Statistics, Common Core of Data: https://nces.ed.gov/ccd/.

urban school districts, and represented a range of contexts for teacher preparation and retention policy contexts.[5] Further, each of the four states had full and available annual datasets of teacher employment that included demographic and teaching-assignment fields. Pennsylvania and Wisconsin published their staffing lists as spreadsheets on state websites. New Jersey's data was not publicly available but was obtained through the process within the state's Open Public Records Act. North Carolina stores all education data with the North Carolina Education Research Data Center (NCERDC), which was made available to us for a fee. Notably, data from North Carolina did not include teacher names, only unique numerical identifiers. Although we acknowledge that a larger study with more states would likely have enriched our investigation, given the constraints of time, funding, and data availability, we felt that the four states selected were likely to yield sufficient answers to the research questions.

For each of the four states, we sought to identify teachers who had been retained for four out of their first five years. As described in chapter 1, we identified the five-year metric as the most beneficial unit of analysis in characterizing individual teachers' employment trajectories from our state-level datasets. To account for mid-year hires, breaks in service, and long-term substitute assignments that turned into permanent hires, we considered a teacher retained if they were in the same district for four out of their first five years. Because staffing data was compiled at the beginning of each state's academic year, six years of data were required. Additionally, we aimed to examine the retention of multiple cohorts of novice science teachers who all began teaching in the same year. Given that complete data was available for each of the four states beginning in 2007 and this project began in 2018, we were able to analyze six full cohorts, as shown in figure A.1. Therefore, in order for us to complete our analysis, we required eleven years of annual staffing data from each state, spanning from 2007 to 2018.

Creating a Master Table for Each State

The first step in this analysis was to construct a master list for each state that included the employment status of each novice science teacher who was a member of the 2007–2012 cohorts. Each dataset was trimmed to include only secondary science teachers who were in their first six years of teaching within this time frame, and each individual was assigned a unique project identifier that

FIGURE A.1 Annual staffing data required for each cohort of novice science teachers

included their state and cohort year (e.g., NJ2007-001). All of the datasets for a given state were then merged and cleaned. This process entailed ensuring consistency in fields, inputting any missing data, and double checking to ensure that first-year teachers were properly identified as such. This process was painstaking and time consuming because it could not be automated, particularly in ensuring that each first-year science teacher was identified with a unique identifier. One final trim of the data excluded any teacher who was not a member of the 2007–2012 cohorts and in their first six years of teaching.

This process ultimately resulted in four master state datasets, consisting of every teacher in the novice-science-teacher cohorts and their employment history. Additional data tags were assigned to each individual to characterize their "real" years of experience and whether they were retained four of their first five years in the same LEA. Ultimately, each teacher in the dataset was designated with a binary indicator for their "Retained-in-district 4 out of their first 5 years" status.

The race and ethnicity data within the original staffing reports were inconsistently reported across states and cohorts, therefore we elected to create a binary category in order to capture whether or not a given individual was from a minoritized demographic. The overwhelming majority of teachers in the dataset were characterized as White and non-Hispanic, not unlike the demographic makeup of the teacher workforce in the United States.[6] The second group included all individuals identified as either Hispanic or non-White or both. Though we acknowledge that these categories are problematic in many ways—certainly, the imprecision of the phrase "teachers of color" held the possibility of introducing new errors—we did ultimately assign teachers to a binary category of whether they were White *and* non-Hispanic (0) or not (1).[7] This approach seemed reasonable given our purpose of analyzing the data through the lens of race and ethnicity so as to identify districts that were successfully retaining teachers of color. However, as we know much of the data was entered by administrators and not by teachers themselves, there is no guarantee that individual teachers were consulted about their ethnicity or race data that was entered in the data we used for this analysis, which is a potential source of error in our analysis.

As an aside, it is worth mentioning one aspect of our project, undertaken at this time, that was unsuccessful. We had hoped to be able to provide state departments of education with a database tool for use in calculating categorical retention rates for their state datasets. The idea was that such a tool could be fed clean and well-ordered state-level data, which would then permit the production of retention reports for any given group of districts, schools, or teachers for a specified time frame. This tool could have also provided a much clearer picture of vacancies, shortage areas, and sites of high retention to inform policymakers and educational stakeholders on future courses of action.

A database expert worked on the first year of the grant as part of our team, and together we built prototype database tools using MySQL that were quite promising. The problem, however, was the data. With our small subset of novice-science-teacher data, we were able—at great effort—to arrive at a clean dataset that could be standardized for analysis. However, when we tried to run queries on the full staffing dataset from each state, there were just too many missing fields and clearly incorrect data. Some records had no unique teacher identification record, some salary entries were comically incorrect, and many records were duplicated in cases where a teacher had a split assignment. Issues of data incongruence also plagued the project, such as the changes to race and ethnicity data collection in 2012. During our second year, with new appreciation for the work of the Workforce Data Quality Campaign, we decided to cut our losses and terminate this part of the project.[8]

PHASE TWO: DISTRICT—CASE STUDY DISTRICT SELECTION & INVITATION

In this section, we discuss the second phase of our study, which included the selection of focus districts and their subsequent recruitment into the study. Our research team created a retention index measure as a first step in identifying potential districts of interest. Six factors were weighted equally in this index and were considered in comparison to all other public local educational agencies in that state: the top 10 percent in a rank of the total number of novice science teachers retained, the top 10 percent in a rank of the ratio of novice science teachers retained to student population, the retention of three or more novice science teachers in eleven years, the retention of at least one novice science teacher of color, greater than 50 percent of students receiving free or reduced lunch, and the top 10 percent in a ranking of districts by percentage of students identified as limited English proficient (LEP). Each of these factors was worth one point on the index. Districts that did not retain more than 50 percent of their novice teachers were excluded, as were districts that only retained one novice science teacher in eleven years.

From this initial index, we identified a subset of districts in each state that demonstrated high retention rates of novice science teachers for possible further qualitative study. In selecting this subset of districts, we sought to balance our opportunity to learn by including a number of factors, such as the district's geographic location in the state, districts that demonstrated success in retaining science teachers of color, and the demographic profile of the school, which included the percentage of students receiving free/reduced lunch or were designated Limited English Proficiency.[9] This process was repeated for each state, and the entire research team was involved in constructing the final lists.

For each state we selected five target districts for invitation, each with distinct characteristics from the other, and another five districts as suitable backups in the event that an invited district declined to participate in the study. After an initial email and/or phone call invitation to the study, the principal investigator and project manager typically met with district leadership to discuss the study and begin the process of local project approval, typically through a director of research or review board prior to full school board approval. Though we aimed for a total of twenty cases (five in each state), our district recruitment happened to coincide with the peak of the COVID-19 pandemic in 2020 and 2021. Many districts were focused on essential functions and declined participation. However, we still obtained a total of thirteen districts in all four states that agreed to participate in the study, which produced a sufficiently robust dataset for analysis.

Phase Three: Qualitative Data Collection

Once districts were established, the research team scheduled site visits and interviews with teachers, science area supervisors, administrators, and other district personnel involved in supporting novice science teachers (e.g., induction coaches). In each district, a liaison typically aided in arranging and scheduling the interviews. Site visits prior to March 2020 and after April 2022 were conducted at schools in person, while those during the intervening time were conducted virtually over the Zoom online video application.

In preparation for our site visits, we developed a series of tools, which included consent forms and interview guides for each type of participant (e.g., novice teacher, retained teacher, administrator, etc.). Additionally, we developed publicly available documents housed on our IMPREST website for future participants to review prior to our visit, which included information related to what to expect from a site visit, sample site visit agendas, and site permission letters. Some tools were later modified to better accommodate an online site-visit format. Sites received pseudonyms upon the confirmation of a visit, which was subsequently used for all data collection and subsequent analysis.[10]

Interviews took place at the convenience of the interviewees, and the consent form promised both individual and institutional confidentiality. While the majority of the interviews were individual, a number of group interviews took place by necessity. These were grouped by experience level (e.g., novice teachers or experienced teachers), though we intentionally did not mix teachers and administrators in order to permit them to speak freely.

Interviews typically lasted thirty to forty-five minutes and were recorded, transcribed, and then analyzed using NVIVO12 software. All active members of the research team collaborated on the data collection and construction of case narratives. Other data collected included publicly available district documents on district websites. We also welcomed any other documentation related to the mentoring and induction efforts that districts wished to provide. This additional information was used primarily for corroboration, accuracy, and further detail for the written case studies.

All interviews were recorded and transcribed, then imported into qualitative analysis software—first NVIVO12, and later Taguette—for further analysis. At least three members of the research team independently coded data for each case prior to a meeting so as to identify emerging themes related to the salient factors influencing novice-science-teacher retention in the district. Additionally, the mentoring and induction efforts within the district were added as a focus for each case in order to characterize the relationship between these efforts and teacher retention in the district, as portrayed in the data.

Phase Four: Case Study Construction and Cross-Case Analysis

Active members of the research team then collaborated on constructing the narrative of each case, with a single author taking the lead on the writing of each case. When a draft of the case was ready for member checking, a copy was sent to each person in that district who was interviewed, along with a link to a feedback form. Participant feedback was generally affirmative and helpful and occasionally necessitated modifying the case study text to reflect any participant's concerns about accuracy or confidentiality. A total of thirteen cases were completed over the course of the project, four of which are found in their entirety in chapters 4–7.

The case studies sought to identify the most salient factors related to novice-science-teacher retention in each district, and the cross-case analysis aimed to synthesize the findings across the completed cases. Following the procedure suggested by Robert Stake for multiple case study analysis, our research team analyzed the findings of each particular district case using the *a priori* categories' retention factors identified within each of the individual cases.[11] Though case study researchers sometimes caution against generalizing findings, we felt that the focus on successful practices in one context for possible use in another made the effort at producing actionable suggestions from a broader analysis worth the risk of overgeneralization.

Our multiple case study analysis was conducted by first establishing interrater reliability, which involved independent coding by team members on three cases and a consultation before the remaining cases were coded individually. This analysis yielded the ten distinct factors that influenced teacher retention across all of the case study districts, which we presented in chapter 1 and again in chapter 8.

factors influencing novice science-teacher retention in the district. Additionally, the mentoring and induction efforts within the district were added as a focus for each case in order to characterize the relationship between these efforts and teacher retention in the district, as portrayed in the data.

Phase Four: Case Study Construction and Cross-Case Analysis

Active members of the research team then collaborated on constructing the narrative of each case, with a single author taking the lead on the writing of each case. When a draft of the case was ready for member checking, a copy was sent to each person in that district who was interviewed, along with a link [illegible]

[illegible]

APPENDIX B

The National Teacher Policy Context

The federal and state contexts for teacher policies during the period between 2007 and 2018 are an important part of the framing of our study. In this brief appendix we present an overview of the relevant federal legislation that served to both influence state-level policies as well as shape the environment that working teachers and administrators experienced during this time.

A ROLE FOR NATIONAL POLICY IN STATE-RUN EDUCATION

Article 10 of the Constitution leaves the responsibility for education as a power devolved to the states, and the constitution of each state contains language mandating the creation and operation of a public education system.[1] Yet, the federal government does play a significant role in education through other policies that impact schools. For example, federal antipoverty legislation has targeted schools since the 1960s because schools are the place where the children these policies are intended to help can be found.

Though the federal government does not exert direct control over education in the states, providing incentives for the adoption of certain policies at the state level is a longstanding practice. The introduction of the National Minimum Drinking Age Act in 1984 is a good example, because setting a minimum age for the purchase and consumption of alcohol is also a power devolved to the states.[2] States could not actually be compelled to raise the drinking age from eighteen to twenty-one by this act, but if they did not do so, they would lose federal highway transportation funds. Consequently, every state now has a minimum drinking age of twenty-one and receives highway funding.

The same sort of policy carrot and stick approach has been used by the US Department of Education and other federal agencies to advance various priorities impacting schools. Here we only touch on the few that are salient in our study of teacher retention and leave the state policy details that affect teachers, such as initial certification, teacher evaluation, and teacher tenure (where applicable), to be addressed in each chapter.

In examining the landscape of state teacher education policy from 2007 through 2018—the time period of our data collection—it is important to take into account three important US federal policy efforts that had an impact both on state-level education policy and the underlying data on which that policy was based. The first was Title II of the Higher Education Act of 1965, the second was No Child Left Behind of 2001/2002 (later replaced by the Every Student Succeeds Act in 2015), and the third was the Race To the Top grant program that was created as part of the American Recovery and Reinvestment Act of 2009. Each of these national efforts played an important role in shaping state-level policies.

TITLE II OF THE HIGHER EDUCATION ACT

Federal legislation and funding have long been a part of the landscape of teacher education in the US. One such piece of legislation was the Higher Education Act (HEA) of 1965, established with intentions to "strengthen the educational resources of our colleges and universities and to provide financial assistance for students in postsecondary and higher education."[3] Specifically, this legislation aimed to increase the educational opportunities for lower- and middle-income families as well as provide assistance at the college and university level to deal with the issue of national poverty.

As it pertains to our study, teacher quality was addressed as one component of this new legislation. Originally designated under Title V in 1965 but reorganized and placed under Title II in the amendment of 1968, the Higher Education Act awarded "fellowships for graduate study at institutions of higher education" in addition to the development and advancement of teacher preparation programs at the postsecondary level. The Higher Education Act has been amended seven times since 1965. The amendment of 1998 was designed to increase the type and amount of data collected from the universities who received funding. Specifically, the Title II amendment required three annual reports in regards to teacher candidates, including rates of passing on state certification and licensure examinations, additional reports from teacher preparation programs at institutions, as well as reports from state departments of education. The reports from states needed to include certification and licensure requirements for both traditional- and alternate-route teacher candidates, passing rates on the state certification assessments aligned to the college or university program in which the candidate participated, as well as additional pieces of data regarding the size and structure of the teacher preparation program.[4]

In 2008, the Higher Education Act was amended to address the disproportionate retention rates of novice teachers in low-income schools across the US by introducing the Teacher Quality Partnership program. This amendment provided federal funding through Title II to programs that sought to prepare teachers for high-need schools and high-need subject areas and encouraged innovation in the development of teaching residency programs. Requirements for the recipients of these grants included a focus on supporting novice teachers by requiring all programs to provide rigorous year-long clinical teacher preparation as well as include at least two years of induction support. All four states in our study (North Carolina, New Jersey, Pennsylvania, and Wisconsin) have benefited from the Teacher Quality Partnership program funding of their teacher preparation programs.

NO CHILD LEFT BEHIND

The No Child Left Behind Act of 2002 (NCLB) was a reauthorization of the Secondary and Elementary Education Act of 1965, and the majority of the funds provided to the US Department of Education by Congress were designated for local educational authorities (school districts) as a component of the antipoverty supports of the original legislation. Most of this support took the form of so-called Title I Funds, which was aimed at students, teachers, and schools in a range of programs. The NCLB also mandated public reporting requirements for a variety of student, school, and district performance indicators, including student achievement. The influence of the NCLB legislation on teacher education policy, the focus of our study, primarily involved the development of plans by states to ensure that teachers of academic subjects were highly qualified. The NCLB defined a highly qualified teacher as someone with a bachelor's degree, a state teacher certification, and subject area competency typically demonstrated by one or more approved standardized tests.[5]

After the passage of the legislation, all new hires in schools with Title I programs had to meet these requirements, and current teachers were required to become highly qualified by the end of the 2005–06 school year. There were clear consequences in terms of withholding federal funds if certain targets set forth for states and districts were not attained. Another feature of this legislation was that districts were required to report annually how many of their teachers met the highly qualified teacher goals set forth in the NCLB. The requirement that teachers were expected to obtain certification for the subject areas they were teaching in order to meet highly qualified teacher status placed additional demands on districts with existing shortages of teachers in certain subject areas, including science, mathematics, special education, and world languages. Republican and Democratic administrations alike recognized that the ambitious goals for staffing schools fully with highly qualified teachers had run up against the hard realities of the labor pool. In the successor to the NCLB, The Every Students Succeeds Act (ESSA) of 2015, the highly qualified teacher requirements were eliminated, and districts simply had to certify that their teachers satisfied state certification requirements.

RACE TO THE TOP

The American Recovery and Reinvestment Act of 2009, developed in the wake of the 2008 global financial crisis, was created to provide an economic stimulus to multiple areas within the US economy. The Race to the Top (RTTT) competitive grant program sought to leverage the federal government's ability to provide economic stimulus while simultaneously creating a policy incentive aimed at modernizing each state's department of education.

In an effort to achieve this goal, one of the RTTT grant requirements focused on improving the preparation of K–12 students for college and the workforce. States were asked to submit competitive proposals in order to receive a share of the limited funding, and their applications were evaluated in light of six major categories. One category of the proposal criteria required states to implement improved data systems intended to "measure student growth and success, and inform teachers and principals about how they can improve instruction."[6] This category built on previous federal efforts to strengthen state data systems under the earlier Education Sciences Reform Act of 2002 and the Educational Technical Assistance Act of 2007. These data collection reforms actually had the greatest impact on the design and operation of our study.

As a whole, the RTTT program was designed to increase the amount, type, and quality of data collected with respect to teachers and students, expanding upon and standardizing the data already being collected as a result of the NCLB.[7] Three of the four states under consideration in this current study (New Jersey, North Carolina, and Pennsylvania) were awarded grants in the RTTT program. Wisconsin submitted an application for each round, and though it was not a finalist, its already robust educational data systems were improved as part of the grant effort.

APPENDIX C

The Role of State Context in Teacher Retention

The following sections describe important aspects of our study, but including them in the main body of the book would have meant straying from our central inquiry concerning the reasons teachers stayed in high-retention school districts. Yet many readers may find these details interesting, hence their inclusion. Here we present two brief discussions drawing upon our study's data, the first about teacher retention across states and the second on the role of salary in teacher retention.

TEACHER RETENTION ACROSS STATES

It was evident throughout our study that state policies played a critical role in determining teachers' classroom experiences as well as their professional trajectories. One question that arose fairly early on in our research was whether there were categorical differences between the two groups of teachers—those who were retained in district and those who were not—both within and across each state. We had retention data for all of the novice science teachers hired between 2007 and 2012 in each of the four states and decided to approach this question systematically. As noted in appendix A, we assigned teachers one of two designations: those who stayed with an employer at least four out of their first five years were designated as *retained* and everyone else was labeled as *not retained*. This binary variable would be the distinction between the two groups we compared.

We then examined how demographic indicators—such as race, gender, education attainment, and age—varied between the two groups. Given the importance of connections with coworkers in the findings of this study, we used the staffing data sets to create a count of people with equivalent subject certifications to our sample (secondary science) in each school and district as a proxy for school science department size and district science department size.

We also conducted a base starting salary analysis to see if there were identifiable differences between the salaries retained and nonretained teachers were offered. Only the New Jersey data included information we could use for comparisons of teachers' preparation pathway, with *alternate-route* teachers being those who enrolled in teacher preparation programs concurrently with being a teacher of record and *traditional*-pathway teachers who completed their initial certification before taking a teaching position.

DIFFERENCES BETWEEN RETAINED AND NOT-RETAINED TEACHERS

The full set of descriptive statistics of the data from all four states are shown in table C.1. New Jersey, Pennsylvania, and North Carolina had somewhat similar five-year novice-teacher retention rates in the 40–50 percent range, but Wisconsin had a much higher rate of retention of 68 percent, as discussed in chapter 9.

Across all four states, there was no significant relationship between highest degree attained and retention. Within states, there was no significant difference in retention between men and women. Neither was there a difference in the age demographic profile of retained versus not-retained teachers. In New Jersey, teachers who earned their teacher certification through the alternate-route program had a slightly lower retention rate than those who went through traditional certification, and this was the case for all demographic categories examined.

When compared to the overall retention rate in each state, teachers of color were retained at a lower rate in New Jersey and Wisconsin, a higher rate in Pennsylvania, and the same rate in North Carolina. North Carolina and New Jersey hired many more teachers of color than Pennsylvania, and Wisconsin, where the total number was quite low. In North Carolina, teachers of color were retained at the same rate as all teachers but at a much lower rate than the teachers of color in Wisconsin and Pennsylvania. We note that only 4 of the 182 districts in Wisconsin hired one or more novice science teachers of color between 2007–2018.

There appeared to be no significant relationship between a district's department size and retention, though the larger urban districts with over 150 science teachers did demonstrate slightly lower rates of science teacher retention. We saw a slightly lower rate of retention in schools with a science department size of between five to seventeen people, as compared with those that were smaller or

TABLE C.1 Descriptive statistics of retained-in-district (4 out of first 5 years) and nonretained first-year secondary science teachers hired between 2007–2012 in North Carolina, New Jersey, Pennsylvania, and Wisconsin

		New Jersey		*Pennsylvania*		*Wisconsin*		*North Carolina*	
		Count	*%*	*Count*	*%*	*Count*	*%*	*Count*	*%*
Number of new science teachers	**Total**	**1691**	(100%)	**1679**	(100%)	**845**	(100%)	**1645**	(100%)
	Retained	728	*(43%)*	803	*(48%)*	573	*(68%)*	701	*(43%)*
	Not Retained	962	*(57%)*	875	*(52%)*	272	*(32%)*	944	*(57%)*
Teachers of color (Hispanic or non-White)	**Total**	**282**	(17%)	**60**	(4%)	**24**	(3%)	**265**	(16%)
	Retained	100	*35%*	34	*(57%)*	11	*(46%)*	112	*(42%)*
	Not Retained	182	*65%*	26	*(43%)*	13	*(54%)*	153	*(58%)*
Not teachers of color (white & non-Hispanic)	**Total**	**1408**	(83%)	**1618**	(96%)	**821**	(97%)	**1292**	(79%)
	Retained	628	*(45%)*	769	*(48%)*	562	*(68%)*	542	*(42%)*
	Not Retained	780	*(55%)*	849	*(52%)*	259	*(32%)*	750	*(58%)*
Women	**Total**	**983**	(58%)	**945**	(56%)	**473**	(56%)	**1101**	(67%)
	Retained	431	*(44%)*	441	*(47%)*	312	*(66%)*	477	*(43%)*
	Not Retained	552	*(56%)*	504	*(53%)*	161	*(34%)*	624	*(57%)*
Men	**Total**	**707**	(42%)	**733**	(44%)	**372**	(44%)	**544**	(33%)
	Retained	297	*(42%)*	362	*(49%)*	261	*(70%)*	224	*(41%)*
	Not Retained	410	*(58%)*	371	*(51%)*	111	*(30%)*	320	*(59%)*
Bachelor's degree	**Total**	**802**	(61%)	**1140**	(71%)	**718**	(85%)	**1294**	(90%)
	Retained	348	*(43%)*	518	*(45%)*	495	*(69%)*	542	*(42%)*
	Not Retained	454	*(57%)*	622	*(55%)*	223	*(31%)*	752	*(58%)*
Master's degree	**Total**	**400**	(31%)	**453**	(28%)	**111**	(13%)	**148**	(10%)
	Retained	168	*(42%)*	224	*(49%)*	69	*(62%)*	78	*(53%)*
	Not Retained	232	*(58%)*	229	*(51%)*	42	*(38%)*	70	*(47%)*
PhD or equivalent	**Total**	**106**	(8%)	**22**	(1%)	**16**	(2%)	**0**	0%
	Retained	39	*(37%)*	15	*(68%)*	9	*(56%)*	-	-
	Not Retained	67	*(63%)*	7	*(32%)*	7	*(44%)*	-	-
Alternate route	**Total**	**684**	(42%)	-	-	-	-	-	-
	Retained	265	*(39%)*	-	-	-	-	-	-
	Not Retained	419	*(61%)*	-	-	-	-	-	-
Traditional route	**Total**	**964**	(58%)	-	-	-	-	-	-
	Retained	444	*(46%)*	-	-	-	-	-	-
	Not Retained	520	*(54%)*	-	-	-	-	-	-
Age mean(SD)	**Total**	46.57 (SD = 11.389)		43.19 (SD = 8.870)		43.66 (SD = 8.879)		n/a	
	Retained	*44.68 (SD = 10.124)*		*43.70 (SD = 9.051)*		*43.15 (SD = 7.908)*		n/a	
	Not Retained	*48.01 (SD = 12.068)*		*41.94 (SD = 8.288)*		*44.75 (SD = 10.572)*		n/a	

larger, but this difference was not significant. We interpret this result in light of our broader study findings to mean that the number of colleagues is less important than what those colleagues actually do with one another.

As we showed previously (in table 8.2), the average starting salary was quite different across the four states. When degree level was taken into consideration, we found no correlation between a teacher's starting salary and whether or not they would be retained in any of the four states. It is quite likely that salary differences across districts did influence teacher attrition, transfer, and retention in various ways that were not measurable in our study. Yet, it also seems fairly clear, at least in the aggregate, that salary has little to no predictive power over five-year retention in district. We provide a more detailed discussion of salary below.

This analysis ultimately found few differences between populations of teachers who were retained and those who were not. The generally lower retention rates for teachers of color and teachers who earned their certification on the job were consistent with the retention literature we discussed in chapter 2. Certainly, the categorical differences we found imply possible areas of future research. This includes the startlingly low numbers of science teachers of color hired in Wisconsin, the policy implications of the cost of living on starting salaries, and a more rigorous examination of the ways in which large-scale shocks affect the retention of teachers.

THE ROLE OF SALARY

It is worth recalling that the study of teacher retention is rooted in an effort to understand—and perhaps influence—the choices that individuals make about the provision of their labor. We were interested in investigating both retention for a specific setting and retention in the teaching profession. In the early days of negotiating the parameters of this study with the funding agency, we received a clear message that there was great interest in an examination of the determinants of science teacher retention that included the possible impact of salary. This, of course, made perfect sense to us, and we readily accepted, knowing that salary was one of the key pieces of data to which we had access.

In the United States, public school teachers are salaried employees, meaning that they are not paid an hourly wage for their primary job assignment but instead provided with a contract that stipulates the terms and conditions of their work, as well as the amount to be paid over a set pay schedule by their district. Typically, in order to satisfactorily discharge the responsibilities of the job, teachers spend additional time outside of the hours they are contracted to be present in order to work directly with students. This is why teachers often stay after the school day ends, take home student work to grade, and spend evenings and weekends planning lessons. By signing a contract, the teacher agrees to exchange labor for payment. As is common in many professions, achieving a sufficient level of quality in one's work and managing the multiple demands of the job can be a steeper challenge for novices. Over time, there is likely a built-in survival bias for experienced teachers who have figured out how to do both.

Public school teacher salaries vary widely across the United States for a variety of reasons and may differ not just in gross pay but in how a starting salary is determined. Some states, like North Carolina, have a statewide salary scale set by the legislature, with districts permitted to supplement pay through local taxation, allowing for regional differences in the cost of living. Other school systems rely on the collective bargaining of contracts between school districts and teachers' associations. There has even been some experimentation in school reform efforts—such as in the case with charter schools—where schools directly negotiate salaries with individual teachers. Teachers' salaries may also take into account experience level, education (in the form of graduate degrees or credits), or other benchmarks of teacher quality—such as earning a National Board Certification from the National Board of Professional Teaching Standards. Some districts may offer signing bonuses to new teachers in an effort to attract teachers in shortage area certifications or high-need schools or offer performance bonuses or merit pay for meeting certain targets for student achievement.

From year to year, depending on where they work, teachers' base salaries may change in clearly defined increments over time or remain static until changed by legislative action or a renegotiation of a contract. Further, teachers often take on additional work for their employer as coaches, curriculum writers, club advisors, summer tutors, teaching an extra class to cover for a teacher on leave, etc. Such work may be salaried or paid at a negotiated hourly rate, and the opportunity to accept these additional jobs may vary greatly both across and within districts. Therefore, the question of how a teacher's pay correlates to retention within a district is linked to how that pay is determined, how it changes over time, and what opportunities there are to supplement one's base pay or advance on the salary guide.

TABLE C.2 Average starting teacher salary in New Jersey, Pennsylvania, Wisconsin, and North Carolina from 2007–2012

	2007	*2008*	*2009*	*2010*	*2011*	*2012*
New Jersey average starting salary with a bachelor's degree	**$45,364**	**$46,427**	**$47,713**	**$48,432**	**$49,098**	**n/a**
NJ RPP	107.563	111.124	108.867	109.277	109.42	n/a
NJ relative salary index	421.74	417.79	438.27	443.20	448.71	n/a
Pennsylvania average starting salary with a bachelor's degree	**$39,195**	**$41,147**	**$41,102**	**$42,749**	**$42,485**	**$43,931**
PA RPP	92.409	91.214	92.813	93.521	93.471	93.683
PA relative salary index	424.15	451.10	442.85	457.11	454.53	468.93
Wisconsin average starting salary with a bachelor's degree	**$32,643**	**$32,589**	**$30,622**	**$31,615**	**$33,553**	**$33,632**
WI RPP	99.232	99.598	99.069	98.473	98.025	97.858
WI relative salary index	328.96	327.21	309.10	321.05	342.29	343.68
North Carolina average starting salary with a bachelor's degree	**$29,750**	**$30,430**	**$30,430**	**$30,430**	**$30,430**	**$30,795**
NC RPP	93.276	94.224	94.858	93.773	94.356	93.911
NC relative salary index	318.95	322.95	320.80	324.51	322.50	327.92

Source: US Department of Commerce, "*Regional Price Parities by State and Metro Area* (U.S. Department of Commerce," news release, December 12, 2024, https://www.bea.gov/news/2024/real-personal-consumption-expenditures-state-and-real-personal-income-state-and.

Note: Regional Price Parities (RPPs) are a measure of relative purchasing power in a region in a given year, relative to the overall national price level, set by convention to 100.

In table C.2, we show the starting salary for a teacher with a bachelor's degree in each of the states we studied. Note that in New Jersey and Pennsylvania, the average salary increased yearly. In Wisconsin this did so until 2012, after the passage of Act 10 ended collective bargaining and many teacher contract salary increases statewide were curtailed in district-budget cost-cutting measures. In North Carolina, the state legislature only increased the salary a total $1000 over a period of six years, and the ongoing stagnation in teacher salaries produced sharp and frequent public criticism.

In practice, it may be difficult to compare the salary of one state or metropolitan region with that of another due to variations in the cost of living, particularly in housing and transportation. The Bureau of Economic Analysis, part of the U.S. Department of Commerce, publishes Regional Price Parities (RPP) annually to measure such regional differences in price levels in a given year. For example, the RPP measures shown in Table C.2 show that prices in New Jersey were about seven percent higher and those in North Carolina were about seven percent lower than the national average in 2007. In figure C.1, we use this measure to calculate the relative purchasing power of salary in each state. Even with this adjustment, New Jersey and Pennsylvania salaries remain higher in cost-of-living adjusted dollars than those in Wisconsin and North Carolina.

One methodological note to future researchers is that salary data is difficult to work with for a few reasons. The main issue is that salary is determined by a mix of experience, longevity, and education level in many places in the US, so salary is more properly considered a matrix or table rather than a single number. Salary guides need not be internally consistent either—sometimes there can be a large difference between step 3 and 4, and then a small difference between step 4 and 5. Public reports of teachers' salaries can be misleading, even if they report only median or average salaries. Then there is the issue that salary tables regularly change from year to year (except in cases such as North Carolina, when

FIGURE C.1 Relative salary adjusted for regional costs in New Jersey, Pennsylvania, Wisconsin, and North Carolina from 2007–2012

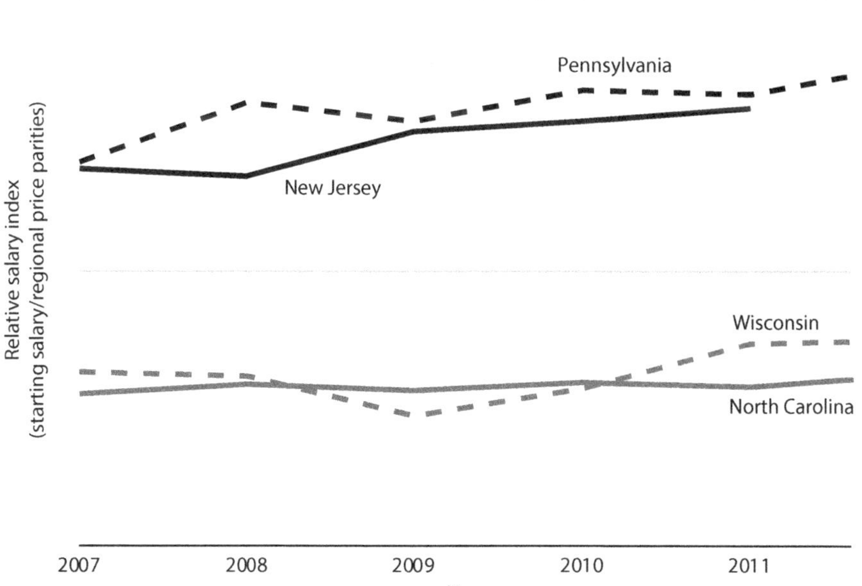

the state legislature is in charge of setting salaries and may do so infrequently), as well as the fact that not every new teacher starts at the lowest salary. A district may offer a new kindergarten teacher a contract that begins on step 1 of the pay scale, while in an effort to be competitive with other districts, they may offer a new chemistry teacher step 4. Some people may have worked as an educator elsewhere (say, as a teacher in the U.S. Peace Corps) and be given credit for that experience upon hire. While all of this makes it difficult to make any comparative claims or predictions about the impact of salary on retention, it also remains the case that teacher compensation is an integral part of recruiting and retaining a qualified and diverse teacher workforce.[1]

What we do know from recent research is that overall patterns in teacher compensation closely follow the overall status of the teaching profession and have done so for at least the past forty years.[2] Teacher pay also closely follows economic trends, and most reports say that the real value of teacher wages and compensation has been falling in recent years, likely discouraging new teachers from entering the profession.[3]

Clearly, a teacher's salary matters for retention. What may matter less is tinkering with small adjustments to teacher compensation in order to influence retention. A recent report from the Economic Policy Institute noted that average pay was 26 percent less than that of their similarly educated peers in other professions.[4] Therefore, the teacher-compensation policy intervention that would probably have the greatest impact on teacher retention would be to increase teachers' pay to the level of the jobs they could be holding instead.

Notes

Introduction

1. A detailed description of the study methodology may be found in appendix A. This material is based upon work supported by the National Science Foundation under Award No. 1758282.
2. The underrepresentation and retention of non-White or non-Latina/o teachers (a group we loosely term "teachers of color" in our study) in US classrooms is an ongoing concern, particularly given the emerging consensus that K–12 students of color are negatively impacted if they do not have at least one teacher with whom they share a racial or ethnic identity. See: Travis J. Bristol, and Javier Martin-Fernandez, "The Added Value of Latinx and Black Teachers for Latinx and Black Students: Implications for Policy," *Policy Insights from the Behavioral and Brain Sciences* 6, no. 2 (2019): 147–53, https://doi.org/10.1177/2372732219862573; Christopher Redding, "A Teacher Like Me: A Review of the Effect of Student-Teacher Racial/Ethnic Matching on Teacher Perceptions of Students and Student Academic and Behavioral Outcomes," *Review of Educational Research* 89, no. 4 (2019): 499–535, https://doi.org/10.3102/0034654319853545; Monica Hernández-Johnson, Valerie Taylor, Ravijot Singh, Norma A. Marrun, Tara J. Plachowski, and Christine Clark, "'Like Where Are Those Teachers?': A Critical Race Theory Analysis of Teachers of Color Who Have 'Left' Teaching," *International Journal of Qualitative Studies in Education* 36, no. 10 (2023): 1924–44, https://doi.org/10.1080/09518398.2021.1956634; J. L. Young, and D. Easton-Brooks, "The Impact of Teachers of Color on School Belonging: A Conceptual Framework," in *Handbook of Research on Teachers of Color and Indigenous Teachers*, eds. Conra D. Gist and Travis J. Bristol (American Educational Research Association, 2022), 637–44.
3. The organization of this book takes into account the busy lives of those most likely to read it. Readers with limited time may safely jump ahead to chapters 8 and 9 to read the findings and recommendations without taking in the details of the individual cases.
4. Charter schools, vocational schools, and other nonstandard organizational structures for public education were included in our inquiry. We use "district" as a colloquial substitute for the more technically correct term Local Educational Authority (LEA) throughout this study.
5. Robert E. Stake, *The Art of Case Study Research* (Thousand Oaks: Sage Publications, 1995); Robert E. Stake, "Qualitative Case Studies," in *Handbook of Qualitative Research*, eds. N. Denzin and Y. Lincoln (Sage, 2005), 443–66.
6. Examples of such case studies include: Sara Lawrence-Lightfoot, *The Good High School: Portraits of Character and Culture* (Basic Books, 1983); Catherine Cornbleth, *Diversity and the New Teacher: Learning from Experience in Urban Schools* (Teachers College Press, 2008); Maria Ong, *The Double Bind in Physics Education: Intersectionality, Equity, and Belonging for Women of Color* (Harvard Education Press, 2023).

7. Jonathan Kozol, *An End to Inequality: Breaking down the Walls of Apartheid Education in America* (The New Press, 2024); Gloria Ladson-Billings. *Justice Matters* (Bloomsbury Publishing, 2023).

Chapter 1

1. Geert Kelchtermans, "'Should I Stay or Should I Go?': Unpacking Teacher Attrition/Retention as an Educational Issue," *Teachers & Teaching* 23, no. 8 (2017): 961–77, https://doi.org/10.1080/13540602.2017.1379793.
2. These were our own reasons for leaving our respective high school teaching positions.
3. Richard Ingersoll, a renowned teacher retention researcher, whose work we will discuss in in the following chapter, noted the tendency for empirical research to focus on the teachers who leave the teaching profession altogether and do not return. Richard M. Ingersoll, "Teacher Turnover and Teacher Shortages: An Organizational Analysis," *American Educational Research Journal* 38, no. 3 (2001): 499–534, https://doi.org/10.3102/00028312038003499.
4. Nicole S. Simon and Susan Moore Johnson, "Teacher Turnover in High-Poverty Schools: What We Know and Can Do," *Teachers College Record* 117, no. 3 (2015): 1–36, https://doi.org/10.1177/016146811511700305; Brooks C. Holtom, Simon T. Tidd, Terence R. Mitchell, and Thomas W. Lee, "A Demonstration of the Importance of Temporal Considerations in the Prediction of Newcomer Turnover," *Human Relations* 66, no. 10 (2013): 1337–52, https://doi.org/10.1177/0018726713477459; Kohyar Kiazad, Brooks C. Holtom, Peter W. Hom, and Alexander Newman, "Job Embeddedness: A Multifoci Theoretical Extension," *Journal of Applied Psychology* 100, no. 3 (2015), https://doi.org/10.1037/a0038919.
5. This phrase is drawn from the work of noted teacher education scholars who have wrestled with the question of what teacher preparation ought to entail (e.g., Linda Darling-Hammond and Joan C. Baratz-Snowden, *A Good Teacher in Every Classroom: Preparing the Highly Qualified Teachers Our Children Deserve*, 1st ed, National Academy of Education, eds (San Francisco: Jossey-Bass, 2005).; Linda Darling-Hammond and John Bransford, *Preparing Teachers for a Changing World: What Teachers Should Learn and Be Able to Do,* 1st ed, National Academy of Education ed. (San Francisco, CA: Jossey-Bass, 2005).
6. Freddie Cross, *Teacher Shortage Areas Nationwide Listing 1990–1991 through 2016–2017*, 1–184 (Washington, DC.: United States Department of Education, Office of Postsecondary Education, 2016), https://www2.ed.gov/about/offices/list/ope/pol/bteachershortageareasreport201718.pdf; Leib Sutcher, Linda Darling-Hammond, and Desiree Carver-Thomas, "Understanding Teacher Shortages: An Analysis of Teacher Supply and Demand in the United States," *Education Policy Analysis Archives* 27 (2019): 1–36, https://doi.org/10.14507/epaa.27.3696.
7. Gloria Ladson-Billings, *Beyond the Big House: African American Educators on Teacher Education* (New York: Teacher College Press, 2005); Sara Lawrence-Lightfoot and Jessica Hoffmann Davis, *The Art and Science of Portraiture,* 1st ed (San Francisco: Jossey-Bass, 1997); John I. Goodlad, *A Place Called School* (New York: McGraw-Hill, 2004); Gloria Ladson-Billings, *The Dreamkeepers: Successful Teachers of African American Children,* 1st ed (San Francisco: Jossey-Bass Publishers, 1994).
8. The topic of involuntary teacher attrition was not of primary concern in our study, though it certainly is important for an understanding employment trends in the teacher workforce. See for example: Katharine O. Strunk, Dan Goldhaber, David S. Knight, and Nate Brown, "Are There Hidden Costs Associated with Conducting Layoffs? The Impact of Reduction-in-

Force and Layoff Notices on Teacher Effectiveness," *Journal of Policy Analysis & Management* 37, no. 4 (2018): 755–82, https://doi.org/10.1002/pam.22074.

9. For example, in the New Jersey data, we examined for a cohort of 231 secondary science teachers, and we found that after 5 years, 150 (65 percent) of them were still teaching in the US and 20 of them had identifiably left the teaching profession. These former teachers included some from the Teach For America (TFA) program who had completed their service requirements and moved onto other jobs as well as a number of people who had become educational consultants. We note that in this group of twenty, one teacher was deceased and two others had abrupt ends to their careers, with incidents described in public reports that led to their dismissal; Douglas B. Larkin, Suzanne Poole Patzelt, Khadija M. Ahmed, Liz Carletta, and Catherine R. Gaynor, "Portraying Secondary Science Teacher Retention with the Person-Position Framework: An Analysis of a State Cohort of First-Year Science Teachers," *Journal of Research in Science Teaching* 59, no. 7 (2022): 1235–73, https://doi.org/10.1002/tea.21757.
10. Simon and Johnson, "Teacher Turnover in High-Poverty Schools."; Holtom et al., "A Demonstration of the Importance of Temporal Considerations."; Kiazad et al., "Job Embeddedness."
11. Larry Cuban, *Frogs into Princes: Writings on School Reform,* Multicultural Education Series (New York: Teachers College Press, 2008).
12. A great deal of prior teacher retention research that drew upon data in the School and Staffing Survey (SASS) and its successors used this definition; Richard M. Ingersoll and Henry May, "The Magnitude, Destinations, and Determinants of Mathematics and Science Teacher Turnover," *Educational Evaluation and Policy Analysis* 34, no. 4 (2012): 435–64, https://doi.org/10.3102/0162373712454326; Richard M. Ingersoll and David Perda, "Is the Supply of Mathematics and Science Teachers Sufficient?" *American Educational Research Journal* 47, no. 3 (2010): 563–94, https://doi.org/10.3102/0002831210370711.
13. Data for May 2023 occupational and employment wages, U.S. Bureau of Labor Statistics, https://www.bls.gov/oes/2023/may/featured_data.htm.
14. James Cowan, Dan Goldhaber, Kyle Hayes, and Roddy Theobald, "Missing Elements in the Discussion of Teacher Shortages," *Educational Researcher* 45, no. 8 (2016): 460–62, https://doi.org/10.3102/0013189X16679145; Dan Goldhaber, Cyrus Grout, and Kristian Holden, "Public Pension Reform and Teacher Turnover: Evidence from Washington State," Working Paper 142, (National Center for Analysis of Longitudinal Data in Education Research, 2015), https://caldercenter.org/sites/default/files/2024-11/WP%20142%20Policy%20Brief.pdf; Eric A. Hanushek, John F. Kain, and Steven G. Rivkin, "Why Public Schools Lose Teachers," *Journal of Human Resources* 39, no. 2 (2004): 326–54, https://doi.org/10.3368/jhr.XXXIX.2.326; Matthew Ronfeldt, Susanna Loeb, and James Wyckoff, "How Teacher Turnover Harms Student Achievement," *American Educational Research Journal* 50, no. 1 (2013): 4–36, https://doi.org/10.3102/0002831212463813.
15. Kira Baker-Doyle refers to this as the "labor market paradigm." Kira Baker-Doyle, "Beyond the Labor Market Paradigm: A Social Network Perspective on Teacher Recruitment and Retention," *Education Policy Analysis Archives* 18 (2010): 1–17, https://doi.org/10.14507/epaa.v18n26.2010.
16. Thomas M. Smith and Richard M. Ingersoll, "What Are the Effects of Induction and Mentoring on Beginning Teacher Turnover?" *American educational research journal* 41, no. 3 (2004): 681–714, http://www.jstor.org/stable/3699442.

17. George Lakoff and Mark Johnson, *Metaphors We Live By* (Chicago: University of Chicago Press, 1980); Douglas R. Hofstadter and Emmanuel Sander, *Surfaces and Essences: Analogy as the Fuel and Fire of Thinking* (New York, NY: Basic Books, 2013); Allison Creed and Susan Nacey, "Qualitative and Quantitative Examination of Metaphorical Language Use in Career-Life Preparedness," in *Handbook of Research Methods in Careers*, Wendy Murphy and Jennifer Tosti-Kharas ed., 299–316 (Edward Elgar Publishing, 2021).
18. Guili Zhang and Nancy Zeller, "A Longitudinal Investigation of the Relationship between Teacher Preparation and Teacher Retention," *Teacher Education Quarterly* 43, no. 2 (2016): 73–92, https://www.jstor.org/stable/teaceducquar.43.2.73; Marcy B. Wood, Lisa M. Jilk, and Lynn W. Paine, "Moving Beyond Sinking or Swimming: Reconceptualizing the Needs of Beginning Mathematics Teachers," *Teachers College Record* 114, no. 8 (2012): 1–44, https://doi.org/10.1177/016146811211400804.
19. Ingersoll, "Teacher Turnover and Teacher Shortages."
20. Ingersoll and Perda, "Supply of Mathematics and Science Teachers Sufficient?"
21. Conra D. Gist, Margarita Bianco, and Marvin Lynn, "Examining Grow Your Own Programs Across the Teacher Development Continuum: Mining Research on Teachers of Color and Nontraditional Educator Pipelines," *Journal of Teacher Education* 70, no. 1 (2019): 13–25, https://doi.org/10.1177/0022487118787504.
22. Martin Haberman, *Star Teachers of Children in Poverty* (West Lafayette, Ind.: Kappa Delta Pi, 1995); Marilyn Cochran-Smith, "Stayers, Leavers, Lovers, and Dreamers," *Journal of Teacher Education* 55, no. 5 (2004): 387–92, https://doi.org/10.1177/0022487104270188.
23. American Psychological Association, *Publication Manual of the American Psychological Association,* 7th ed. (Washington, DC: American Psychological Association, 2020).
24. We debated about introducing two relatively new and different frameworks in this book and hope that neither overshadows the other. Our view is that the person-position framework shared in this chapter is primarily descriptive and conceptual, while the teacher embeddedness framework introduced in chapter 3 draws upon theory to offer significant explanatory power for understanding teacher retention. Larkin et al., "Portraying Secondary Science Teacher Retention."
25. Ingersoll and Perda, "Supply of Mathematics and Science Teachers Sufficient?"
26. For similar reasons, we suggest that the term *veteran teacher* ought to be reserved to describe military veterans who enter the teacher workforce and not as a synonym for experienced teachers.
27. Cochran-Smith, "Stayers, Leavers, Lovers, and Dreamers."; Sonia Nieto, *What Keeps Teachers Going?* (New York: Teachers College Press, 2003).
28. Wood, et al., "Moving Beyond Sinking or Swimming."; Smith and Ingersoll, "What Are the Effects of Induction and Mentoring on Beginning Teacher Turnover?"; Matthew Ronfeldt and Kiel McQueen, "Does New Teacher Induction Really Improve Retention?" *Journal of Teacher Education* 68, no. 4 (2017): 394–410. https://doi.org/10.1177/0022487117702583.
29. EunJin Bang, Anne L. Kern, Julie A. Luft, and Gillian H. Roehng, "First-Year Secondary Science Teachers," *School Science and Mathematics* 107, no. 6 (2007): 258–61, https://doi.org/10.1111/j.1949-8594.2007.tb18287.x; Karen Zumwalt, Gary Natriello, Judy Randi, Alison Rutter, and Richard Sawyer, "Learnings from a Longitudinal Study of New Jersey Alternate Route and College-Prepared Elementary, Secondary English, and Secondary Math Teachers," *Teachers College Record* 119, no. 14 (2017): 122–44, https://doi.org/10.1177/016146811711901406.

30. For example, Judi Randi's retention study examines "career teachers" who have remained in the profession for eleven years or more: Judy Randi, "Exploring Options: From Preparation to Placements," *Teachers College Record* 119, no. 14 (2017): 66–78, https://doi.org/doi.org/10.1177/016146811711901402; Similarly, Guili Zhang and Nancy Zeller, noting a gap in the research about long-term teacher retention, suggest that studies should direct their attention to retention of over eight to twenty years or even longer: Zhang and Zeller, "A Longitudinal Investigation."
31. Thomas Smith and Richard Ingersoll describe turnover as "normal, inevitable, and even beneficial.": Smith and Ingersoll, "What Are the Effects of Induction and Mentoring on Beginning Teacher Turnover?"; Julie A. Luft, Jonah B. Firestone, Sissy S. Wong, Ira Ortega, Krista Adams, and EunJin Bang, "Beginning Secondary Science Teacher Induction: A Two-Year Mixed Methods Study," *Journal of Research in Science Teaching* 48, no. 10 (2011): 1199–224, https://doi.org/10.1002/tea.20444.
32. See appendix A for more detail about our methodology.
33. Such a label might also apply to teacher education researchers in the academy who still hold valid teaching licenses and feel like they are still in the teaching profession!

Chapter 2

1. W. E. Hatch, "The Superintendent," *The Journal of Education* 54, no. 11 (1901): 183–84, http://www.jstor.org/stable/44053816.
2. H. V. Holloway, "Pretty Teachers: How to Keep Them Is Delaware's Problem," *Journal of Education* 118, no. 17 (1935): 489–89, https://doi.org/10.1177/002205743511801717.
3. The definition of "high-need local educational agency (or high-need LEA/high-need school district)" comes from section 201 of the Higher Education Act of 1965 (20 U.S.C.1021); it means a US local educational agency (e.g., school district) that has at least one school that meets at least one of the following criteria:
   i. not less than 20% of the children served by the agency are from low income families;
   ii. serves at least 10,000 children from low-income families;
   iii. is eligible for funding under the Small, Rural School Achievement Program under 20 U.S.C. 7345(b); or
   iv. is eligible for funding under the Rural and Low-Income School Program under 20 U.S.C. 7351(b) and meets at least one of the following criteria:
      i. has a high percentage of teachers not teaching in the academic subject areas or grade levels in which the teachers were trained to teach; or
      ii. has a high teacher turnover rate or a high percentage of teachers with emergency, provisional, or temporary certification
4. See for example R. H. Eliassen and Earl W. Anderson, "Teacher Supply and Demand," *Review of Educational Research* 4, no. 3 (1934): 257–60, https://doi.org/10.2307/1167468; R. H. Eliassen and Earl W. Anderson, "Teacher Supply and Demand," *Review of Educational Research* 1, no. 2 (1931): 69–72, https://doi.org/10.2307/1168121.
5. For example, Ward S. Mason and Robert Ketcham Bain, *Teacher Turnover in the Public Schools, 1957-58* (US Office of Education, 1959); Werrett W. Charters Jr., "What Causes Teacher Turnover?" *The School Review* 64, no. 7 (1956): 294–99, https://doi.org/10.1086/442335.
6. Crist H. Costa, "The Prediction of Teacher Turnover Employing Time Series Analysis," Paper presented at the annual meeting of the American Educational Research Association, Chicago, IL, ERIC, 1972.

7. As reported in Costa, "The Prediction of Teacher Turnover," 1972.
8. Werrett W. Charters Jr., "Some Factors Affecting Teacher Survival in School Districts," *American Educational Research Journal* 7, no. 1 (1970): 1–27, https://doi.org/10.3102/00028312007001001.
9. Charters Jr., "Some Factors Affecting Teacher Survival".; Jerome James Ryscavage, Jr., "An Investigation of the Relationship Between a Set of Economic Concerns and Teacher Withdrawal in the State of Maryland from 1960 to 1970," (unpublished dissertation from the University of Maryland, 1972); Joy E. Whitener, "An Actuarial Approach to Teacher Turnover," (unpublished doctoral dissertation, St. Louis, Missouri, Washington University, 1965).
10. Jonathan H. Mark and Barry D. Anderson, "Teacher Survival Rates—a Current Look," *American Educational Research Journal* 15, no. 3 (1978): 379–83, https://doi.org/10.3102/00028312015003379. Mark and Anderson repeated this analysis in 1985 with fourteen years of teacher staffing data for the St. Louis, Missouri region, and their conclusion was that the "survival rates" were consistent with earlier studies. They reported rapid dropouts for new teachers, with the remainder tending to stay in teaching for much longer. Jonathan H. Mark and Barry D. Anderson, "Teacher Survival Rates in St. Louis, 1969–1982," *American Educational Research Journal* 22, no. 3 (1985): 413–21, https://doi.org/10.3102/00028312022003413.
11. United States National Commission on Excellence in Education, *A Nation at Risk: The Imperative for Educational Reform. A Report to the Nation and the Secretary of Education*, (Washington, DC: United States Department of Education, 1983), http://www2.ed.gov/pubs/NatAtRisk/index.html.
12. One might be forgiven for thinking that one logical response at the national level would have been to fortify the profession of teaching by providing substantial federal resources to solve teacher shortage and curb the loss of teaching jobs, something that did happen at the state level later that decade in places like New Jersey and California. However, it must be remembered that teachers represented one of the largest unionized labor forces in the country at the time (which they still do) and the Reagan administration, which had fired over 11,000 unionized air traffic controllers on strike in 1981, was loathe to make any move that would bolster labor as a political force. We will show that similar state-level political considerations were important in the case studies that we share in this book, particularly in Wisconsin in the 2010s.
13. The SASS and TFS instruments were constructed by the National Center for Education Statistics and underwent only minor changes during the twenty-three years they were used. There were four linked surveys: one for the district, one for the administration, one for the school, and one for a sample of teachers in each selected school. The SASS teacher questionnaire sought a rich array of information about teacher's perceptions of support, school climate, and overall experiences teaching in the school. For example, respondents to the version of the questionnaire for teachers were asked to indicate the extent to which they agreed or disagreed with dozens of statements like: "I am satisfied with my teaching salary"; "I am given the support I need to teach students with special needs"; and "Most of my colleagues share my beliefs and values about what the central mission of the school should be." Personal contact information was collected in this teacher questionnaire, and a follow-up survey was sent out a year later. There were two versions of this survey, one for those who were currently teachers (even if they had moved to a new school) and another for those who were no longer in the position of a K–12 teacher. Both surveys had questions asking respondents

to rate the level of importance of various reasons for their decisions. In 2015, the survey was redesigned and retitled as the National Teacher and Principal Survey and has since continued to be administered every few years to a sample of schools and districts. All of the SASS and TFS materials may be found at: *Schools and Staffing Survey* (2025) National Center for Educational Statistics. https://nces.ed.gov/surveys/sass/index.asp.

14. Richard M. Ingersoll, "Teacher Turnover and Teacher Quality: The Recurring Myth of Teacher Shortages," *Teachers College Record* 99, no. 1 (1997): 1–3, https://doi.org/10.1177/016146819709900118; Richard M. Ingersoll, "Four Myths About America's Teacher Quality Problem," *Yearbook of the National Society for the Study of Education (Wiley-Blackwell)* 103, no. 1 (2004): 1–33, https://doi.org/10.1177/016146810410601301; Richard M. Ingersoll and Henry May, "The Magnitude, Destinations, and Determinants of Mathematics and Science Teacher Turnover," *Educational Evaluation and Policy Analysis* 34, no. 4 (2012): 435–64, https://doi.org/10.3102/0162373712454326.
15. Ingersoll and May, "The Magnitude, Destinations, and Determinants."
16. Lucinda Gray and Soheyla Taie, *Public School Teacher Attrition and Mobility in the First Five Years: Results from the First through Fifth Waves of the 2007–08 Beginning Teacher Longitudinal Study* (Washington, DC: US Department of Education, 2015), https://eric.ed.gov/?id=ED556348.
17. Douglas B. Larkin, Suzanne Poole Patzelt, Khadija M. Ahmed, Liz Carletta, and Catherine R. Gaynor, "Portraying Secondary Science Teacher Retention with the Person-Position Framework: An Analysis of a State Cohort of First-Year Science Teachers," *Journal of Research in Science Teaching* 59, no. 7 (2022): 1235–73, https://doi.org/10.1002/tea.21757.
18. Organisation for Economic Co-operation and Development, *Education at a Glance 2021: OECD Indicators* (OECD Publishing, Paris, 2021), https://doi.org/10.1787/b35a14e5-en.
19. Geoffrey D. Borman and N. Maritza Dowling, "Teacher Attrition and Retention: A Meta-Analytic and Narrative Review of the Research," *Review of Educational Research* 78, no. 3 (2008): 367–409, https://doi.org/10.3102/0034654308321455; Tuan D. Nguyen, Lam Pham, Matthew G. Springer, and Michael Crouch, "The Factors of Teacher Attrition and Retention: An Updated and Expanded Meta-Analysis of the Literature," Working Paper no. 19-149(Annenberg Institute at Brown University, 2019), https://edworkingpapers.com/sites/default/files/ai19-149.pdf.
20. Desiree Carver-Thomas and Linda Darling-Hammond, "The Trouble with Teacher Turnover: How Teacher Attrition Affects Students and Schools," *Education Policy Analysis Archives* 27 (2019): 36, https://doi.org/10.14507/epaa.27.3699; Ingersoll, "Teacher Turnover and Teacher Quality."; R. M. Ingersoll, *Out-of-Field Teaching and the Limits of Teacher Policy* (The Center for the Study of Teaching and Policy and The Consortium for Policy Research in Education, 2003), https://repository.upenn.edu/cgi/viewcontent.cgi?article=1143&context=gse_pubs; Richard M. Ingersoll, "Is There Really a Teacher Shortage?" (Seattle, WA: The Consortium for Policy Research in Education and The Center for the Study of Teaching and Policy, 2003), https://repository.upenn.edu/gse_pubs/133; Richard M. Ingersoll and David Perda, "Is the Supply of Mathematics and Science Teachers Sufficient?" *American Educational Research Journal* 47, no. 3 (2010): 563–94, https://doi.org/10.3102/0002831210370711.
21. Nguyen et al. actually have three categories for their correlates: personal, school, and external. However, the external category included salary and other attributes that we decided fit better in the "school" category. In the next chapter, we will introduce our own "external"

category of community, which played a large role in the factors related to teacher retention in our study.

22. Nguyen et al. calculated the odds of a twenty-nine-year-old teacher leaving is 30% less than one who is younger.
23. In 2007, following similar changes to the US Census, US Secretary of Education Margaret Spellings announced changes to US Department of Education's guidelines for demographic data collection. Given that states must report race and ethnicity data to the federal government, in the years that followed, many state data systems adopted federal guidelines that permitted respondents to choose more than one race and presented ethnicity as a separate category. See: Margaret Spellings. *Final Guidance on Maintaining, Collecting, and Reporting Racial and Ethnic Data to the U.S. Department of Education* (Federal Register: US Department of Education, 2007), https://title2.ed.gov/Public/TA/Guidance.pdf.
24. Given their underrepresentation in the teaching labor force, it is quite likely that it is simply more noticeable when a teacher of color leaves. In the psychological literature, this is known as a "figure-ground effect." See Daniel Kahneman, *Attention and Effort,* Prentice-Hall Series in Experimental Psychology (Englewood Cliffs, NJ: Prentice-Hall, 1973).
25. This finding was presented in a study by Cara M. Djonko-Moore that was included in the meta-analysis by Nguyen et al. Cara M. Djonko-Moore, "An Exploration of Teacher Attrition and Mobility in High Poverty Racially Segregated Schools," *Race Ethnicity and Education* 19, no. 5 (2016): 1063–87, https://doi.org/10.1080/13613324.2015.1013458.
26. Cassandra M. Guarino, Lucrecia Santibanez, and Glenn A. Daley, "Teacher Recruitment and Retention: A Review of the Recent Empirical Literature," *Review of Educational Research* 76, no. 2 (2006): 173–208, https://doi.org/10.3102/00346543076002173.
27. See also Tuan D. Nguyen, "Linking School Organizational Characteristics and Teacher Retention: Evidence from Repeated Cross-Sectional National Data," *Teaching and Teacher Education* 97 (2021): 103–220, doi.org/10.1016/j.tate.2020.103220; Thomas M. Smith and Richard M. Ingersoll, "What Are the Effects of Induction and Mentoring on Beginning Teacher Turnover?" *American educational research journal* 41, no. 3 (2004): 681–714, http://www.jstor.org/stable/3699442; Matthew A. Kraft, William H. Marinell, and Darrick Shen-Wei Yee, "School Organizational Contexts, Teacher Turnover, and Student Achievement: Evidence from Panel Data," *American Educational Research Journal* 53, no. 5 (2016): 1411–49, https://doi.org/10.3102/0002831216667478.
28. See for example: Susan J. Rosenholtz, "Effective Schools: Interpreting the Evidence," *American Journal of Education* 93, no. 3 (1985): 352–88, https://doi.org/10.1086/443805; Benjamin Scafidi, David L. Sjoquist, and Todd R. Stinebrickner, "Race, Poverty, and Teacher Mobility," *Economics of Education Review* 26, no. 2 (2007): 145–59, https://doi.org/10.1016/j.econedurev.2005.08.006; Djonko-Moore, "An Exploration of Teacher Attrition and Mobility."
29. Carver-Thomas and Darling-Hammond, "The Trouble with Teacher Turnover," 13.
30. Nguyen et al., "The Factors of Teacher Attrition and Retention," 25.
31. Samantha Viano, Luis A. Rodriguez, and Seth B. Hunter, "Principal and Teacher Shared Race and Gender Intersections: Teacher Turnover, Workplace Conditions, and Monetary Benefits," *AERA Open* 9, no. 1 (2023). https://doi.org/10.1177/23328584221148156; Wesley Edwards and Cornelius Q. Anderson, "Teacher-Principal Ethnoracial Matching, Geography, and Novice Teacher Career Outcomes," *AERA Open* 9 (2023), https://doi.org/10.1177/23328584231213344.
32. Issues concerning salary and retention are discussed more thoroughly in appendix C.

33. This example is somewhat oversimplified. For example, Tuan D. Nguyen, J. Cameron Anglum, and Michael Crouch found that changes to teacher salary that were driven by school finance reforms indeed had a measurable impact on retention but over a very long time span. Tuan D. Nguyen, J. Cameron Anglum, and Michael Crouch, "The Effects of School Finance Reforms on Teacher Salary and Turnover: Evidence from National Data," *AERA Open* 9, no. 1 (2023). https://doi.org/10.1177/23328584231174447.
34. See for example: Richard M. Ingersoll and Gregory J. Collins, "Accountability and Control in American Schools," *Journal of Curriculum Studies* 49, no. 1 (2017): 75–95, https://doi.org/10.1080/00220272.2016.1205142; Richard Ingersoll, Lisa Merrill, and Henry May, *What Are the Effects of Teacher Education and Preparation on Beginning Teacher Attrition? Research Report (#RR-82)* (Philadelphia: Consortium for Policy Research in Education, University of Pennsylvania, 2014), https://www.cpre.org/sites/default/files/researchreport/2018_prepeffects2014.pdf; L. Bartlett and L. S. Johnson, "The Evolution of New Teacher Induction Policy Support, Specificity, and Autonomy," *Educational Policy* 24, no. 6 (2010): 847–71, https://doi.org/10.1177/0895904809341466.
35. Lynnette Mawhinney and Carol R. Rinke, *There Has to Be a Better Way: Lessons from Former Urban Teachers* (New Brunswick, New Jersey: Rutgers University Press, 2019); Lynnette Mawhinney and Carol R. Rinke, "I Just Feel So Guilty: The Role of Emotions in Former Urban Teachers' Career Paths." *Urban Education* 53, no. 9 (2018): 1079–101, https://doi.org/10.1177/0042085917741726; Carol R. Rinke, *Why Half of Teachers Leave the Classroom: Understanding Recruitment and Retention in Today's Schools* (Lanham: Rowman & Littlefield, 2014); Lynnette Mawhinney, Leana Cabral, and Jill C. Pierce, "When We Know Better, We Do Better: Educators' Storied Reflections on Black Teacher Attrition and Retention," *Journal of Black Studies* 56, no. 1 (2025): 42–64, https://doi.org/10.1177/00219347241286262.
36. Rita Kohli, "Behind School Doors: The Impact of Hostile Racial Climates on Urban Teachers of Color," *Urban Education* 53, no. 3 (2018): 307–33, https://doi.org/10.1177/0042085916636653; Travis J. Bristol, "A Tale of Two Types of Schools: An Exploration of How School Working Conditions Influence Black Male Teacher Turnover," *Teachers College Record* 122, no. 3 (2020): 1–24, https://doi.org/10.1177/016146812012200312; Monica Hernández-Johnson, Valerie Taylor, Ravijot Singh, Norma A. Marrun, Tara J. Plachowski, and Christine Clark, "'Like Where Are Those Teachers?': A Critical Race Theory Analysis of Teachers of Color Who Have 'Left' Teaching," *International Journal of Qualitative Studies in Education* 36, no. 10 (2023): 1924–44, https://doi.org/10.1080/09518398.2021.1956634. https://doi.org/10.1080/09518398.2021.1956634.
37. Doris A. Santoro, *Demoralized: Why Teachers Leave the Profession They Love and How They Can Stay* (Cambridge, Massachusetts: Harvard Education Press, 2018); Doris A. Santoro, "Good Teaching in Difficult Times: Demoralization in the Pursuit of Good Work," *American Journal of Education* 118, no. 1 (2011): 1–23, https://doi.org/10.1086/662010.
38. Viewing teacher attrition and retention from the perspective of the teacher, rather than the employer, is a relatively recent turn in the scholarship that parallels the rise of the teacher professionalism movement beginning in the 1980s. See: Kenneth M. Zeichner, "The Adequacies and Inadequacies of Three Current Strategies to Recruit, Prepare, and Retain the Best Teachers for All Students," *Teachers College Record* 105, no. 3 (2003): 490–519, https://doi.org/10.1111/1467-9620.00248.

39. The field of education and educational research has a long history of pathologizing individuals for systemic problems. Gloria Ladson-Billings and William Tate, in discussing the early twentieth century work of W. E. B. DuBois and Carter Woodson, noted the revolutionary nature of reframing pathological perspectives about race and African Americans in particular into a multitextured cultural and political analysis. Gloria Ladson-Billings and William F. Tate IV, "Toward a Critical Race Theory of Education," *Teachers College Record* 97, no. 1 (1995): 47–68, https://doi.org/10.1177/016146819509700104.
40. Lisa Scherff, "Disavowed: The Stories of Two Novice Teachers," *Teaching and Teacher Education* 24, no. 5 (2008): 1317–32, https://doi.org/10.1016/j.tate.2007.06.002. The opening lines of Leo Tolstoy's *Anna Karenina* seem relevant here: "All happy families resemble one another; each unhappy family is unhappy in its own way." There is a thematic congruence between reasons for leaving teaching and Tolstoy's unhappy families. To overextend the analogy, this book is about studying what makes the happy families happy.
41. A great counter example to this claim is the report produced by Doris Santoro, Julia Hazel, and Alberto Morales for the Portland Public School District in Maine. The report included both the documentation of problematic practices of the district that were contributing to teacher attrition as well as tangible recommendations for the administrators and employees—including teachers themselves—on how to begin addressing issues of racism and microaggressions in the district. This report will be discussed further in chapter 8. Doris A. Santoro, Julia Hazel, and Alberto Morales, "Cultivating Anti-Racist Professional Cultures That Support Educators of Color," *Phi Delta Kappan* 104, no. 1 (2022): 22–27, https://doi.org/10.1177/00317217221123645; Doris A. Santoro, Julia Hazel, and Alberto Morales, *Educators of Color Insights Report: What Will It Take for Educators of Color to Thrive in PPS?* (Bowdoin College and Portland Public Schools, 2021), https://drive.google.com/file/d/1_tIjd7XXabmueG8SP5rTFIUY2bvJDGqW/view.
42. Geert Kelchtermans, "'Should I Stay or Should I Go?': Unpacking Teacher Attrition/Retention as an Educational Issue," *Teachers & Teaching* 23, no. 8 (2017): 961–77, https://doi.org/10.1080/13540602.2017.1379793; Corey R. Sell, "Why Teachers Move: School Context Influences on Teachers' Experiences," in *Opportunities and Challenges in Teacher Recruitment and Retention: Teachers' Voices across the Pipeline*, Carol R. Rinke and Lynnette Mawhinney ed. (Charlotte, NC: Information Age Publishing, Inc., 2019), 93–119.
43. Edward J. Fuller and Andrew Pendola, *Teacher Preparation and Teacher Retention: Examining the Relationship for Beginning STEM Teachers* (2019), https://aaas-arise.org/wp-content/uploads/2020/01/Fuller-Pendola-Teacher-Preparation-and-Teacher-Retention-Examining-the-Relationship-for-Beginning-STEM-Teachers.pdf; Guili Zhang and Nancy Zeller, "A Longitudinal Investigation of the Relationship between Teacher Preparation and Teacher Retention," *Teacher Education Quarterly* 43, no. 2 (2016): 73–92, https://www.jstor.org/stable/teaceducquar.43.2.73; Karen Zumwalt, Gary Natriello, Judy Randi, Alison Rutter, and Richard Sawyer, "Recruitment, Preparation, Placement, and Retention of Alternate Route and College-Prepared Teachers: An Early Study of a New Jersey Initiative," *Teachers College Record* 119, no. 14 (2017), https://doi.org/10.1177/016146811711901408.
44. Monica Grillo and Meredith Kier, "Why Do They Stay? An Exploratory Analysis of Identities and Commitment Factors Associated with Teaching Retention in High-Need School Contexts," *Teaching & Teacher Education* 105 (2021), https://doi.org/10.1016/j.tate.2021.103423; Argun Saatcioglu, "Teacher Persistence as a Function of Teacher-Job Fit: Evidence from a Large Suburban District, 2010–2015," *Teaching & Teacher Education* 94 (2020), https://doi.org/10.1016/j.tate.2020.103121.

45. For example, Katie M. Tricarico, Jennifer Jacobs, and Diane Yendol-Hoppey, "Reflection on Their First Five Years of Teaching: Understanding Staying and Impact Power," *Teachers & Teaching* 21, no. 3 (2015): 237–59, https://doi.org/10.1080/13540602.2014.953821.
46. Mario I. Suárez and Kim B. Wright, "Investigating School Climate and School Leadership Factors That Impact Secondary STEM Teacher Retention," *Journal for STEM Education Research* 2, no. 1 (2019): 55–74, https://doi.org/https://doi.org/10.1007/s41979-019-00012-z; Catherine Whalen, Elizabeth Majocha, and Shirley Van Nuland, "Novice Teacher Challenges and Promoting Novice Teacher Retention in Canada," *European Journal of Teacher Education* 42, no. 5 (2019): 591–607, https://doi.org/10.1080/02619768.2019.1652906; Sissy S. Wong, Jonah B. Firestone, Richard L. Lamb, and Julie A. Luft, "Perceived Support and Retention of First Year Secondary Science Teachers," in *Newly Hired Teachers of Science* (Rotterdam, Netherlands: SensePublishers, 2015), 31-42; Erez Zavelevsky and Orly Shapira Lishchinsky, "An Ecological Perspective of Teacher Retention: An Emergent Model," *Teaching & Teacher Education* 88 (2020): 1–15, https://doi.org/10.1016/j.tate.2019.102965; Andrew Brantlinger, "Entering, Staying, Shifting, Leaving, and Sometimes Returning: A Descriptive Analysis of the Career Trajectories of Two Cohorts of Alternatively Certified Mathematics Teachers," *Teachers College Record* 123, no. 9 (2021): 28–56, https://doi.org/10.1177/01614681211051996; Zumwalt et al., "Recruitment, Preparation, Placement, and Retention of Alternate Route and College-Prepared Teachers."; Tray Geiger and Margarita Pivovarova, "The Effects of Working Conditions on Teacher Retention," *Teachers & Teaching* 24, no. 6 (2018): 604–25, https://doi.org/10.1080/13540602.2018.1457524.
47. Brantlinger, "Entering, Staying, Shifting, Leaving, and Sometimes Returning: A Descriptive Analysis of the Career Trajectories of Two Cohorts of Alternatively Certified Mathematics Teachers."; Carycruz Bueno and Tim R. Sass, "The Effects of Differential Pay on Teacher Recruitment and Retention," *Andrew Young School of Policy Studies Research Paper Series*, no. 18–07 (2018); Dongwoo Kim, Cory Koedel, Wei Kong, Shawn Ni, Michael Podgursky, and Weiwei Wu, "Pensions and Late-Career Teacher Retention," *Education Finance and Policy* 16, no. 1 (2021): 42–65, https://doi.org/10.1162/edfp_a_00293. https://doi.org/10.1162/edfp_a_00293.
48. Brantlinger, "Entering, Staying, Shifting, Leaving, and Sometimes Returning."; Mike Coldwell, "Exploring the Influence of Professional Development on Teacher Careers: A Path Model Approach," *Teaching & Teacher Education* 61 (2017): 189–98, https://doi.org/10.1016/j.tate.2016.10.015.
49. Wong et al., "Perceived Support and Retention of First Year Secondary Science Teachers."
50. Jason M. Miller and Peter Youngs, "Person-Organization Fit and First-Year Teacher Retention in the United States," *Teaching & Teacher Education* 97 (2021): 1–14, https://doi.org/10.1016/j.tate.2020.103226; Peter Youngs, Kristen Bieda, and Jihyun Kim, *Teacher Induction Programs That Lead to Retention in the STEM Teaching Workforce* (American Association for the Advancement of Science, 2019), https://aaas-arise.org/wp-content/uploads/2020/01/Youngs-Bieda-Kim-Teacher-Induction-Programs-that-Lead-to-Retention-in-the-STEM-Teaching-Workforce.pdf; Jennifer Moradian Watson, "Job Embeddedness May Hold the Key to the Retention of Novice Talent in Schools," *Educational Leadership and Administration: Teaching and Program Development* 29, no. 1 (2018): 26–43, https://www.csueastbay.edu/el/files/docs/arriaza-2018-journal.pdf#page=35.
51. The question of whether it was advantageous or a weakness for a teacher to hire its own graduates as teachers, or "home girls" as they were termed, was a regularly debated issue

throughout the early history of public schools in the United States. Reasons for this varied widely, and there were strong feelings on opposing sides of the matter. One report from 1933 notes that about a third of the schools in Mississippi would not accept its graduates as applicants for teaching positions, while another quarter of schools in the state *only* hired "home girls." Robert L. Williams, "The Bases for Selection and Retention of Teachers in Mississippi," *Peabody Journal of Education* 10, no. 6 (1933): 366–76, https://www.jstor.org/stable/1487658.

52. Wesley Edwards, J. Jacob Kirksey, Kafarra Q. L. Burden, and Alexis Miller, "Teaching Close to Home: Exploring New Teachers' Geographic Employment Patterns and Retention Outcomes," *Teaching & Teacher Education* 145 (2024): 1–13, https://doi.org/10.1016/j.tate.2024.104606; Christopher Redding, "Are Homegrown Teachers Who Graduate from Urban Districts More Racially Diverse, More Effective, and Less Likely to Exit Teaching?" *American Educational Research Journal* 59, no. 5 (2022): 939–74, https://doi.org/10.3102/00028312221078018.
53. Christopher Hurst and Andrew Brantlinger, "Patterns in Critical Incidents: Understanding Teacher Retention through Career Decision Making," *Teaching & Teacher Education* 109 (2022): 1–12, https://doi.org/10.1016/j.tate.2021.103557; Brady K. Jones, "A Special Kind of Ambition: The Role of Personality in the Retention of Academically Elite Teachers," *Teachers College Record* 120, no. 9 (2018): 1–28, https://doi.org/10.1177/016146811812000902; Richard M. Ingersoll, Lisa Merrill, and Henry May, "Do Accountability Policies Push Teachers Out? Sanctions Exacerbate the Teacher Turnover Problem in Low-Performing Schools–but Giving Teachers More Classroom Autonomy Can Help Stem the Flood," *Educational Leadership* 73, no. 8 (2016): 46, https://repository.upenn.edu/gse_pubs/551; Susan Moore Johnson and Sarah E. Birkeland, "Pursuing a 'Sense of Success': New Teachers Explain Their Career Decisions," *American Educational Research Journal* 40, no. 3 (2003): 581–617, https://doi.org/10.3102/00028312040003581.
54. Bristol, "A Tale of Two Types of Schools."; Stacy Olitsky, Amy Perfetti, and Allyson Coughlin, "Filling Positions or Forging New Pathways? Scholarship Incentives, Commitment, and Retention of STEM Teachers in High-Need Schools," *Science Education* 104, no. 2 (2020): 113–43, https://doi.org/10.1002/sce.21552; Erez Zavelevsky, Pascale Benoliel, and Orly Shapira-Lishchinsky, "Retaining Novice Teachers: The Meaning and Measure of Ecological School Culture Construct," *Teaching & Teacher Education* 117 (2022): 1–11, https://doi.org/10.1016/j.tate.2022.103783; Zavelevsky and Lishchinsky, "An Ecological Perspective of Teacher Retention."; Zumwalt et al., "Recruitment, Preparation, Placement, and Retention of Alternate Route and College-Prepared Teachers."; Brantlinger, "Entering, Staying, Shifting, Leaving, and Sometimes Returning."
55. Grillo and Kier, "Why Do They Stay?"; Zavelevsky, Benoliel, and Shapira-Lishchinsky, "Retaining Novice Teachers."; Zavelevsky and Lishchinsky, "An Ecological Perspective of Teacher Retention."; Brantlinger, "Entering, Staying, Shifting, Leaving, and Sometimes Returning."; Kelchtermans, "'Should I Stay or Should I Go?'"
56. Daisy Rooks, "The Unintended Consequences of Cohorts: How Social Relationships Can Influence the Retention of Rural Teachers Recruited by Cohort-Based Alternative Pathway Programs," *Journal of Research in Rural Education* 33, no. 9 (2018): 1–22, https://doi.org/10.18113/P8JRRE3309.
57. Richard M. Ingersoll, and Michael Strong, "The Impact of Induction and Mentoring Programs for Beginning Teachers: A Critical Review of the Research," *Review of Educational*

Research 81, no. 2 (2011): 201–33, https://doi.org/10.3102/0034654311403323; Smith and Ingersoll, "What Are the Effects of Induction and Mentoring on Beginning Teacher Turnover?"; T. Voss, W. Wagner, U. Klusmann, U. Trautwein, and M. Kunter, "Changes in Beginning Teachers' Classroom Management Knowledge and Emotional Exhaustion During the Induction Phase," *Contemporary Educational Psychology* 51 (2017): 170–84, https://doi.org/10.1016/j.cedpsych.2017.08.002; Todd D. Reeves, Valerie Hamilton, and Yasemin Onder, "Which Teacher Induction Practices Work? Linking Forms of Induction to Teacher Practices, Self-Efficacy, and Job Satisfaction," *Teaching & Teacher Education* 109 (2022), https://doi.org/10.1016/j.tate.2021.103546; Kevin C. Bastian, and Julie T. Marks, "Connecting Teacher Preparation to Teacher Induction: Outcomes for Beginning Teachers in a University-Based Support Program in Low-Performing Schools," *American Educational Research Journal* 54, no. 2 (2017): 360–94, https://doi.org/10.3102/0002831217690517.

58. Whalen, Majocha, and Van Nuland, "Novice Teacher Challenges and Promoting Novice Teacher Retention in Canada."; Youngs, Bieda, and Kim, *Teacher Induction Programs That Lead to Retention in the STEM Teaching Workforce*; Matthew Ronfeldt and Kiel McQueen, "Does New Teacher Induction Really Improve Retention?" *Journal of Teacher Education* 68, no. 4 (2017): 394–410, https://doi.org/10.1177/0022487117702583.

59. Julie A. Luft, Shannon L. Navy, Sissy S. Wong, and Kathleen M. Hill, "The First 5 Years of Teaching Science: The Beliefs, Knowledge, Practices, and Opportunities to Learn of Secondary Science Teachers," *Journal of Research in Science Teaching* 59, no. 9 (2022): 1692–725, https://doi.org/10.1002/tea.21771; Julie A. Luft, Jonah B. Firestone, Sissy S. Wong, Ira Ortega, Krista Adams, and EunJin Bang, "Beginning Secondary Science Teacher Induction: A Two-Year Mixed Methods Study," *Journal of Research in Science Teaching* 48, no. 10 (2011): 1199–224, https://doi.org/10.1002/tea.20444; Julie A. Luft, Shannon L. Dubois, Ryan S. Nixon, and Benjamin K. Campbell, "Supporting Newly Hired Teachers of Science: Attaining Teacher Professional Standards," *Studies in Science Education* 51, no. 1 (2015): 1–48, https://doi.org/10.1080/03057267.2014.980559.

60. Rod Paige, "Meeting the Highly Qualified Teachers Challenge: The Secretary's Annual Report on Teacher Quality," in *Handbook of Research on Teacher Education: Enduring Questions in Changing Contexts*, Marilyn Cochran-Smith, Sharon Feiman-Nemser and D. John McIntyre ed. (New York: Routledge, copublished by the Association of Teacher Educators, 2008), 492–500; Keffrelyn D. Brown, "Teaching in Color: A Critical Race Theory in Education Analysis of the Literature on Preservice Teachers of Color and Teacher Education in the US," *Race, Ethnicity & Education* 17, no. 3 (2014): 326–45, https://doi.org/10.1080/13613324.2013.832921; Betty Achinstein and Julia Aguirre, "Cultural Match or Culturally Suspect: How New Teachers of Color Negotiate Sociocultural Challenges in the Classroom," *Teachers College Record* 110, no. 8 (2008): 1505–40, https://doi.org/10.1177/016146810811000802; Kohli, "Behind School Doors."; Michèle Foster, *Black Teachers on Teaching* (New York: New Press, 1997).

61. Dorinda J. Carter Andrews, Eliana Castro, Christine L. Cho, Emery Petchauer, Gail Richmond, and Robert Floden, "Changing the Narrative on Diversifying the Teaching Workforce: A Look at Historical and Contemporary Factors That Inform Recruitment and Retention of Teachers of Color," *Journal of Teacher Education* 70, no. 1 (2019): 6–12, https://doi.org/10.1177/0022487118812418; Desiree Carver-Thomas, *Diversifying the Teaching Profession: How to Recruit and Retain Teachers of Color* (Palo Alto, CA: Learning Policy Institute, 2018), https://learningpolicyinstitute.org/product/diversifying-teaching-

profession-report; Conra D. Gist, Margarita Bianco, and Marvin Lynn, "Examining Grow Your Own Programs across the Teacher Development Continuum: Mining Research on Teachers of Color and Nontraditional Educator Pipelines," *Journal of Teacher Education* 70, no. 1 (2019): 13–25, https://doi.org/10.1177/0022487118787504; Richard Ingersoll, Henry May, and Gregory Collins, "Recruitment, Employment, Retention and the Minority Teacher Shortage," *Education Policy Analysis Archives* 27, no. 34–39 (2019): 1–42, https://doi.org/10.14507/epaa.27.3714.

62. Andrew Morgan Brantlinger and Ashley Anne Grant, "The First-School Retention of Black and Latinx Community-Insiders and Elite College Graduates: Implications for the Recruitment, Selection, and Training of Urban Mathematics Teachers," *Educational Policy Analysis Archives* 30, no. 111–113 (2022): 1–25, https://doi.org/10.14507/epaa.30.7235; Gist, Bianco, and Lynn, "Examining Grow Your Own Programs across the Teacher Development Continuum."; A. R. Griffin, R. Davis Dixon, and H. N. Tackie, "Perspectives of Black Teachers' Experiences in the Field and the Connection to Retention," in *Handbook of Research on Teachers of Color and Indigenous Teachers*, Conra D. Gist and Travis J. Bristol ed. (American Educational Research Association, 2022), 909–22.
63. Ayana Kee Campoli, "Supportive Principals and Black Teacher Turnover: ESSA as an Opportunity to Improve Retention," *Journal of School Leadership* 27, no. 5 (2017): 675–700, https://doi.org/10.1177/105268461702700504; Ingersoll, May, and Collins, "Recruitment, Employment, Retention and the Minority Teacher Shortage."; Mawhinney, Cabral, and Pierce, "When We Know Better, We Do Better."
64. Min Sun, "Black Teachers' Retention and Transfer Patterns in North Carolina: How Do Patterns Vary by Teacher Effectiveness, Subject, and School Conditions?"*AERA Open* 4, no. 3 (2018), https://doi.org/10.1177/233285841878491.
65. Griffin, Davis Dixon, and Tackie, "Perspectives of Black Teachers' Experiences in the Field and the Connection to Retention."
66. Bristol, "A Tale of Two Types of Schools: An Exploration of How School Working Conditions Influence Black Male Teacher Turnover."
67. Ain A. Grooms, Duhita Mahatmya, and Eboneé T. Johnson, "The Retention of Educators of Color Amidst Institutionalized Racism," *Educational Policy* 35, no. 2 (2021): 180–212, https://doi.org/10.1177/0895904820986765.
68. James D. Anderson, *The Education of Blacks in the South, 1860-193.* (University of North Carolina Press, 1988); Jarvis R. Givens, *Fugitive Pedagogy: Carter G. Woodson and the Art of Black Teaching* (Cambridge, Massachusetts: Harvard University Press, 2021); Richard Kluger, *Simple Justice: The History of Brown V. Board of Education and Black America's Struggle for Equality* (New York: Knopf, 2004); Vanessa Siddle Walker, *The Lost Education of Horace Tate: Uncovering the Hidden Heroes Who Fought for Justice in Schools* (New York: The New Press, 2018).
69. Geiger and Pivovarova, "The Effects of Working Conditions on Teacher Retention."; Kari Kokka, "Urban Teacher Longevity: What Keeps Teachers of Color in One under-Resourced Urban School?" *Teaching & Teacher Education* 59 (2016): 169–79, https://doi.org/10.1016/j.tate.2016.05.014; Grillo and Kier, "Why Do They Stay?"; Olitsky, Perfetti, and Coughlin, "Filling Positions or Forging New Pathways?"; Jennifer Whitfield, Manjari Banerjee, Hersh C. Waxman, Timothy P. Scott, and Mary Margaret Capraro, "Recruitment and Retention of STEM Teachers through the Noyce Scholarship: A Longitudinal Mixed Methods Study," *Teaching & Teacher Education* 103 (2021), https://doi.org/10.1016/j.tate.2021.103361.

Chapter 3

1. This account of the origin of the theory of job embeddedness comes from two papers on which Lee and Mitchell are coauthors: Thomas W. Lee and Terence R. Mitchell, "Working in Research Teams: Lessons from Personal Experiences," *Management and Organization Review* 7, no. 3 (2011): 461–69, https://doi.org/10.1111/j.1740-8784.2011.00224.x; Thomas W. Lee, Tyler C. Burch, and Terence R. Mitchell, "The Story of Why We Stay: A Review of Job Embeddedness," *Annual Review of Organizational Psychology and Organizational Behavior* 1, no. 1 (2014): 199–216, https://doi.org/10.1146/annurev-orgpsych-031413-091244.
2. Terrence R. Mitchell, Brooks C. Holtom, Thomas W Lee, Chris J. Sablynski, and Miriam Erez, "Why People Stay: Using Job Embeddedness to Predict Voluntary Turnover," *Academy of Management Journal* 44, no. 6 (2001): 1102–21, https://doi.org/10.5465/3069391.
3. In addition to the 2001 paper, which has over 5000 citations on Google Scholar as of this writing, a number of other papers from the University of Washington group have formed the nucleus of job-embeddedness scholarship, including: Thomas W. Lee, Terence R. Mitchell, Chris J. Sablynski, James P. Burton, and Brooks C. Holtom, "The Effects of Job Embeddedness on Organizational Citizenship, Job Performance, Volitional Absences, and Voluntary Turnover," *Academy of Management Journal* 47, no. 5 (2004): 711–22, https://doi.org/10.5465/20159613.; Brooks C. Holtom, Terence R. Mitchell, and Thomas W. Lee, "Increasing Human and Social Capital by Applying Job Embeddedness Theory," *Organizational Dynamics* 35, no. 4 (2006): 316–31, https://doi.org/10.1016/j.orgdyn.2006.08.007.
4. William H. Mobley, "Intermediate Linkages in the Relationship between Job Satisfaction and Employee Turnover," *Journal of Applied Psychology* 62, no. 2 (1977): 237–40, https://doi.org/10.1037/0021-9010.62.2.237.
5. Thomas W. Lee and Terence R. Mitchell, "An Alternative Approach: The Unfolding Model of Voluntary Employee Turnover," *Academy of Management Review* 19, no. 1 (1994): 51–89, https://doi.org/10.5465/amr.1994.9410122008.
6. We debated on whether or not to include an image of this model but decided not to do so because it might be as confusing and unhelpful to readers as it was for the University of Washington group.
7. Thomas W. Lee, Terence R. Mitchell, Brooks C. Holtom, Linda S. McDaneil, and John W. Hill, "The Unfolding Model of Voluntary Turnover: A Replication and Extension," *Academy of Management Journal* 42, no. 4 (1999): 450–62, https://doi.org/10.5465/257015; Thomas W. Lee, Terence R. Mitchell, Lowell Wise, and Steven Fireman, "An Unfolding Model of Voluntary Employee Turnover," *Academy of Management Journal* 39, no. 1 (1996): 5–36, https://doi.org/10.5465/256629.
8. Our use of Kuhnian language here is intentional. Kuhn also discussed the way that a paradigm shift permits the re-examination of old problems in new ways. It is notable that the construct of embeddedness has found much wider application beyond research on employee turnover and has provided fruitful explanations in fields as diverse as military re-enlistment, repatriation to home countries, and innovation-related behaviors. Thomas S. Kuhn, *The Structure of Scientific Revolutions*, International Encyclopedia of Unified Science: Foundations of the Unity of Science (Chicago: University of Chicago Press, 1970); Lee, Burch, and Mitchell, "The Story of Why We Stay."
9. Holtom, Mitchell, and Lee, "Increasing Human and Social Capital by Applying Job Embeddedness Theory," 319.
10. The web metaphor comes from Brooks C. Holtom, Simon T. Tidd, Terence R. Mitchell, and Thomas W. Lee, "A Demonstration of the Importance of Temporal Considerations in the

Prediction of Newcomer Turnover," *Human Relations* 66, no. 10 (2013): 1337–52, https://doi.org/10.1177/0018726713477459. In our own group of researchers, populated by former high school science teachers as it was, we found the analogy to a gravity well to be much more useful. Strong embeddedness is like a person walking on the earth, and weak embeddedness is the same person walking on a small asteroid. Jumping up on the earth returns the person to their starting point, but a jump on the asteroid might turn into a trajectory that just keeps going. In public presentations, we have often represented strong embeddedness with an image of a marble at the bottom of a large bowl, juxtaposed with the weak embeddedness of a marble in the shallow indentation of a child's puzzle game.

11. Mitchell et al., "Why People Stay."
12. Frank Siedlok, Paul Hibbert, and Fiona Whitehurst, "Employee Responses to Organizational Demise: The Influence of Network Embedding," *Academy of Management Proceedings* 2015, no. 1 (2015): 10848, https://doi.org/10.5465/ambpp.2015.10848abstract.
13. Amy L. Kristof, "Person-Organization Fit: An Integrative Review of Its Conceptualizations, Measurement, and Implications," *Personnel Psychology* 49, no. 1 (1996): 1–9; Michelle L. Verquer, Terry A. Beehr, and Stephen H. Wagner, "A Meta-Analysis of Relations between Person–Organization Fit and Work Attitudes," *Journal of Vocational Behavior* 63, no. 3 (2003): 473–89, https://doi.org/10.1016/S0001-8791(02)00036-2.
14. Holtom, Mitchell, and Lee, "Increasing Human and Social Capital by Applying Job Embeddedness Theory."
15. Holtom, Mitchell, and Lee, "Increasing Human and Social Capital by Applying Job Embeddedness Theory," 320.
16. Carlos M. Mallol, Brooks C. Holtom, and Thomas W. Lee, "Job Embeddedness in a Culturally Diverse Environment," *Journal of Business and Psychology* 22, no. 1 (2007): 35–44, https://doi.org/10.1007/s10869-007-9045-x; Imran Ahmed Shah, Tamas Csordas, Umair Akram, Amit Yadav, and Hassan Rasool, "Multifaceted Role of Job Embeddedness within Organizations: Development of Sustainable Approach to Reducing Turnover Intention," *SAGE Open* 10, no. 2 (2020): 2158244020934876, https://doi.org/10.1177/2158244020934876; Siedlok, Hibbert, and Whitehurst, "Employee Responses to Organizational Demise."; Xuguang Sun and Ailing Huang, "Development of a Scale of Chinese Primary School Teachers' Job Embeddedness," *Palgrave Communications* 6, no. 1 (2020): 38, https://doi.org/10.1057/s41599-020-0413-8. https://doi.org/10.1057/s41599-020-0413-8; Christian Tröster, Andrew Parker, Daan Van Knippenberg, and Ben Sahlmüller, "The Coevolution of Social Networks and Thoughts of Quitting," *Academy of Management Journal* 62, no. 1 (2019): 22–43.
17. One drawback of the proliferation of job-embeddedness research is that the difference between staying and *intent* to stay is not always recognized. One of the hallmarks of the research done by Lee, Mitchell, Holtom, and their colleagues over the years is that they have always been very clear about this distinction and have even been able to compare intention to stay with actual employee attrition in many of their studies.
18. According to the loss aversion theory, the psychological impact of losing job assets is often felt more profoundly than the potential gains of moving to another position. Even the prospect of losing those assets is likely to activate emotional, noncognitive responses. Carroll E. Izard, "Four Systems for Emotion Activation: Cognitive and Noncognitive Processes," *Psychological Review* 100, no. 1 (1993): 68–90, https://doi.org/10.1037/0033-295X.100.1.68; Daniel Kahneman and Amos Tversky, "Prospect Theory: An Analysis of Decision Under Risk." *Econometrica: Journal of the Econometric Society* (1979): 263–91, https://doi.org/10.1142/9789814417358_0006.

Chapter 4

1. Richard Vespucci, *Public Education in New Jersey* (New Jersey Department of Education, 2001), https://www.njsba.org/wp-content/uploads/2016/02/public-education-in-new-jersey.pdf
2. Allan Odden and Larry Picus, *School Finance: A Policy Perspective* (McGraw-Hill New York, 2000); National Research Council, *Equity and Adequacy in Education Finance: Issues and Perspectives* (National Academies Press, 1999); "The History of Abbott v. Burke" Education Law Center, 2020, https://edlawcenter.org/litigation/abbott-history/.
3. NJDOE, *New Jersey's Teacher Equity Plan: Updated 2009* (New Jersey Department of Education, 2009), https://www.nj.gov/education/rpi/diversityandequity/educatorequity/Plan09.pdf.
4. Joseph van der Naald and Todd E. Vachon, *The State of Labor in New Jersey, 2021–2023: A Profile of Organized Labor in the Garden State.* Labor Education Action Research Network (Rutgers University, 2024), https://smlr.rutgers.edu/sites/default/files/Documents/LEARN/State_of_Labor_Report_May2024.pdf.
5. New Jersey schools must simply self-certify each year that they have a mentoring and induction plan for new teachers. There is no other external assessment of the presence or quality of mentoring by the state's department of education. New Jersey Department of Education, *Educator Mentoring and Induction Support*, Nj.gov, 2021, https://www.nj.gov/education/profdev/mentor/.
6. Of course, the history of the United States (and humanity as a whole) shows that there is a wide interpretation of "just cause" for land dispossession.
7. Thomas A. Kersten, "Teacher Tenure: Illinois School Board Presidents' Perspectives and Suggestions for Improvement," *Planning and Changing* 37 (2006): 234–57; Susanna Loeb, Luke C. Miller, and James Wyckoff, "Performance Screens for School Improvement: The Case of Teacher Tenure Reform in New York City," *Educational Researcher* 44, no. 4 (2015): 199–212, https://doi.org/10.3102/0013189X15584773; van der Naald and Vachon, *The State of Labor in New Jersey, 2021-2023.*
8. Richard D. Kahlenberg, "Teacher Tenure Has a Long History and, Hopefully, a Future," *Phi Delta Kappan* 97, no. 6 (2016): 16–21, https://doi.org/10.1177/0031721716636866.
9. Douglas B. Larkin and Joseph O. Oluwole, "The Opportunity Costs of Teacher Evaluation: A Labor and Equity Analysis of the Teach-NJ Legislation," *West's Education Law Reporter* 308 (2014): 1–24.
10. Bruce D. Baker and Mark Weber, *Separate and Unequal: Racial and Ethnic Segregation and the Case for School Funding Reparations in New Jersey* (New Jersey Policy Perspective, 2021), https://www.njpp.org/publications/report/separate-and-unequal-racial-and-ethnic-segregation-and-the-case-for-school-funding-reparations-in-new-jersey/.
11. A nondistrict charter school is also colocated on the property but is not included in the Mulberry case study, as it operates essentially as an independent school district.
12. Douglas B. Larkin, Suzanne Poole Patzelt, Khadija M. Ahmed, Liz Carletta, and Catherine R. Gaynor, "Portraying Secondary Science Teacher Retention with the Person-Position Framework: An Analysis of a State Cohort of First-Year Science Teachers," *Journal of Research in Science Teaching* 59, no. 7 (2022): 1235–73, https://doi.org/10.1002/tea.21757; US Bureau of Labor Statistics, *Highlights of Women's Earnings in 2017*, Bls.gov, August 2018, https://www.bls.gov/opub/reports/womens-earnings/2017/.
13. In fact, one teacher expressed some frustration that the union was not active *enough* in terms of job actions, noting that the most recent contract had taken over two years to finalize after the expiration of the previous one.

14. As is common in New Jersey, the administrators were members of their own union, separate from teachers. They negotiated their compensation, benefits, and terms and conditions of work collectively with the board of education in the same manner as the teachers' union.
15. Odden and Picus, *School Finance: A Policy Perspective.*
16. Vanessa Siddle Walker, "Valued Segregated Schools for African American Children in the South, 1935–1969: A Review of Common Themes and Characteristics," *Review of Educational Research* 70, no. 3 (2000): 276, https://doi.org/10.3102/00346543070003253.
17. Melanie M. Acosta, Michele Foster, and Diedre F. Houchen, "'Why Seek the Living among the Dead?' African American Pedagogical Excellence: Exemplar Practice for Teacher Education," *Journal of Teacher Education* 69, no. 4 (2018): 341–53, https://doi.org/10.1177/0022487118761881; Michèle Foster, *Black Teachers on Teaching* (New York: New Press, 1997).
18. Travis J. Albritton, "Educating Our Own: The Historical Legacy of HBCUs and Their Relevance for Educating a New Generation of Leaders," *The Urban Review* 44, no. 3 (2012): 311–31, https://doi.org/10.1007/s11256-012-0202-9; Sandra Edmonds Crewe, "Education with Intent—the HBCU Experience," *Journal of Human Behavior in the Social Environment* 27, no. 5 (2017): 360–66, https://doi.org/10.1080/10911359.2017.1318622.
19. Richard M. Ingersoll, Lisa Merrill, and Henry May, "Do Accountability Policies Push Teachers Out?" *Education Leadership* 73, no. 8 (2016): 46, http://www.ascd.org/publications/educational-leadership/may16/vol73/num08/Do-Accountability-Policies-Push-Teachers-Out%C2%A2.aspx.
20. Linda Darling-Hammond, Maria E. Hyler, and Madelyn Gardner, *Effective Teacher Professional Development* (Palo Alto, CA: Learning Policy Institute, 2017), https://learningpolicyinstitute.org/sites/default/files/product-files/Effective_Teacher_Professional_Development_REPORT.pdf.

Chapter 5

1. Uriah Stephens and nine other Philadelphia garment workers founded the Knights of Labor in 1869, which later became the first successful national labor union in the 1890s. With its farm, mining, and steel industries, union activity and membership in the state was high until the late twentieth century. See: Nathaniel J. Donato, Charles L. Lumpkins, and Kenneth Wolensky, "A Bibliography of Labor History in Pennsylvania," *Pennsylvania History* 78 (2011): 323–54, https://pa-history.org/wp-content/uploads/2017/05/LaborhistoryBib2015.pdf.
2. Barry Hirsch, David Macpherson, and William Even "Union Membership, Coverage, and Earnings from the CPS," Unionstats.com, 2024, https://unionstats.com/.
3. Nicholas Toloudis, "Pennsylvania's Teachers and the Tenure Law of 1937," *Journal of Policy History* 31, no. 2 (2019): 217–241, https://doi.org/10.1017/S0898030619000034; Act of March 29, 1996, Pub. L. 47, No. 16, Cl. 24 (1996).
4. Charlotte Danielson, *Enhancing Professional Practice: A Framework for Teaching* (Alexandria, VA: Association for Supervision and Curriculum Development, 1996).
5. Pennsylvania Department of Education, *Educator Effectiveness Administrative Manual* (PDE, 2014), https://www.education.pa.gov/Documents/Teachers-Administrators/Educator%20Effectiveness/Educator%20Effectiveness%20Administrative%20Manual.pdf.
6. Pennsylvania Department of Education, *Educator Induction Plan Guidelines* (PDE, 2019), https://www.education.pa.gov/Documents/Teachers-Administrators/Act%2048-PERMS/Educator%20Induction%20Plan%20Guidelines.pdf.

7. Teachers Pay Teachers (https://www.teacherspayteachers.com) is a website created in 2006, where teachers may sell or purchase original self-created instructional materials. An alternate view on the website is that it helps to protect teacher-created materials from commercial exploitation and demonstrates value for the intellectual labor of teachers.
8. A similar "founders' effect" was noted in the science department described in a study on departmental curriculum collaboration. Douglas B. Larkin, Scott C. Seyforth, and Holly J. Lasky, "Implementing and Sustaining Science Curriculum Reform: A Study of Leadership Practices among Teachers within a High School Science Department," *Journal of Research in Science Teaching* 4, no. 7 (2009): 813–35, https://doi.org/10.1002/tea.20291.

Chapter 6

1. For example, the first kindergarten in the US was started in Watertown, Wisconsin in 1856, and the first school voucher program in the US was enacted in Milwaukee in 1989.
2. Act 10 was ultimately found unconstitutional by the Wisconsin Supreme Court in December 2024.
3. Katy Swalwell, Simone Schweber, Kristin Sinclair, Jennifer Gallagher, and Eleni Schirmer, "In the Aftermath of Act 10: The Changed State of Teaching in a Changed State," *Peabody Journal of Education* 92, no. 4 (2017): 486–504, https://doi.org/10.1080/0161956X.2017.1349485; Barbara Biasi and Heather Sarsons, "Flexible Wages, Bargaining, and the Gender Gap," *The Quarterly Journal of Economics* 137, no. 1 (2022): 215–66, https://doi.org/10.1093/qje/qjab026; Dave Umhoefer and Sarah Hauer, "From Teacher 'Free Agency' to Merit Pay, the Uproar over Act 10 Turns into Upheaval in Wisconsin Schools," *Milwaukee Journal Sentinel*, October 9, 2016, https://projects.jsonline.com/news/2016/10/9/from-teacher-free-agency-to-merit-pay-the-uproar-over-act-10.html.
4. Anne Chapman and Ari Brown, *A Teacher Who Looks Like Me: Examining Racial Diversity in Wisconsin's Teacher Workforce and the Student-to-Teacher Pipeline*, (Wisconsin Policy Forum, 2020), https://wispolicyforum.org/wp-content/uploads/2020/06/TeacherWhoLooksLikeMe_FullReport.pdf; Tony Evers, *State Superintendent's Working Group on School Staffing Issues*, (Wisconsin Department of Public Instruction, 2016), https://dpi.wi.gov/sites/default/files/imce/tepdl/pdf/FINALReport-StateSuperintendentsWorkingGrouponSchoolStaffingIssues.pdf; David Madland and Alex Rowell, "Attacks on Public-Sector Unions Harm States: How Act 10 Has Affected Education in Wisconsin," Center for American Progress Action Fund, November, 15 2017, americanprogressaction.org/content/uploads/sites/2/2017/11/15074954/ImpactofWisconsinAct10-brief.pdf.
5. Shelly Hadley and David Trechter, *Wisconsin Education Act 31: 2014 Administrator and Teacher Survey Report.* (University of Wisconsin-River Falls, 2014), https://dpi.wi.gov/sites/default/files/imce/amind/pdf/2014-act31surveyreport.pdf; The text of the legislation may be seen here: "State Statutes for American Indian Studies (Wisconsin Act 31)," Wisconsin Department of Public Instruction, https://dpi.wi.gov/amind/state-statues; For more on the history of Act 31, see J P Leary, *The Story of Act 31: How Native History Came to Wisconsin Classrooms*, (Wisconsin Historical Society Press, 2018).
6. Anne Chapman, *Opening Doors: Strategies for Advancing Racial Diversity in Wisconsin's Teacher Workforce*, (Wisconsin Policy Forum, 2021), https://wispolicyforum.org/wp-content/uploads/2021/03/OpeningDoors_FullReport.pdf.
7. Wisconsin Department of Public Instruction, *State Superintendent's Working Group on School Staffing Issues.*

8. The Master Educator or Tier IV Lifetime License was designated for teachers who had successfully completed a rigorous assessment of their professional practice, such as National Board Certification by the National Board of Professional Teaching Standards (NBPTS) or the Wisconsin Master Educator Assessment Process (WMEAP). Current license types in Wisconsin are listed at: "Educator Licensing General Information," Wisconsin Department of Public Instruction, https://dpi.wi.gov/licensing/general.
9. Specifically (Wis. Stat. § 121.02 (1)(q), Wis. Admin. Code § PI 8.01(2)(q)). This description of the evaluation comes from Wisconsin's 2010 Race to the Top application; it is worth noting that the bipartisan scrutiny on teacher evaluation practices leading to Act 166 preceded the consequential 2010 election and was largely driven by the availability of significant federal funding toward this end through the US Department of Education's Race to the Top grant proposal process.
10. Individual districts had the option of using the state-developed model based on Danielson or using an equivalent model approved by the Department of Public Instruction. Charlotte Danielson, *The Framework for Teaching Evaluation Instrument: 2013 Edition*, 2nd ed. (Alexandria, Va.: Association for Supervision and Curriculum Development, 2013).
11. Isabel Wilkerson, *The Warmth of Other Suns: The Epic Story of America's Great Migration*, 1st ed. (New York: Random House, 2010).
12. Note: This respondent was the only person to mention a loan forgiveness program as a rationale for retention in Pompano. Though the specific program was not named, it was likely the Teacher Loan Cancellation program available for teachers with Federal Perkins Loans. Pompano Regional School District would have qualified as meeting the low-income school requirement for this loan forgiveness program, provided the individual has taught there for "five complete and consecutive academic years." Cited in "Teacher Loan Forgiveness," Federal Student Aid, effective 2016, https://studentaid.gov/manage-loans/forgiveness-cancellation/teacher.
13. Michelle Reininger, "Hometown Disadvantage? It Depends on Where You're From: Teachers' Location Preferences and the Implications for Staffing Schools," *Educational Evaluation and Policy Analysis* 34, no. 2 (2012): 127–45, https://doi.org/10.3102/0162373711420864.

Chapter 7

1. Kenneth M. Zeichner, "The Adequacies and Inadequacies of Three Current Strategies to Recruit, Prepare, and Retain the Best Teachers for All Students," *Teachers College Record* 105, no. 3 (2003): 490–519, https://doi.org/10.1111/1467-9620.00248.
2. National Board Certification is a voluntary advanced credential offered by the National Board of Professional Teaching Standards, designed to be a mechanism for professional regulation akin to similar credentials in law and medicine. According to the organization's website, as of 2025, over 140,000 teachers have earned National Board Certification; "National Board Certification," National Board for Professional Teaching Standards, https://www.nbpts.org/.
3. Currently, tenure does not exist in North Carolina, and teachers serve as at-will employees, though they have many of the same basic workplace protections as other workers; Harvard Law Review, "North Carolina Ass'n of Educators, Inc. V. State," *Harvard Law Review,* 3, no. 28 (2015), https://harvardlawreview.org/2015/01/north-carolina-assn-of-educators-inc-v-state
4. Vijay Gondhalekar, Lara Kessler, and Julia Hofmann, "Right-to-Work Laws: A Brief Review," *JL Bus. & Ethics* 29 (2023): 1.

5. The most commonly joined North Carolina teacher association is the NCAE. NCAE Homepage, https://www.ncae.org/.
6. North Carolina State Statute § 143C-5-4
7. *Teacher Pay Issue Brief* (NCSBA, 2016), https://www.ncsba.org/wp-content/uploads/2016/08/NCSBA-Teacher-Pay-Brief.pdf.
8. Bruce D. Baker, Matthew Di Carlo, and Mark Weber, *The Adequacy and Fairness of State School Finance Systems. Findings from the School Finance Indicators Database, School Year 2015-2016* (Albert Shanker Institute, 2019), https://eric.ed.gov/?id=ED596199.
9. Teachers who were already receiving this supplement continued to do so, but anyone earning an advanced degree after 2014 did not.
10. For example, at this writing, one county is offering a $10,000 bonus for new teachers in certain subject areas who commit to two years and $20,000 to teachers who commit to three years and achieve two years of "exceeds expected growth" in the Student Growth Measure of their teaching evaluation.
11. Thomas Ahn and Jacob L. Vigdor, *Making Teacher Incentives Work: Lessons from North Carolina's Teacher Bonus Program. Education Outlook. No. 5.* (American Enterprise Institute for Public Policy Research, 2011); T. Smith and B. Hassel, *Retaining and Extending the Reach of Excellent Educators: Current Practices, Educator Perceptions, and Future Directions* (Chapel Hill, NC: Public Impact, 2019), https://everychildnc.org/wp-content/uploads/2021/01/Leandro-Retain-Extend-Report.pdf.
12. In 1987, in collaboration with Carnegie Corporation of New York, Governor Hunt helped establish The National Board for Professional Teaching Standards (NCPTS). During his second term, Governor Hunt promoted National Board Certification through legislation. He provided financial incentives to teachers with three years or more teaching experience that received certification by awarding them a salary increase of 12 percent, as well as covering the cost of the application, a key expenditure in the state's education budget.
13. NC Data on National Board Certification for 2020, North Carolina Department of Public Instruction, retrieved September 30, 2021, https://www.dpi.nc.gov/educators/national-board-certification/nc-data-national-board-certification.
14. Phillip Scott Riner, "A Study of the Criterion-Related Validity of North Carolina Teacher Performance Appraisal Instrument," (unpublished dissertation, The University of North Carolina at Greensboro, 1988); David Holdzkom, "Teacher Performance Appraisal in North Carolina: Preferences and Practices," *The Phi Delta Kappan* 72, no. 10 (1991): 782–85, https://www.jstor.org/stable/20404535.
15. Javaid Siddiqi, Patrick C. Sims, and Allison L. Goff, *Connecting the Continuum: Longitudinal Data Systems in North Carolina* (Hunt Institute, 2019), http://www.hunt-institute.org/wp-content/uploads/2019/06/Hunt-Institute-Connecting-the-Continuum.pdf.
16. Shanique Lee, *Policy Brief: Putting North Carolina's Beginning Teacher Support Program Policy into Practice* (University of North Carolina, 2018), https://thecollaborative.charlotte.edu/wp-content/uploads/sites/1073/2024/01/Shanique-Lee-Putting-NC-Beginning-Teacher-Policy-Brief.pdf.
17. "Beginning Teach Support," NC.gov, https://www.dpi.nc.gov/educators/recruitment-support/beginning-teacher-support#BTCoordinatorResources-758.
18. In North Carolina, villages, towns, and cities are incorporated and have local governments, while townships are unincorporated and without local government, though their boundaries are used for voting and legislative purposes.

19. In order to maintain the anonymity promised to participants and school districts in this study, we have refrained from naming the specific tribe. Certain details about this tribe and its history are relevant and interesting but would be identifying and so have been omitted out of respect and caution; Linda Tuhiwai Smith, *Decolonizing Methodologies: Research and Indigenous People* (New York: St Martin's Press, 1999).
20. For example, see Carol R. Rinke, *Why Half of Teachers Leave the Classroom: Understanding Recruitment and Retention in Today's Schools* (Lanham: Rowman & Littlefield, 2014); Doris A. Santoro, *Demoralized: Why Teachers Leave the Profession They Love and How They Can Stay* (Cambridge, Massachusetts: Harvard Education Press, 2018).
21. This pathway is similar to those in other states labeled as alternate route, where teachers become certified while working as a teacher of record. North Carolina has recently renamed this pathway as the "Residency Licensure" program, though the description of such programs as "lateral entry" was still in wide use during.
22. Michelle Reininger, "Hometown Disadvantage? It Depends on Where You're From: Teachers' Location Preferences and the Implications for Staffing Schools," *Educational Evaluation and Policy Analysis* 34, no. 2 (2012): 127–45. https://doi.org/10.3102/0162373711420864.
23. Jay Miller, "Kinship, Family Kindreds, and Community," in *A Companion to American Indian History*, ed. Neal Salisbury and Philip J. Deloria (Blackwell Malden, MA, 2002),139–53:
24. Vine Deloria, *Custer Died for Your Sins: An Indian Manifest.* (University of Oklahoma Press, 1988); Jacqueline Fear-Segal and Susan D. Rose, *Carlisle Indian Industrial School: Indigenous Histories, Memories, and Reclamations* (U of Nebraska Press, 2016).
25. Leo Kevin Killsback, "A Nation of Families: Traditional Indigenous Kinship, the Foundation for Cheyenne Sovereignty," *AlterNative: An International Journal of Indigenous Peoples* 15, no. 1 (2019): 34, https://doi.org/10.1177/1177180118822833.
26. Cornel D. Pewewardy, Anna Lees, and Hyuny Clark-Shim, "The Transformational Indigenous Praxis Model: Stages for Developing Critical Consciousness in Indigenous Education," *Wicazo Sa Review* 33, no. 1 (2018): 42, https://doi.org/10.5749/wicazosareview.33.1.0038; This is similar to the "ethnic epistemology" of *Ubuntu* described in Gloria Ladson-Billings, "Racialized Discourses and Ethnic Epistemologies," in *Handbook of Qualitative Research*, ed. N. Denzin and Y. Lincoln (Thousand Oaks, CA: Sage, 2000).
27. We were told that the cancellation of the retreat was one of the many impacts of the COVID-19 pandemic. At this writing, it is not clear whether the district will resume this practice.
28. Achieve Inc, *Next Generation Science Standards: For States, by States* (Washington, DC: National Academies Press, 2013).
29. The school district had multiple relationships with this university. For example, high school students could also obtain college credits by taking courses there. The district also partnered with the university for teacher certification, and the administrator noted that the schools receive "a lot of student teachers or students observing."
30. It appears that mentors were assigned by school administrators, but like any paid position, required approval by the school board.
31. Currently there is no in-person mentor training.

Chapter 8

1. Our use of the term *factor* here to describe why teacher retention occurred at a higher rate in these districts may strike some readers and researchers as an overreach. Qualitative-methods

experts Norman K. Denzin and Yvonna S. Lincoln note that the central question of validity is, "How do we know when we have specific social inquiries that are faithful enough to some human construction that we may feel safe in acting upon them, or more important, that members of the community in which the research is conducted may act on them?" Given our qualitative approach in this study, it is simply not possible to make the same sort of correlational, let alone causational, claims that are made in quantitative research on teacher attrition and retention. Such is the nature of case studies. Our findings are empirically derived and interpretively rigorous, and the colleagues, practitioners in our own professional communities, and study participants with whom we have shared these findings with the response have all reported a high degree of face validity. That is, these factors seem plausible to those in the best position to evaluate their plausibility. Therefore, we believe that we are justified in claiming that the items we list are indeed likely factors for teacher retention in the districts we studied; Yvonna. S. Lincoln and Egon G. Guba, "Paradigmatic Controversies, Contradictions, and Emerging Confluences," in *Handbook of Qualitative Research*, ed. N. Denzin and Y. Lincoln: (Thousand Oaks, CA: Sage, 2000),163–88.

2. For the sake of convenience in this chapter, we refer to each district by a shortened pseudonym label rather than the full pseudonym of the school district (e.g., Hickory instead of Hickory Island School District). All of the original written cases are available on our project website. Induction and Mentoring Programs for the Retention of Science Teachers (2024). http://www.montclair.edu/IMPREST
3. We feel obligated to note that Chestnut was not a high-need school district, and that the example of rhetoric presented here concerning support for education is often rooted in different socioeconomic conceptions about education. See for example: Annette Lareau, *Unequal Childhoods: Class, Race, and Family Life,* 2nd ed. (Berkeley: University of California Press, 2011).
4. In the 1970s, organizational theorist Karl Weick described schools as "loosely-coupled" institutions, where administrators and teachers did their work separately but in ways that were still connected. Another organizational theorist, Richard Elmore, later observed that "in a loosely-coupled system, administrators buffer instructional practice from outside interference." That is precisely what happened in our case with this district; Richard F. Elmore, Building a New Structure for School Leadership (Albert Shanker Institute, 2000), https://files.eric.ed.gov/fulltext/ED546618.pdf; Karl E. Weick, "Administering Education in Loosely Coupled Schools," *The Phi Delta Kappan* 63, no. 10 (1982): 673–76, http://www.jstor.org/stable/20386508.
5. Richard M. Ingersoll, Lisa Merrill, and Henry May, "Do Accountability Policies Push Teachers Out?" *Education Leadership* 73, no. 8 (2016): 46, http://www.ascd.org/publications/educational-leadership/may16/vol73/num08/Do-Accountability-Policies-Push-Teachers-Out%C2%A2.aspx.
6. Anneli Eteläpelto, Katja Vähäsantanen, Päivi Hökkä, and Susanna Paloniemi have produced a useful definition of professional agency, situated in a socio-cultural perspective: "Professional agency is practiced when professional subjects and/or communities exert influence, make choices and take stances in ways that affect their work and/or their professional identities."; Anneli Eteläpelto, Katja Vähäsantanen, Päivi Hökkä, and Susanna Paloniemi, "What Is Agency? Conceptualizing Professional Agency at Work," *Educational Research Review* 10 (2013): 45–65, https://doi.org/10.1016/j.edurev.2013.05.001.
7. Albert Bandura, "Perceived Self-Efficacy in Cognitive Development and Functioning," *Educational Psychologist* 28, no. 2 (1993): 117–48.

8. The relationship between teacher autonomy and collegial collaboration is an interesting one, but for our purposes here, we simply note that they are not mutually exclusive. Geert Kelchtermans' conception of "collaborative autonomy" seems particularly apt for a number the districts we studied; Geert Kelchtermans, "Teacher Collaboration and Collegiality as Workplace Conditions. A Review," *Zeitschrift für Pädagogik* 52, no. 2 (2006): 220–37, https://doi.org/10.25656/01:4454; See also: Katrien Vangrieken, Ilke Grosemans, Filip Dochy, and Eva Kyndt, "Teacher Autonomy and Collaboration: A Paradox? Conceptualising and Measuring Teachers' Autonomy and Collaborative Attitude," *Teaching and Teacher Education* 67 (2017): 302–15, https://doi.org/10.1016/j.tate.2017.06.021.
9. This "benign neglect" in Rivuline may be one finding where extrapolating from secondary science teacher participants to the wider population may be misleading, because the science teachers saw their autonomy as a consequence of the district's focus on teachers in other subject areas, such as language arts and mathematics, who reportedly faced more scrutiny and micromanagement in their work because of high-stakes testing. Science teachers believed that were able to reap the benefit of not being the object of district-level attention and valued this highly. For many teachers we interviewed, this form of autonomy served as a way for them to more easily share their passion for science with their students. Each interviewee, including those at the science curriculum office, used their autonomy to experiment with novel or unconventional ideas to improve the science experiences of their students in ways that they described as pedagogically sound. One experienced science teacher gave the example of being given permission to build an aquaponics lab. The teacher said to us, "She didn't need to know why I wanted my kids to raise tilapia… I didn't have to fight very hard. So, if you want to try something new, sometimes it's nice to be that forgotten subject that nobody argues with."
10. Harold M. Proshansky, "The City and Self-Identity," *Environment and Behavior* 10, no. 2 (1978): 147–69, https://doi.org/10.1177/0013916578102002.
11. In Wallago—a small town near a military base in a mostly rural community—the shortage of available housing in the area was of great concern precisely because it made it more difficult for teachers to live in the community.
12. In a foundational study on educational equity in K–12 school districts located in "college towns," Robert Maranto and Jeffery Dean describe a number of their common features:

> College towns typically have considerable financial resources, so they can afford to serve advantaged and disadvantaged students alike… College towns have vast human resources as well, in recent graduates and the family members of professors and administrators, who may want to teach near the college or university… Third, college towns should be relatively tolerant and inclusive, with political elites making it a public priority to education all children, and not merely their own… Fourth, the large number of university-based intellectuals in a college town will pressure the school system to maintain quality, as is true of upper-income communities generally… Fifth, to attract new faculty, universities may pressure the local school systems to maintain quality. Finally, the very presence of a college or university may enable schools to partner with higher education, particularly regarding curricula, measurement, and tutoring.
>
> (p. 986)

Maranto and Dean's depiction of such school districts certainly resembles what our research team heard from educators in Linnet; Robert Maranto and Jeffery Dean, "Not Separate and Not Equal? Achievement and Attainment Equity in College Towns," *Social Science Quarterly* 96, no. 4 (2015): 985–95, https://doi.org/10.1111/ssqu.12174.

13. For a comprehensive and well-documented summary of the research on the impact of funding on education, see: Bruce D. Baker and David S. Knight, *Does Money Matter in Education?* (Albert Shanker Institute, 2025), https://www.shankerinstitute.org/sites/default/files/2025-01/moneymatters3rdedition_final.pdf.
14. Carleton H. Brown and David Knight, "Staffing Schools to Support the Classroom: Examining Student-to-School-Counselor Ratios and Academic Student Outcomes in Texas," *Professional School Counseling* 27, no. 1 (2023), https://doi.org/10.1177/2156759X231165497.
15. The practice of carving out time for teacher professional development through the weekly and regular early dismissal of students has been documented throughout the United States but appears more widely adopted in Wisconsin than elsewhere. Documents on Wisconsin's State Department of Public Instruction website encourage administrators to consider early release one day a week as a tool for providing teachers with time for collaboration. For example, see: "Wisconsin Professional Development Model: Tools and Resources," Wisconsin Department of Public Instruction, https://dpi.wi.gov/sites/default/files/imce/sped/pdf/wpdmtools.pdf; See also longitudinal examples from Florida and Connecticut: Nancy Ames Slabine, "841 Square Miles of Commitment: Districtwide Plan Makes Professional Learning a Priority," *The Learning Professional* 33, no. 1 (2012): 22, https://learningforward.org/wp-content/uploads/2012/02/slabine331.pdf; Catherine Buchholz and Karen L. List, "A Place for Learning," *Principal Leadership* 9, no. 7 (2009): 38–42.
16. Substitute teachers play an important role in school settings that remains understudied. See: Andrea Reupert, Anna Sullivan, Neil Tippett, Simone White, Stuart Woodcock, Lingling Chen, and Michele Simons, "An Exploration of the Experiences of Substitute Teachers: A Systematic Review," *Review of Educational Research* 93, no. 6 (2023): 901–41, https://doi.org/10.3102/00346543221149418.
17. Michael Omi and Howard Winant, *Racial Formation in the United States: From the 1960s to the 1990s*, 2nd ed. (New York: Routledge, 1994); Ian F. Haney Lopez, "The Social Construction of Race," in *Critical Race Theory: The Cutting Edge* (Temple University Press, 2000).
18. Gloria Ladson-Billings and William F. Tate IV, "Toward a Critical Race Theory of Education," *Teachers College Record* 97, no. 1 (1995): 47–68, https://doi.org/10.1177/016146819509700104.
19. Karen Manheim Teel and Jennifer E. Obidah, *Building Racial and Cultural Competence in the Classroom: Strategies from Urban Educators* (New York, NY: Teachers College Press, 2008).
20. H Richard MilnerIv, "Beyond a Test Score: Explaining Opportunity Gaps in Educational Practice," *Journal of Black Studies* 43, no. 6 (2012): 693–718, https://doi.org/10.1177/0021934712442539. https://doi.org/10.1177/0021934712442539.
21. Subini Ancy Annamma, Darrell D. Jackson, and Deb Morrison, "Conceptualizing Color-Evasiveness: Using Dis/Ability Critical Race Theory to Expand a Color-Blind Racial Ideology in Education and Society," *Race Ethnicity and Education* 20, no. 2 (2017): 147–62, https://doi.org/10.1080/13613324.2016.1248837.
22. Doris A. Santoro, Julia Hazel, and Alberto Morales, *Educators of Color Insights Report: What Will It Take for Educators of Color to Thrive in PPS?* (Bowdoin College and Portland Public Schools, 2021), https://drive.google.com/file/d/1_tIjd7XXabmueG8SP5rTFIUY2b-vJDGqW/view.
23. The influence of behaviorist ideas on the field of education over the last century cannot be overstated. See: Alfie Kohn, *Punished by Rewards: The Trouble with Gold Stars, Incentive Plans, A's, Praise, and Other Bribes* (Boston: Houghton Mifflin Co., 1993).

24. For example, see: Zachary Griffen and Aaron Panofsky, "Ambivalent Economizations: The Case of Value Added Modeling in Teacher Evaluation," *Theory and Society* 50, no. 3 (2021): 515–39, https://doi.org/10.1007/s11186-020-09417-x; Sangyub Ryu and Yusuke Jinnai, "Effects of Monetary Incentives on Teacher Turnover: A Longitudinal Analysis," *Public Personnel Management* 50, no. 2 (2021): 205–31, https://doi.org/10.1177/0091026020921414; Madhu Narayanan, A. L. Shields, and T. J. Delhagen, "Autonomy in the Spaces: Teacher Autonomy, Scripted Lessons, and the Changing Role of Teachers," *Journal of Curriculum Studies* 56, no. 1 (2024): 17–34, https://doi.org/10.1080/00220272.2023.2297229; Luis A. Rodriguez, Walker A. Swain, and Matthew G. Springer, "Sorting Through Performance Evaluations: The Influence of Performance Evaluation Reform on Teacher Attrition and Mobility," *American Educational Research Journal* 57, no. 6 (2020): 2339–77, https://doi.org/10.3102/0002831220910989.

Chapter 9

1. This result seemed so anomalous that our team felt it necessary to reanalyze the data starting from the very beginning, and we did so twice. We found the same result each time, and did not appear to be the result of a measurement effect. For example, if alternate route teachers in Wisconsin had not been counted as certified teachers until they completed their probationary period, they might have been masked as third-year teachers. This was not the case. However, we cannot rule out the possibility that some other economic, cultural, or measurement effect was responsible for this finding.
2. This is a simplified account events, but one important detail that was to become the basis of renewed legal challenges in 2023 was the exemption of certain labor unions (e.g., fire and police) from the law.
3. Katy Swalwell, Simone Schweber, Kristin Sinclair, Jennifer Gallagher, and Eleni Schirmer, "In the Aftermath of Act 10: The Changed State of Teaching in a Changed State," *Peabody Journal of Education* 92, no. 4 (2017): 486–504, https://doi.org/10.1080/0161956X.2017.1349485.
4. See: Kevin C. Bastian, and Sarah C. Fuller, "Educator Attrition and Mobility during the Covid-19 Pandemic," *Educational Researcher* 52, no. 8 (2023): 516–20, https://doi.org/10.3102/0013189X231187890.
5. In this study, we drew upon Philip Dawson's framework, which describes a set of design elements that can be used to make decisions about mentoring relationships. Phillip Dawson, "Beyond a Definition: Toward a Framework for Designing and Specifying Mentoring Models," *Educational Researcher* 43, no. 3 (2014): 137–45, https://doi.org/10.3102/0013189X14528751.
6. Richard M. Ingersoll and Michael Strong, "The Impact of Induction and Mentoring Programs for Beginning Teachers: A Critical Review of the Research," *Review of Educational Research* 81, no. 2 (2011): 201–33, https://doi.org/10.3102/0034654311403323.
7. This replicates similar findings in the literature. See, for example: L. M. Desimone, E. D. Hochberg, A. C. Porter, M. S. Polikoff, R. Schwartz, and L. J. Johnson, "Formal and Informal Mentoring: Complementary, Compensatory, or Consistent?" *Journal of Teacher Education* 65, no. 2 (2014): 88–110, https://doi.org/10.1177/0022487113511643; Stéphane Colognesi, Catherine Van Nieuwenhoven, and Simon Beausaert, "Supporting Newly-Qualified Teachers' Professional Development and Perseverance in Secondary Education: On the Role of Informal Learning," *European Journal of Teacher Education* 43, no. 2 (2020): 258–76, https://doi.org/10.1080/02619768.2019.1681963; Amy Auletto, "Making Sense of Early-Career Teacher Support, Satisfaction, and Commitment," *Teaching & Teacher Education* 102 (2021), https://doi.org/10.1016/j.tate.2021.103321

8. Multi-level marketing, perhaps. Or sports.
9. Julie Luft's body of scholarship on recruitment, induction, and mentoring of newly hired science teachers has been instrumental to us in the conception and execution of this project. In particular: Julie A. Luft, and Shannon L. Dubois, *Newly Hired Teachers of Science: A Better Beginning* (Rotterdam, The Netherlands: Brill, 2015); Julie A. Luft, Deborah Hanuscin, Linda Hobbs, and Günter Törner, "Out-of-Field Teaching in Science: An Overlooked Problem," *Journal of Science Teacher Education* 31, no. 7 (2020): 719–24, https://doi.org/10.1080/1046560X.2020.1814052; Julie A. Luft, Sissy S. Wong, and Steve Semken, "Rethinking Recruitment: The Comprehensive and Strategic Recruitment of Secondary Science Teachers," *Journal of Science Teacher Education* 22, no. 5 (2011): 459–74, https://doi.org/10.1007/s10972-011-9243-2.
10. For example, see: Robert M. O'Neil, "Politics, Patronage and Public Employment," *University of Cincinnati Law Review* 44, no. 4 (1975): 725–40, https://heinonline.org/HOL/LandingPage?handle=hein.journals/ucinlr44&div=41; Lucy Maynard Salmon, *Patronage in the Public Schools* (Women's Auxiliary of the Massachusetts Civil Service Reform Association, 1908).
11. In places like Indonesia and Brazil, however, these are contemporary concerns. For example: Jan H. Pierskalla and Audrey Sacks, "Personnel Politics: Elections, Clientelistic Competition and Teacher Hiring in Indonesia," *British Journal of Political Science* 50, no. 4 (2020): 1283–305, https://doi.org/10.1017/S0007123418000601; Guillermo Toral, "How Patronage Delivers: Political Appointments, Bureaucratic Accountability, and Service Delivery in Brazil," *American Journal of Political Science* 68, no. 2 (2024): 797–815, https://doi.org/https://doi.org/10.1111/ajps.12758.
12. U.S. Department of Education, Office of Postsecondary Education. (2016). Preparing and Credentialing the Nation's Teachers: The Secretary's 10th Report on Teacher Quality. https://files.eric.ed.gov/fulltext/ED565683.pdf The Education Commission of the States maintains a website with licensure and reciprocity information for all 50 states and the District of Columbia at https://reports.ecs.org/comparisons/teacher-license-reciprocity-01.
13. Critical race theorists like Cheryl Harris and Kimberlee Crenshaw have written about Whiteness as property. Cheryl I. Harris, "Whiteness as Property" *Harvard Law Review* 106 (1993): 1707–91, https://doi.org/10.2307/1341787; Kimberlé Crenshaw, "Demarginalizing the Intersection of Race and Sex: A Black Feminist Critique of Antidiscrimination Doctrine," *University of Chicago Legal Forum* (1989): 139–68.
14. Jacqueline M. Nowicki, *K–12 Education: Student Population Has Significantly Diversified, but Many Schools Remain Divided Along Racial, Ethnic, and Economic Lines* (US Government Accountability Office, 2022), https://www.gao.gov/assets/gao-22-104737.pdf.
15. For a broader discussion of the role of segregation in contemporary schooling, see: Jonathan Kozol, *An End to Inequality: Breaking down the Walls of Apartheid Education in America* (New York: The New Press, 2024).
16. For example: Cassandra M. D. Hart and Constance A. Lindsay, "Teacher-Student Race Match and Identification for Discretionary Educational Services," *American Educational Research Journal* 61, no. 3 (2024): 474–507, https://doi.org/10.3102/00028312241229413; Travis J. Bristol and Javier Martin-Fernandez, "The Added Value of Latinx and Black Teachers for Latinx and Black Students: Implications for Policy," *Policy Insights from the Behavioral and Brain Sciences* 6, no. 2 (2019): 147–53, https://doi.org/10.1177/2372732219862573; Michael Gottfried, J. Jacob Kirksey, and Tina L. Fletcher, "Do High School Students with a Same-Race Teacher Attend Class More Often?" *Educational Evaluation and Policy*

Analysis 44, no. 1 (2021): 149–69, https://doi.org/10.3102/01623737211032241; Seth Gershenson, Cassandra M. D. Hart, Joshua Hyman, Constance A. Lindsay, and Nicholas W. Papageorge, "The Long-Run Impacts of Same-Race Teachers," *American Economic Journal: Economic Policy* 14, no. 4 (2022): 300–42, https://doi.org/10.1257/pol.20190573.

17. Christopher Redding, "A Teacher Like Me: A Review of the Effect of Student-Teacher Racial/Ethnic Matching on Teacher Perceptions of Students and Student Academic and Behavioral Outcomes," *Review of Educational Research* 89, no. 4 (2019): 499–535, https://doi.org/10.3102/0034654319853545.
18. Gloria Ladson-Billings notes that, "In a racialized society where whiteness is positioned as normative, *everyone* is ranked and categorized in relation to these points of opposition. These categories fundamentally sculpt the extant terrain of possibilities even when other possibilities exist." Gloria Ladson-Billings, "Just What Is Critical Race Theory and What's It Doing in a Nice Field Like Education?" *International Journal of Qualitative Studies in Education* 11, no. 1 (1998): 7–24, https://doi.org/10.1080/095183998236863.
19. For example: Christine E. Sleeter, "Preparing Teachers for Culturally Diverse Schools: Research and the Overwhelming Presence of Whiteness," *Journal of Teacher Education* 52, no. 2 (2001): 94–106, https://doi.org/10.1177/0022487101052002002; Sharon M Chubbuck, "Whiteness Enacted, Whiteness Disrupted: The Complexity of Personal Congruence," *American Educational Research Journal* 41, no. 2 (2004): 301–33, https://doi.org/10.3102/00028312041002301; Edward W. Morris, *An Unexpected Minority: White Kids in an Urban School* (New Brunswick, N.J.: Rutgers University Press, 2006.)
20. Martin Luther King Jr., *Letter from Birmingham City Jail*, April 16, 1963, letter, in Research and Education Institute, Stanford University, http://okra.stanford.edu/transcription/document_images/undecided/630416-019.pdf.
21. David B. Tyack and Larry Cuban, *Tinkering Toward Utopia: A Century of Public School Reform* (Cambridge, Mass.: Harvard University Press, 1995); James W. Fraser, *Preparing America's Teachers: A History,* Reflective History Series (New York: Teachers College Press, 2007).
22. E.g. Conra D. Gist, Margarita Bianco, and Marvin Lynn, "Examining Grow Your Own Programs Across the Teacher Development Continuum: Mining Research on Teachers of Color and Nontraditional Educator Pipelines," *Journal of Teacher Education* 70, no. 1 (2019): 13–25, https://doi.org/10.1177/0022487118787504.
23. A number of the induction efforts described by Julie Luft and her colleagues noted earlier have been such programs. See: Julie A. Luft, Jonah B. Firestone, Sissy S. Wong, Ira Ortega, Krista Adams, and EunJin Bang, "Beginning Secondary Science Teacher Induction: A Two-Year Mixed Methods Study," *Journal of Research in Science Teaching* 48, no. 10 (2011): 1199–224, https://doi.org/10.1002/tea.20444; Julie A. Luft, Shannon L. Navy, Sissy S. Wong, and Kathleen M. Hill, "The First 5 Years of Teaching Science: The Beliefs, Knowledge, Practices, and Opportunities to Learn of Secondary Science Teachers," *Journal of Research in Science Teaching* 59, no. 9 (2022): 1692–725, https://doi.org/10.1002/tea.21771.

Appendix A

1. Recall that we are using *school district* and *local educational authority (LEAs)* synonymously, even though technically they are not the same.
2. For example: Kevin C. Bastian and Julie T. Marks, "Connecting Teacher Preparation to Teacher Induction: Outcomes for Beginning Teachers in a University-Based Support Program in Low-Performing Schools," *American Educational Research Journal* 54,

no. 2 (2017): 360–94, https://doi.org/10.3102/0002831217690517; Zoe Rose Mandel, Edward Fuller, and Andrew Pendola, "Production, Placement, and Retention of Secondary STEM Teachers of Color: A Case Study of Texas," Paper presented at the annual meeting of the American Educational Research Association, New York, NY, 2018; Nicole S. Simon and Susan Moore Johnson, "Teacher Turnover in High-Poverty Schools: What We Know and Can Do," *Teachers College Record* 117, no. 3 (2015): 1–36, https://doi.org/10.1177/016146811511700305; W. H. Marinell and V. M. Coca, *Who Stays and Who Leaves? Findings from a Three Part Study of Teacher Turnover in Nyc Middle School* (The Research Alliance for NYC Schools, 2013), https://files.eric.ed.gov/fulltext/ED540818.pdf.

3. William G. Howell and Asya Magazinnik, "Presidential Prescriptions for State Policy: Obama's Race to the Top Initiative," *Journal of Policy Analysis and Management* 36, no. 3 (2017): 502–31, https://doi.org/10.1002/pam.21986.
4. Margaret Spellings, *Final Guidance on Maintaining, Collecting, and Reporting Racial and Ethnic Data to the U.S. Department of Education* (US Department of Education, 2007), https://www.federalregister.gov/documents/2007/10/19/E7-20613/final-guidance-on-maintaining-collecting-and-reporting-racial-and-ethnic-data-to-the-us-department
5. Our data included other public school LEAs, such as county-level vocational schools and charter schools. "Regular local public school district" is a data category used by the National Center of Educational Statistics (NCES). US Department of Education, National Center for Educational Statistics, (n.d.) School and District Glossary, https://nces.ed.gov/ccd/commonfiles/glossary.asp.
6. J. McFarland et al., *The Condition of Education 2019* (US Department of Education, 2019), https://nces.ed.gov/pubs2019/2019144.pdf.
7. Robert T. Teranishi, Bach Mai Dolly Nguyen, Cynthia M. Alcantar, and Edward R. Curammeng, *Measuring Race: Why Disaggregating Data Matters for Addressing Educational Inequality,* (Teachers College Press, 2020).
8. Workforce Data Quality Campaign, *Mastering the Blueprint: State Progress on Workforce Data* (WDQC, 2016), https://www.dol.gov/sites/dolgov/files/ETA/Performance/pdfs/WDQC-Mastering-the-Blueprint.pdf.
9. Robert E. Stake, *The Art of Case Study Research* (Sage Publications, 1995); Robert K. Yin, "Case Study Methods," in *Handbook of Complementary Methods in Education Research*, ed. Judith L. Green, Gregory Camilli, and Patricia B. Elmore, (Lawrence Erlbaum Associates, 2006), 111–22; Bedrettin Yazan, "Three Approaches to Case Study Methods in Education: Yin, Merriam, and Stake," *The Qualitative Report* 20, no. 2 (2015): 134–52, https://doi.org/10.46743/2160-3715/2015.2102; Robert E. Stake, "Qualitative Case Studies," in *Handbook of Qualitative Research*, ed. N. Denzin and Y. Lincoln, 443–66 (Sage, 2005).
10. To select the pseudonyms we used trees for New Jersey, minerals for Pennsylvania, fish for Wisconsin, and birds for North Carolina and were careful to ensure that each began with a unique letter of the alphabet to avoid possible confusion.
11. Robert E. Stake, *Multiple Case Study Analysis* (The Guilford Press, 2006).

Appendix B

1. Emily Parker, *50-State Review: Constitutional Obligations for Public Education* (Education Commission of the States, 2016), https://www.ecs.org/wp-content/uploads/2016-Constitutional-obligations-for-public-education-1.pdf.
2. Post-Prohibition, of course, after the repeal of the 18th Amendment by the 21st amendment in 1933.

3. The Higher Education Act, Pub. L. No. 89-329 (1965).
4. Rod Paige, "Meeting the Highly Qualified Teachers Challenge: The Secretary's Annual Report on Teacher Quality," in *Handbook of Research on Teacher Education: Enduring Questions in Changing Contexts*, ed. Marilyn Cochran-Smith, Sharon Feiman-Nemser, and D. John McIntyre (Routledge; Co-published by the Association of Teacher Educators, 2008), 492–500.
5. United States Department of Education, *No Child Left Behind: A Desktop Reference* (US Department of Education, Office of the Under Secretary, Office of Elementary and Secondary Education, 2002), http://purl.access.gpo.gov/GPO/LPS23531.
6. United States Department of Education, *State and Local Implementation of the No Child Left Behind Act Volume VIII: Teacher Quality Under NCLB: Final Report* (United States Department of Education, 2009), https://www2.ed.gov/rschstat/eval/teaching/nclb-final/report.pdf.
7. The Race to the Top effort was designed to maximize the diversity of state-level approaches to ensuring better student outcomes while maintaining a level of methodological rigor in the collection of data. One use of such data was for teacher quality purposes, which included both rewards and sanctions. The performance data collected could be used for the purposes of offering additional compensation, or so-called merit pay, as a way to reward high-quality teachers, but it could also be used as justification for the removal of "ineffective tenured and untenured teachers." It is beyond the scope of this book to provide a detailed analysis of this effort, but to summarize, it was much harder to put into practice than many people thought; US Dept. of Education, *Volume VIII: Teacher Quality,* 2009; Lam D. Pham, Tuan D. Nguyen, and Matthew G. Springer, "Teacher Merit Pay: A Meta-Analysis," *American Educational Research Journal* 58, no. 3 (2020): 527–66, https://doi.org/10.3102/0002831220905580; MET Project, *Ensuring Fair and Reliable Measures of Effective Teaching: Culminating Findings from the Met Project's Three-Year Study* (Bill & Melinda Gates Foundation, 2013), https://usprogram.gatesfoundation.org/-/media/dataimport/resources/pdf/2016/12/met-ensuring-fair-and-reliable-measures-practitioner-brief.pdf.

Appendix C

1. Desiree Carver-Thomas and Susan Patrick, *Understanding Teacher Compensation: A State-by-State Analysis* (Learning Policy Institute, 2022), https://files.eric.ed.gov/fulltext/ED622832.pdf.
2. Matthew A. Kraft and Melissa Arnold Lyon, "The Rise and Fall of the Teaching Profession: Prestige, Interest, Preparation, and Satisfaction over the Last Half Century," *American Educational Research Journal* 61, no. 6 (2024): 1192–236, https://doi.org/10.3102/00028312241276856.
3. Sylvia Allegretto, *The Teacher Pay Penalty Has Hit a New High: Trends in Teacher Wages and Compensation through 2021* (Economic Policy Institute, 2022), https://files.eric.ed.gov/fulltext/ED622883.pdf.
4. Sylvia Allegretto, *Teacher Pay Penalty Still Looms Large: Trends in Teacher Wages and Compensation through 2022* (Economic Policy Institute, 2023), https://policycommons.net/artifacts/4941069/teacher-pay-penalty-still-looms-large/5770572/.

Acknowledgments

In the original proposal for this project, we stated that one of our main aims was to lift up the work of teachers and administrators who were doing amazing things and to make their efforts visible to a wider audience. Therefore, our first and most heartfelt thanks goes to the teachers, administrators, and school leaders who welcomed us into their workplaces and shared their experiences with us. We promised anonymity, but you know who you are, and we are grateful for your generosity and openness. This book is dedicated to you.

A project like this is necessarily a collaborative effort and was supported in many different ways by many different people. This work would not have been at all possible without the steadfast collaboration and support of Dr. Sandra Adams from Montclair State University, who served as coprincipal investigator on the grant and whose virology research and public health advocacy was proven to be so vital during the COVID-19 pandemic.

The core of the IMPREST research team at Montclair State University was Liz Carletta, Khadija Ahmed, Mayra Muñoz, along with the two of us. We met weekly—much like the group in chapter three—to shape this study, select districts, develop research tools, and respond to the impediments imposed by the global pandemic. This team not only collected and analyzed the data but collectively helped give shape to the case studies, and we are grateful for their efforts that ultimately helped give this book shape. Other Montclair graduate students contributed to this project, including Divya Vasarla, Manar Hussein, Catherine Gaynor, Erika Oliveros, Stephenie Tidwell, Robert Heintjes, Cheyenne Chmara, Sophia Giudici, Mitch Peters, Sami Jo Freeman, and Amy Sloat.

We are grateful for the various forms of administrative and collegial support we received at Montclair State University throughout this project from: Tamara Lucas, Katrina Bulkley, Vincent Alfonso, Lora Billings, Sumi Hagiwara, Carolina Gonzalez, Linda Wise, Jennifer Robinson, Marilyn Davis, Eden

Kyse, April Serfass, Mark Heimerdinger, Dana Natale, Rhena Jasey-Goodman, Mika Munakata, Jason Francis, Jesse Ryan Miller, Scott Kight, Rebecca Swann-Jackson, Tina Seaboch, Heather Kugelmass, Provost Junius Gonzalez, and President Jonathan Koppell. We acknowledge the sponsorship of Montclair State University in making this book possible through its provision of sabbatical leave for Doug Larkin in the spring of 2025. At Touro University, we thank Laurie Bobley, Nelly Lejter Morales, Charity Dacey, Provost Patricia Salkin, and President Alan Kadish for their support.

We appreciate the efforts of those at the National Science Foundation and the American Association for the Advancement of Science that supported and championed this project, with special thanks to Kathleen Bergin, Sandra Richardson, Betty Calinger, Lauren Manier, Chantal Fuqua, and Jennifer Carinci. This material is based upon work supported by a grant from the National Science Foundation under Award No. 1758282.

We also acknowledge the support provided by individuals at the New Jersey Department of Education, the Pennsylvania Department of Education, the Wisconsin Department of Public Instruction, and the North Carolina Education Research Data Center. Other valuable forms of support were provided by David Stroupe, Jennifer C. Murphy, John Rudolph, Edna Tan, Christy Marhatta, Tuan Nguyen, Meredith Kier, Julia Hazel, Alberto Morales, Doris Santoro, John Settlage, Jeff Rozelle, and Meltem Alemdar.

We are grateful for the valuable contributions of Mark Windschitl, Melissa Braaten, and Julie Luft, who served as the project's advisory board throughout the duration of the grant. Their wise counsel helped keep this project on track, while their thoughtful questions sent us in new directions.

At Harvard Educational Press, we are indebted to Jess Fiorillo, Jayne Fargnoli, and Emma Struebing, and Cole Bowman at KnowledgeWorks Global for their support. An extra measure of that to our editor, Shannon Davis, whose feedback and suggestions along the way strengthened this manuscript tremendously.

Finally, we wish to thank our families for their support. Doug's mom, Barbara Ryan Larkin, carefully read and edited every word of this book—though any errors remain attributable to the authors—and his dad, John Larkin, offered his continued encouragement. We also wish to acknowledge the "children" in our lives for their patience and understanding while we disappeared for periods of time to research and write this book: Casey and Amani (who are actually human adults), and Morocco, Oscar, and Cosmo (canine). As teachers who have stayed in the classroom, our spouses Melissa and Kurt have also served as sounding boards and reality checks for our ideas, and we are deeply grateful for their ongoing love and support.

About the Authors

Douglas B. Larkin is a professor in the Department of Teaching and Learning at Montclair State University in New Jersey. His research concerns the preparation of science teachers for culturally diverse classrooms, issues of equity and justice in teacher education, and science teacher recruitment, preparation, and retention.

Suzanne Poole Patzelt is an assistant professor in the Department of Alternative Programs and University Partnerships at Touro University in New York. Her research concerns Research Experiences for Teachers (RETs), science teachers' conceptions of the nature of science, science teacher identities, and sustainable and equitable approaches for recruiting and retaining science teachers. She is equally passionate about science and education as well as working to make both fields more equitable and justice centered.

Index